The Global Silicon Valley Home

ASIAN AMERICA

A series edited by Gordon H. Chang

The increasing size and diversity of the Asian American population, its growing significance in American society and culture, and the expanded appreciation, both popular and scholarly, of the importance of Asian Americans in the country's present and past—all these developments have converged to stimulate wide interest in scholarly work on topics related to the Asian American experience. The general recognition of the pivotal role that race and ethnicity have played in American life, and in relations between the United States and other countries, has also fostered this heightened attention.

Although Asian Americans were a subject of serious inquiry in the late nineteenth and early twentieth centuries, they were subsequently ignored by the mainstream scholarly community for several decades. In recent years, however, this neglect has ended, with an increasing number of writers examining a good many aspects of Asian American life and culture. Moreover, many students of American society are recognizing that the study of issues related to Asian America speaks to, and may be essential for, many current discussions on the part of the informed public and various scholarly communities.

The Stanford series on Asian America seeks to address these interests. The series will include works from the humanities and social sciences, including history, anthropology, political science, American studies, law, literary criticism, sociology, and interdisciplinary and policy studies.

The Global Silicon Valley Home

LIVES AND LANDSCAPES

WITHIN TAIWANESE AMERICAN

TRANS-PACIFIC CULTURE

Shenglin Chang

STANFORD UNIVERSITY PRESS

STANFORD, CALIFORNIA

2006

Stanford University Press
Stanford, California
© 2006 by the Board of Trustees of the
Leland Stanford Junior University

Library of Congress Cataloging-in-Publication Data

Chang , Shenglin.
    The global Silicon Valley home : lives and landscapes within
Taiwanese American trans-Pacific culture / Shenglin Chang.
        p. cm.
    Includes bibliographical references and index.
    ISBN 0-8047-5215-x (cloth : alk. paper)
    1. Taiwanese Americans—California—Santa Clara Valley
(Santa Clara County)—Ethnic identity. 2. Taiwanese
Americans—California—Santa Clara Valley (Santa Clara
County)—Social conditions. 3. Immigrants—California—
Santa Clara Valley (Santa Clara County)—Social conditions.
4. Commuters—California—Santa Clara Valley (Santa Clara
County)—Social conditions. 5. Commuters—Taiwan—Hsin-
chu shih—Social conditions. 6. Transnationalism. 7. Santa
Clara Valley (Santa Clara County, Calif.)—Relations—Taiwan—
Hsin-chu shih. 8. Hsin-chu shih (Taiwan)—Relations—
California—Santa Clara Valley (Santa Clara County) .
9. Community life—California—Santa Clara Valley (Santa Clara
County). 10. Santa Clara Valley (Santa Clara County, Calif.)—
Social conditions. I. Title.

F868.S25C47 2006
305.895'1073'079473—dc22

                                          2005022596

Printed in the United States of America
Original printing 2006
Last figure below indicates year of this printing:
15 14 13 12 11 10 09 08 07 06

Typeset at Stanford University Press in 11/14 Garamond

For Grandma, Elijah, and my family

Contents

Homes

Tables and Illustrations

Acknowledgments

This book grew from my doctoral dissertation. My deepest thanks go to Randy Hester, Michael Southworth, Louise Mozingo, and AnnaLee Saxenian. Their guidance and support inspired me throughout my studies at UC Berkeley. I am indebted to John K. C. Liu for his constant encouragement, incisive criticism, sense of humor, and faith in me. His and Shirley's Berkeley-Taiwan family life gave me insights for this volume.

I also want to thank Richard Weismiller and Margarita Hill of the Department of Natural Resource Sciences and Landscape Architecture at the University of Maryland for their generous and continuous support of my research. Several research grants helped me expand the scope of my research: the 2000 Nautilus Institute Research Grants for the Global Accountability Project, the 2002–2003 University of Maryland General Research Board Summer Research Award, the 2005–2006 Research Support Award, and the 2000–2003 University of Maryland start-up research grant. I also wish to thank John Liu and Qindong Liang for involving me in the 2001 Pu-yu Information-based New Town Planning Project (Hsinchu, Taiwan) and the EDAW 2003 Summer Student Workshop (Beijing, China). These opportunities provided me precious data for this book. The invitations that Tianxin Zhang and Jeff Hou extended to me to share my work at Beijing University and the University of Washington, and at "A Center of Women" symposium held at UC Berkeley, respectively, helped me clarify many of my ideas.

I am grateful to In-chuan Chang, Ching-jie Wu, Tianxin Zhang, Sam D.Y. Liu, Grace Hsu, and my brother, Yuhlin Chang, for the help they provided in locating interviewees in Taiwan, China, and the United States. I thank all the interviewees who helped me understand the trans-Pacific home phenomenon. I could not have completed the book without the keen data analysis talents of Yuchuan Ku, Ping Sung, Gaobo Pang, and Paul Rodriguez. I thank Kimmy Chen and Kenya Thompson for their expert graphics contributions. Sharon Wood and John Feneron at Stanford University Press, as well as Jason Young, Mary Jo Dosh, Mike Jones and Hsiu-tzu Chang, have my gratitude for helping me shape a bulky manuscript into an elegant book. The consistent support I received from Muriel Bell and Carmen Borbon-Wu at Stanford University Press is truly appreciated.

I owe a debt of gratitude to Ingrid Chou and Sister Nora Bennett for the joy and peace that they brought to me in the lonely writing journey. I am grateful to my family for their enduring patience and generous support, and I am especially grateful to my mother and father for having my grandmother live with us. Finally, this book could not have been written without the inspiration, transcultural understanding, and poetic insights that I received from my husband, Elijah Mirochnik. I feel blessed to have him in my life.

Preface: All Leaves Fall Back to Their Roots

My family history is a history of diaspora. In the short period of the second half of the twentieth century, three generations of my family migrated twice, first from mainland China to Taiwan, and then from Taiwan to the United States. Each generation struggled with its adopted land's sociohistorical context. Every member's personal desires, fortunes, misfortunes, gains, and losses have been inextricably woven into my family's voyage.

My family's migration started with the Chinese Civil War in 1949, when my grandmother had to flee from her home in mainland China. Her son, who was in Chiang Kai-shek's army, brought his mother and his sister across the Taiwan Strait with him to the island of Taiwan. My grandmother was in her late fifties when she fled from Tienlou, her mainland China hometown. Although she lived in Taiwan for four decades, nostalgia for her beloved hometown and the families she left behind haunted her life in Taiwan.

I grew up with her memories of her previous life in Tienlou, memories that she recalled daily in whatever she did.[1] Although she could not read, she sang many folk poems when her mind was still clear. During my childhood I enjoyed listening to her songs, and I felt the emotion in her voice as she depicted a faraway people and landscape. Even though she sat on the old couch with me as she spun stories of her earlier mainland China experiences, I felt that, in a way, she was not there with me.

As close as I was to my grandmother, I felt that she had never completely left her homeland; her body had been transported to Taiwan, but her mind had remained in her beloved China. Throughout the latter half of her life, she always wanted to go back to her mainland home, but she never returned. She passed away at the age of one hundred. Ironically, the Taiwanese restriction on visiting mainland China was lifted the year after her death. My parents and my uncle carried her ashes back to the home she had left behind. There her life came to a close, as a leaf falls back to its roots.

As my mother began her journey back to her childhood home, carrying her mother's ashes, she was eager to embrace her childhood home and to revisit her mainland identity once again. My grandmother's home had also been my mother's home until she was a teenager. My mother was in her mid-fifties when she made the trip back to Tienlou, almost the same age that her mother had been when she left. But, throughout the trip, my mother felt like an outsider. The village relatives that she had expected would warmly greet her instead alienated her. She discovered many changes that she had not anticipated, and she didn't experience the homecoming she had expected at all. After she returned to Taiwan, she shared the rather heartbreaking story of the trip, and I realized how profoundly frustrating the homecoming must have been for her.

Instead of being a joyous return, the trip destroyed the symbolic meaning that the Tienlou house held for my mother. The way the other family members pejoratively hurled the label "Taiwanese" at her hurt her deeply. Bruised by the experience of visiting the mainland, she expressed her frustration, asking "Where on earth is my home? When I am in Taiwan, people identify me as a mainlander. When I go back to my home village in China, people call me Taiwanese. When I visit America, people say I am a foreigner. Where is my home?" Due to frightening childhood memories involving the civil war, my mother was very fearful about living in Taiwan, and she always hoped that one day our family could migrate to the United States. My father, however, had a different view. He once told me, "Where can we go? Taiwan is our home already. We should just appreciate what the land offers and be thankful for the people we encounter every day."

Meanwhile, my older brother and I ended up going in opposite directions. He was deeply engaged in American literature, movies, and jazz, and he now works as an electrical engineer in Silicon Valley's computer industry. Following traditional Chinese values, he believed that as the eldest son in our family he was obligated to study science, because it was the route to social status and promised a secure income. After fulfilling his Taiwanese military service, he came to the United States to pursue his Master's degree and Ph.D. He decided to remain in the United States after completing his graduate work to build a career and start a family.

I arrived in the United States to pursue an academic career in 1991. At first I lived in Ithaca, New York, for three years, and then I moved to Berkeley, California. In spite of living so far away, I have stayed closely connected to Taiwanese society and life, reading Internet news from Taiwan daily and commuting between the United States and Taiwan up to three times each year. I receive emails, faxes, and phone calls from my Taiwanese friends and colleagues weekly. Together with my colleagues and friends, I have coordinated projects, initiated political movements, and participated in social activism, even though we were separated by the width of the Pacific Ocean. Somehow, in the midst of leading a transnational life, I have been able to overcome time and space, and to satiate my need to stay connected to the social and cultural networks that I came from. However, instead of celebrating the information age that makes all this possible, I feel I have lost my sense of having a home rooted in a place—the place that fostered my grandmother's nostalgia for half a century; the place my parents imagined could provide our family a secure life; the place my brother saw as a location he could never return to.

The picture in my mind of the place I was once so strongly attached to is now fading away. When I arrived in the United States to pursue a graduate degree at Cornell University in 1991, I often missed the mouthwatering Taiwanese *xiaochi* (snacks) that I had enjoyed when I lived in Taipei. When I returned to Taipei, the first place I headed after getting off the plane was the night market to satisfy my uncontrollable urge for the stir-fried rice noodles, seared oyster pancakes, steamed vegetable dumplings, and fish ball bisque topped with coriander that I had acquired a taste for long ago.

During my nine years of student life in upstate New York and the San Francisco Bay Area, I journeyed back and forth between my American and Taiwan homes as frequently as I could. At first, I viewed every trip back to Taiwan as the quick remedy to alleviate my homesickness. But then something peculiar happened. By 1998 I had been at UC Berkeley for five years and in America for eight. During that year's trip back to Taiwan, I was surprised to find that, for the first time, I felt homesick for Berkeley.

I moved to the Washington, D.C., area in the summer of 2000. One rainy afternoon, shortly after settling in D.C., as I was driving and listening to a Joni Mitchell tape, a mixed set of emotions arose (Mitchell 1971). As Joni Mitchell sang "Oh! California, I am coming home," I felt a longing for home. But I did not know where my home was. Was home in Taiwan, in Berkeley, or in D.C.?

As I encountered this ambiguity I wondered if the network of friends and professional colleagues in Taiwan that I was plugged into would always provide me with a way of keeping in touch with the Taiwanese side of myself. As I drove along with Joni Mitchell serenading me, I wondered whether the person that I had become over the years that I had spent in America was still connected to her home and family in Taiwan, and to the memory of her grandmother. Why had my memories of Taiwan and Berkeley been fading away simultaneously? Why had I felt that I was an outsider? How could I have felt alienated in American society after being here for more than a decade?

In the story that I am about to tell, I am not the only outsider. This book shares the story of a group of high-tech Taiwanese engineers who have lived in Silicon Valley for decades. Like me, they are "outsiders" in that they have immigrated to the United States from Taiwan. My brother and his friends are members of this group. Inspired by my brother's migration experience and his reflection on the technological evolution, I decided to take a closer look at how Taiwanese immigrant families who have relocated to Silicon Valley relate their Taiwanese homes in the past to their new American ones. From 1998 to 2004 I conducted fieldwork in Silicon Valley (United States), Hsinchu (Taiwan), and Shanghai and Beijing (China), while I also visited seven high-tech communities outside Silicon Valley.[2] During this period I interviewed 148 people, including the families of high-tech engineers, high-tech production workers, government officials, planning and design professionals, real estate agents, scholars, and researchers.[3] Based on in-depth interviews, I have tried to come to understand how the high-tech families have made sense of the relationship between their previous home in Taiwan and their current home in Silicon Valley. I have found that their ways of making sense of leaving one home and one culture for another say much about how they think about themselves—how they think about who they are, who they were, and who they are becoming.

I have been confronted by these high-tech families' deep admiration for and enjoyment of the American suburban landscape. They also have succeeded in developing a Taiwanese inner-city lifestyle within that suburban landscape. For instance, after my brother had just bought a new house in Fremont, California, he proudly told me that the house was located adjacent to a park and within a five-minute walk of a Ranch 99 Taiwanese shopping center. In that location he can enjoy his suburban detached house while also satisfying his Taiwanese love for urban shopping convenience. More important, his house is also within walking distance of shops that offer good Chinese groceries. My brother's integration of his Taiwanese inner-city identity with his American suburban identity is one example of what I call the trans-Pacific home identity.

In 1998, after six months of conversation with Taiwanese American computer engineers who had relocated to Silicon Valley, I began to realize that many of them actually had two homes, one in California and the other in Hsinchu Science Park in Taiwan. I learned that many of them regularly commuted between their two homes on opposite sides of the Pacific, and that's when I started thinking of them as residents of a trans-Pacific commuter culture. Many of the people I introduce later in this book have homes in both Silicon Valley and Hsinchu Science Park. Others with homes only in Silicon Valley or Hsinchu deeply admire the American suburban landscape while enjoying a California life that re-creates their previous Taiwanese life. I was excited to find that a great number of high-tech engineers and their families had created a unique landscape by taking their California homes and landscapes and transplanting them to Taiwan.

The stories of the trans-Pacific commuters' home identities that I am about to share weave together dream lives, dream careers, and dream houses. This should not, however, be taken as a sign that the lives of these trans-Pacific commuters are perfect or trouble-free. In certain instances the trans-Pacific "dream" has resulted in "nightmare" scenarios, with communities affected by traffic, environmental pollution, and economic segregation. Instead of translating these "dreams" and "nightmares" into theoretical language, I provide a narrative of the commuters' experiences. I prefer to start with the stories that I heard from people whom I studied because these stories enable the reader to become engaged with the storytellers, to find connections with them that relate to the reader's lived experiences. In the approach that I have taken, my theories about my interviewees' lives emerged within a process of coming to understand their stories. This approach emphasizes the power of the voices that the author has interviewed, rather than using those voices to prove the author's theories. Within this approach storytelling allows room for theory to emerge and for the reader to better sense how the theory has emerged through an understanding of those whose stories are often untold.

While I use personal narratives and the self-descriptions of engineers' families throughout this book, I also draw on scholarly theoretical and interdisciplinary literatures concerned with landscapes and home identities. These literatures include those of John Horton (sociology), Peggy Levitt (anthropology), Lucy Lippard (art), Clare Cooper Marcus (environmental design), Richard Rorty and Wolfgang Welsch (philosophy), AnnaLee Saxenian (regional economics), Yi-Fu Tuan (human geography), Edward Soja (cultural geography), and Doreen Massey (cultural geography and feminist study). The work of the scholars named above has helped me to develop the concept of a shifting home identity, a concept that is integrated into and generated from my fieldwork interviews. My reflections on Marcus's and Tuan's home identity research added depth to the shifting home identities concept. The concept of "bi-gration," which I explore in chapters 2 and 5, stems from Soja's *Thirdspace*. Welsch's transculturality profoundly informs my idea of transcultural lifestyles in chapter 5. Leavitt's research on the transnational family and Lippard's writing about multicentered places influence the way I see Taiwanese families' transnational family lives in chapter 4. In addition, Saxenian's investigation into the travel frequency of Asian immigrant engineers in Silicon Valley provides me the solid data to picture the trans-Pacific activities between Silicon Valley and Taiwan in chapter 3. In addition, Horton's Monterey Park research offers a clear picture of Taiwanese Americans' California dreams between 1980 and early 1990, described here in chapters 5 and 6. Finally, Doreen's feminist view of sense of global space and Rorty's concept of de-essentialized selfhood opened up a new window through which I view the mosaic home landscapes that I describe in chapters 2 and 10.

I see the narrative approach that I take as echoing Rorty, who follows Harold Bloom's understanding that the reader's interpretation of text is as important as the author's intended meaning (Bloom 2000; Rorty 2001). Rorty agrees with Bloom's opinion that "reading" is not about the arguments and ideologies that "recontextualize all the books" we previously read (Rorty 2001). To Rorty, "reading" is about the reader's process of understanding how other people (who are different from the reader) think of themselves, construct actions, and create meanings for their lives on their own terms. As Rorty states, "The problem of how to live our own lives then becomes a problem of how to balance our needs against theirs, and their self-descriptions against ours. To have a more educated, developed and sophisticated moral outlook is to be able to grasp more of these needs, and to understand more of these self-descriptions" (ibid.).

In the chapters that follow I attempt to give voice to the untold story of a group of Taiwanese immigrants whose lives inform a newly emerging definition of the relationship between self and place. I had originally thought that immigrants' journeys from Taiwan to Silicon Valley were simply based on a result of their aspirations for a successful life. What I later realized was that their migration stories were as complicated as my grandmother's story. Some of them achieved their dreams and have created a particular way of life for themselves. Others did not. The story I tell in this book is about both their old and new homes and landscapes; it is a story about how their actual or imagined return to their motherland is reflected in the homes they choose to dwell in and the landscapes in which they choose to make their homes. It is a story of how homes and landscapes have enabled an emerging Asian American immigrant population to construct and reconstruct their individual and cultural identities. It is a story of how homes and landscapes express one's departure and return.

In addition to this being a story of departure from homes and landscapes, it is also a story of departure from the traditional lenses through which we see our selves, our homes, and our landscapes. In the process of listening carefully to stories of departure from one's homeland, I began to understand that physical departure engendered a departure from some deeply held conceptions of self and place. My parents' ritual burial of my grandmother's ashes in the landscape in which she was born was their way of enacting a conception of self and place that had been handed down to them through many centuries of Chinese thought, the belief that one's self, one's identity, who one is, is forever tied to one's birthplace.

This traditional concept of self as inextricably wedded to the location of one's birth is captured in the Chinese adage "All leaves fall back to their roots." This adage uses the tree as a metaphor to express the idea that one's identity is always tied to one's place of birth, no matter how far from home one might roam.

The story I tell in this book is about those families who have migrated to California and have constructed for themselves lives that include the experience of commuting back and forth across the Pacific from their new homes to their Taiwanese homeland. In a sense, it is a story of those leaves that the wind has blown far from the tree's roots. Unlike the leaves that fall to the roots, these trans-Pacific commuters fly great distances away from their roots, but their commuting between two homes across vast distances has led them to think in new ways about the relationship between self, home, and landscape. It is a story about how I listened to their stories, and how over time and through many conversations I began to make sense of the home/identity relationship that they had already internalized—a relationship that is less about a return to their roots and more about the fluidity with which they are able to travel from one home to another, from one picture of themselves to another.

Memories and Identities

ONE

Returning Home in the Information Age

Jin-yi-huan-xiang is a Chinese phrase that signifies the act of returning to one's homeland, or to one's hometown, after being gone for a long, long time. Having grown up in Taiwan, I immediately associate this phrase with an image from the movies in which the hero returns victoriously to his home village. Attired in a crisp, clean crimson uniform, he rides into his hometown on a handsome white horse as children form rows to greet him with envious applause and firecrackers. To everyone's surprise, this man who left his village poor and young returns years later as a soaring eagle. Those who return after many years away from their homeland and after achieving great success dress themselves in beautiful clothes that symbolically honor their family. The single succinct phrase "beautiful clothes retuning home" connotes their entire epic journey, from their determination to leave, the changes they undertake, the social recognition they achieve, and their emotional homecoming.

Although I associate the phrase *jin-yi-huan-xiang* with cinematic heroes, it is most often used to describe the act of ordinary people returning home. It implies a reunion ritual that engages the entire family. It also suggests that a choice has been made. When people choose to leave home, they may do so because they want to pursue their dream life, dream career, or dream house. *Jin-yi-huan-xiang* depicts the conclusion of their journey; that journey begins at the moment when they make the choice to depart in search of a better life, and it ends when they finally reunite with their family.

The phrase embodies the various social aspects of the experience of returning home. *Huan-xiang* emphasizes the emotional aspect of the return home. In the past, Chinese often used the phrase when they needed to convey the career achievements of a person with humble origins. Throughout much of China's history, the experiences of both forced and voluntary migration have been shared by many generations of Chinese. Due to wars, poverty, or famine, people left their homes behind to pursue a better life. *Huan-xiang* has always been the most meaningful action to conclude that journey. It is an act of closure, the last act in which the dream of returning home finally comes true.

In Chinese culture the ritual of returning home, theatrically played out by riding back to one's old home on a white horse, is not reserved exclusively for soldiers and warriors. The heroic homecoming is also part of a process of social climbing in which members of various economic classes reach an elite status through higher education and participation in the civil service. In today's Taiwanese society, after excelling in various academic challenges, both men and women are the guests of honor at receptions organized for them when they return home with their diplomas in hand. The high-tech Taiwanese that you will soon meet in this volume have experienced this homecoming ritual. However, the story I tell is not about how they have improved their social status, nor about their return to their old home. It is a story about how today's high-tech lifestyle allows them to keep two homes and two identities simultaneously. Neither is it a story of heroic people, but rather a story of how ordinary husbands, wives, and children have created lives in which they have replaced traditional definitions of home and identity with new ones.

From No Return to Returning as a Stranger

In the Preface, I mentioned that my research interests stem from my family's history of diaspora. My family's migration started with the Chinese Civil War in 1949. My grandmother's experience of having to flee from her home in mainland China is one shared by thousands of others during the mid-twentieth century. She was in her late fifties when she fled Tienlou, her mainland China hometown. Although she lived in Taiwan for four decades, nostalgia for her beloved hometown and the family she left behind haunted her Taiwanese life.

My mother attempted to convince my grandmother that our new home in Taiwan was much better and more comfortable than her old home. But, having been uprooted from her familiar house and the landscape in which she had grown up, my grandmother lost part of her identity. Both she and my mother were uprooted from the same place, but my mother adapted to the new home as her mother never did.

I would attribute my grandmother's loss of identity to her adoption of the traditional belief in the static relationship between one's home and one's identity. She believed she belonged to the place she left behind. The *place* embodied her *self*. So, for her, being removed from her place was equivalent to having her identity taken away. A successful Tang dynasty poet and court bureaucrat named He Zhi-zhang (ninth century A.D.) expressed this traditional static relation between home and identity in a poem in which he described his sense of loss in returning to a hometown that he left long ago. He wrote:

> Departing home since I was young,
> Now returning being old.
> My accent has not changed
> yet my sideburns have grayed.
> The village children thought I am from the distant
>   land,
> They smiled and asked
> "Where did you come from,
> My guest?"

My grandmother and the poet shared the same loss of self. Both of them believed that their identities were permanently intertwined with their home landscapes. The simple question the children of He's village asked, "Where do you come from, my guest?" is indicative of the static home-identity relationship. From the children's point of view, He is a stranger from a "foreign land." The children's question, which catches him off guard, severs the relationship between the landscape he has fixated upon in his memory and himself. When He returns, he realizes that the hometown that he had kept in a static state in his memory was not the hometown of the present.

Although my grandmother never returned to her hometown, and the poet He returned as a stranger, the hometowns in their respective memories never changed, remaining the way they were since the day they departed. In reality, of course, the places and the landscape *had* changed. In their own memories, my grandmother and He imagined themselves to be the insiders, but they found themselves to be outsiders when they returned. Their static memories of their homes were challenged because landscapes are never static.

Mosaic Electronic Return

Perhaps if my grandmother or He were alive today, modern technology would have enabled them to keep up with the changes in their hometowns. In our modern lives we have the technology to help us sustain our sense of connection between home and identity during our absence from home. For example, the home-identity relation is sustained by the modern media through movies, newspapers, TV, photos, and even popular music. Modern media technology has provided us with new approaches to constructing the relationships among our homes, our landscapes, and our selves. Compared to my grandmother's era, the early twentieth century, we have more opportunities to travel away from our homes and still get news of home through media technology. Media technology brings us images of and information about our homes, neighborhoods, and the landscapes we are familiar with, no matter where on the globe we may be.

In the early 1990s I traveled halfway across the globe to pursue a graduate education. My experience of watching television news from Taiwan while at Cornell University is a clear example of how fragmented imagery and information are selected and controlled by the mass media. The only consistent media coverage of events in Taiwan available in Ithaca, New York, was the Channel 57 weekday evening news. So, by 9:45 P.M., all of us Taiwanese students would make our way home to turn on the Channel 57 *Nightly Taiwan Report*. Those of us who did not have cable television would invite ourselves into our Taiwanese neighbors' apartments to get our daily dose of Taiwan news. In those pre-Internet days, a mere twenty-minute, day-old news broadcast satisfied our longing for a connection with our homeland.

Those twenty minutes were powerful for us. For twenty minutes, the images presented to us enabled our imaginations to travel across the globe and construct for ourselves an electronic return home. The travels we undertook through the broadcast news kept our memories alive and helped my Taiwanese friends and I sustain our sense of belonging to our homeland. Most of the events we saw on the news happened in Taiwan's big cities, while we were located in Ithaca's rural environment. Our relationships with our homes were constructed by piecing together fragmented images, stories, and lifestyles from places as varied as the East District Urban Center of Taipei, Ithaca Commons, Kaohsiung Lin-yuan Industrial Park, and the Carousel Center in Syracuse. This mosaic of landscapes and lifestyles became the basis of our Taiwanese home identities. Every night we enthusiastically used our late-night electronic return-trip ticket to go back to Taiwan for less than half an hour, even though we never left our quaint little college town in upstate New York.

Identity Crisis Returns

In the modern era many of us have had times in our lives in which we have experienced what I call the "mosaic home identity," times in which we found ourselves living in a foreign land, adapting to new lifestyles, or connecting with our old home via electronic news and images. During the process of adapting to our new homes, we found it necessary to change so that we might fit in with new landscapes and lifestyles. Some changes may have been minor modifications. For example, I learned what sizes of American clothing fit my Taiwanese body. Other changes might have involved significant struggles that challenged our conceptions of our selves. For example, we may have started a family, switched careers, or changed our relationships with our loved ones. After going through these significant changes, we may have ended up feeling like strangers to ourselves.

The question "Where did you come from, my guest?" posed in He's poem is an example of the type of internal questioning that we find ourselves going through during these times of change. We find ourselves asking our old homes and landscapes to recognize and accept who we have become. We often experience an identity crisis as part of the process of returning.

When the Canadian singer-songwriter Joni Mitchell released the song "California" in 1971, she was expressing the interplay between her mosaic identity and the identity crisis she felt about returning home. In the song Mitchell, a Canadian expatriate who has relocated to California, portrays herself as a romantic world traveler, sitting in a park in Paris or partying in Spain. But despite her vagabond ways, her heart eventually cries out for her adopted home of California. After experiencing numerous new places and encountering many strangers on her European travels, she finds that she has developed a new relationship with her beloved California. Upon her return, she is filled with joy as she realizes just how much she has missed her familiar people and places. The song ends as Mitchell pleads with California to take her back, as one might plead with a lover to take her back. Her inner dialogue with California, in which she expresses the loneliness of separation and humbly pleads for a reunion, signifies her simultaneous discovery of the new self she has become and the discovery that her new self could not live without her old home.

In contrast to the children's question for He, "Where did you come from, my guest?" Mitchell's conversation is with the landscape she feels attached to. In contrast to the question posed to He, asked by an external interlocutor, Mitchell's question emerges from an internal dialogue. By endowing the state of California with human attributes that make it equivalent to a lover, Mitchell is able to express her desire to reconnect with the landscape she has temporarily left behind as she pleads, "California . . . Will you take me as I am? Will you?"

The poet He returned home as a stranger more than a millennium ago, while Joni Mitchell returned home with an identity crisis at the end of the 1960s. Mitchell's identity crisis, it seems to me, is symbolic of her generation's unresolved struggle between the desire to escape from the conformist traditions of rootedness and the conformist longing for a secure and stable home. Like the Woodstock generation she represents, Mitchell struggles to maintain the static relationship between her old home landscape and her new self.

Mitchell's home identity is no longer a static one, but rather a mosaic. She constructs a mosaic home identity by leading a life in which she blends her experiences of numerous exotic lifestyles and adapts to different societies. She enjoys her memories from different travel episodes, and she embraces the changes that she has experienced in different periods of her life.

Mosaic home identity reflects a merger, because it is a type of identity that embraces the dynamic interactions between one's old and new home landscapes. For someone who experiences a mosaic self, new daily experiences that emerge during the process of adapting to a new home gradually transform the relationship with one's old home landscapes. On the one hand, the person who experiences a mosaic self still believes that his or her relationship with the home landscape should remain as it was in "the good old days." On the other hand, even though there is a return to the old home, one carries his or her new mosaic landscape experiences and connects to new friends, new landscapes, and new lifestyles. Those of Mitchell's 1960s Woodstock generation who experienced a mosaic self may have experienced guilt about having both new and old homes. They could never have imagined that some day technology would enable one to reside simultaneously in multiple places and maintain a coherent sense of self while leading a double life.

The Virtual Return

The rapid evolution of information technology (IT) and the proliferation of air travel in the past decade have profoundly impacted how we relate our new homes to the old ones. New technologies and twenty-first-century modes of transportation enable us to shift our homes from one landscape to another, from one part of the globe to another, with ease.

New technologies have enabled some people to maintain double lives at two remote places. You will meet some of these people in this book. These people not only frequently commute between two places, but they also identify both places as their home. Their lives give rise to a new and important reality that has surfaced at the turn of the twenty-first century: it is now possible for us to integrate our new and old lifestyles and social networks in multiple home landscapes, and we can physically and electronically travel within a web of intertwined landscapes, lifestyles, and social networks. When we are at one home, we can choose to virtually return to the other home. In other words, we can simultaneously exist in two homes at once.

In this book the seemingly extraordinary phenomena of virtual returning and shifting home identities will be seen as ordinary aspects of the everyday lives of people who work as engineers within the high-tech computer industry in Silicon Valley. I use the term "high-tech family" to refer to families in which one member is employed in this industry. The families you will meet are of Taiwanese origin and structurally identical to typical nuclear families in Taiwan today, whose primary members include husband, wife, children, and grandparents.

Instead of focusing exclusively on the individual family member engaged in the high-tech profession, this book examines the entire family. Moreover, because my fieldwork indicates that the housewives of high-tech personnel play a central role in the creation of the home's aesthetic identity, they will be discussed extensively. The housewives demonstrate the phenomena that I call "virtual home return" and "shifting home identity." It is their stories and these phenomena that I explore in this book.

Before unfolding the stories of the many women I encountered, I want to introduce Melissa. It was during a conversation I had with Melissa in 1998 that I realized how fascinated I was with how lifestyles, house styles, and landscape styles reflected the identities of Taiwanese American high-tech immigrants. Melissa was once a manager of the Hsinchu Science Park Administration. At the time of our appointment, she was sitting in her office in a skyscraper in Taipei, Taiwan, while writing an email to her daughter in Fremont, California. She sent the email to her daughter's college email address right before our conversation began, and she received a reply message during our talk. Her daughter told her that she and her college pals had recently decided to form a band.

When I asked Melissa where she considered her home to be, she told me that she had two homes, saying, "One is in Silicon Valley, the other in Taiwan."

"How do you relate these two homes to your present life here?" I wondered.

She smiled and replied, "My husband and I live in Taiwan, but my parents and daughters live in Fremont, a city in the so-called Silicon Valley. I shuttle between our Taiwan home and Fremont home five times a year, and exchange emails with my daughter daily. Anyhow, I don't quite feel the distance between Taiwan and Silicon Valley. The reason is simple. I can enjoy my perfect Taiwanese life in Silicon Valley these days, driving my mom to visit our friends in her Fremont neighborhood, shopping at Tawa 99 [Ranch 99] . . . you know, those things you usually can only do in Taiwan. I also can buy all the Taiwanese groceries plus enjoy very good Taiwanese food, trimming and styling my hair in the hair salon at the Tawa 99 mall."[1]

Melissa did not struggle to choose between a static home identity and a mosaic one. Nor did she return home with an identity crisis, like Joni Mitchell did. Unlike Mitchell, the poet He, or my grandmother, Melissa did not construct her home identity as a singular entity, but rather as a melding of several identities. Melissa's home identities constantly shifted between her Taiwanese and Silicon Valley home landscapes. She felt at home in both places. Her two social lives seemed to merge together seamlessly because she traveled extensively, and by utilizing high-tech products she was able to communicate between her two homes with ease.

The blending of the two homes' landscapes and lifestyles in Melissa's experience was illustrated as she described how everyday errands were accomplished in similar ways in both places. She seemed to simultaneously exist in both places and maintain a double life and double identity. Within her suburban Silicon Valley landscape she lived in her Fremont home, visited Taiwanese friends, and enjoyed her Taiwanese food and lifestyle. In her Taiwanese home, emails and information that flowed from her Silicon Valley home created an intimate and instant connection to her home across the Pacific. In other words, whenever she left one home, she virtually returned to the other.

Melissa's experiences are not unique. Hundreds of other Taiwanese high-tech families perform everyday life patterns that reflect their construction of a sense of self that is multiple rather than singular, a sense of self-consciousness that I call a "shifting home identity." I found that the high-tech families I met deeply admire and enjoy the American suburban landscape because they have re-created a Taiwanese inner-city lifestyle within it. They create for themselves shifting identities that enable a virtual return to either of their two homes by transplanting both physical landscape (home, garden) and their residential lifestyle across the Pacific Rim.

Three Identity Patterns

In a book entitled *Minoritized Space: An Inquiry into the Spatial Order of Things*, Michael S. Laguerre describes several important aspects of diaspora: "a dispersed population that has been evicted from its homeland . . . [d]iaspora also refers to re-rooted communities that are extensions of the national community and that maintain ongoing relations with the country of origin. . . . Diasporic communities construct micro and macro spatial niches through which they remain connected to the homeland" (Laguerre 1999, 80). I found that the micro and macro spatial niches that members of the Taiwanese high-tech diaspora created to remain connected to their homeland were not just a matter of constructing physical spaces, but were simultaneously a construction of "psychic spaces" or, as I call them in this book, "shifting home identities." My interviews with Melissa and other Taiwanese high-tech diaspora families helped me understand how dramatic the differences were among my grandmother, Joni Mitchell, and Melissa.

These three women, whose lives span more than a century, take three different approaches toward dealing with the changed sense of self that they encounter once they leave their homelands. Their ways of redefining themselves within their experience of leaving and returning to their homeland are useful in understanding the relationship between one's identity and one's home. First, my grandmother reflects the qualities of a static home identity, even though she never returned to her native home. Second, Joni Mitchell characterizes the mosaic home identity and the identity crisis caused by a return home. And third, Melissa is a representative of shifting home identity and virtual home return. An understanding of the differences between these three patterns of the relationship between landscape and identity has led me to define what I call "transcultural home identity." Before I elaborate on my transcultural home identity theory, however, I would like to describe the three patterns in detail.

Premodern Static Home Identity

My grandmother's story represents the static home identity that results from an inability to return in the pre-media eras, or eras in which electronic media and high-speed travel did not exist. Although my grandmother was born in northeastern China in the nineteenth century, toward the end of her life modern media had become pervasive. I can vividly remember her amazement when she first saw photographs my father had taken. I was a toddler at the time, but I recall her gazing at my father's photos with disbelief. "How wonderful!" she exclaimed. "How can people do this? We don't have this in our hometown! These people are very smart here! We should bring these pictures back to our hometown to show my uncles when we return home!"

As you recall, my grandmother's journeys home consisted of recollections stemming from bodily experiences of the hometown of the past. The Shandong town in which she was born and the Taiwan home where she was relocated were two separate worlds, distinguished by different languages and different physical surroundings.

My grandmother's image of her home in Shandong province in mainland China was generated solely from her memory of the landscape and her daily life experiences there. It was not at all influenced by the mass media she encountered after relocating to Taiwan. She did not understand the Mandarin or Taiwanese dialects that the media used in their broadcasts, and because of the political confrontation across the Taiwan Strait during the Cold War, the Taiwanese government had forbidden all news, information, and images from mainland China. After she left Tienlou, she never saw another image—not even a single photograph—of her former home.

My grandmother did not bring any photos of her hometown or her family with her when she fled to Taiwan. Perhaps this is because she never imagined that she would end up being trapped in Taiwan for forty years, or maybe it was because the photo industry had not, by the time she left the mainland, made its way into her rural town. When she was very old and her memory had faded, she did not even remember that she was living in Taiwan. Every morning when she woke up, she behaved as if she were back in Tienlou with other children and her relatives, following the routines of her old agrarian lifestyle. Her old habits were most apparent at dusk; that's when she requested that we all go to bed because she didn't even remember that we had electricity to provide light after dark.

There were many differences between my grandmother's hometown life and her life in Taiwan. She had never seen plastic bags in Tienlou, and was always amazed by the colorful patterns printed on plastic bags in Taiwan. She told me that she wanted to save them so that when the time came she could take them back with her to her hometown. Eventually she collected dozens of bags and stored them underneath her bed. Every night, in her dreams, she brought those colorful bags with her when she returned home.

Not only did my grandmother not understand the Mandarin or Taiwanese spoken by everyone else, but there were few in her new hometown that understood her. She spoke only Shangdongnese, a folk dialect from Shangdong Province. We spoke Shangdongnese at home with her when she and my father's mother were alive. After we bought our first black-and-white television while I was in kindergarten, she always made up stories that went along with the shows she watched, and I can remember her watching TV news that was spoken in a language completely foreign to her and telling me that what she saw reminded her of her past life in Tienlou. The amazing thing was that even though she could barely hear and couldn't understand a word of what she did hear, her stories often almost exactly corresponded to the storylines of the shows we watched together. After she passed away, the use of Shangdongnese in my home ceased. It seems that my grandmother's native language returned to her home in Shandong Province with her ashes.

Modern Mosaic Home Identity

Joni Mitchell represents the mosaic home identity and the homecoming identity crisis of modern life. Although she has the freedom to fly from one place to another, Mitchell can only be in one place at a time. When she travels away from California, she maintains a partial connection with her home through media sources. However, she senses that she has transformed into a different person during her travels outside California, the place where she ultimately feels rooted.

One important outcome of the modern technological revolution is that our sense of who we are—our identity—is significantly impacted by the visual and verbal messages we receive through the mass media and by our travel experiences. Some of us are lucky enough to possess the resources and freedom required to travel to different lands. News from other countries is readily available to us through print and electronic media. We are instantly gratified with images from movies, newspapers, magazines, or the Internet.

Given all of the media that stimulates us, and all of our travel to places unlike our home, we have adopted a way of constructing our identities in which we see our single self as a mosaic whole composed of many different parts. So, like Joni Mitchell, we believe we have to be in one locale, interact with the local society, and nurture a specific local network in order for the mosaic of the self to remain glued together. We can visit as many different lands as we want, but the glue that holds our identity intact is our connection to a specific home. Following this modern conception of the construction of a mosaic identity, we seek to add foreign pieces to our home identity. So, like Mitchell, we love traveling because it suits our image of a mosaic self that modern media and travel technology allow, but we end up feeling homesick when we leave home for too long. Again, like Mitchell, we end up feeling like outsiders when we are in a foreign land, and because we rely on a singular concept of self, we plead for our local home to embrace us, to give us the psychic glue that we need to adhere the new piece to the existing mosaic when we return.

The Shifting Home Identity in the Postmodern Age

Melissa represents a new prototype for generating one's new identity: the shifting home identity and virtual home return. This is the method of constructing the self that I feel is more appropriate to the twenty-first-century lives that many of us presently lead. We are now able to communicate across the globe with ease, and the ability to travel on jets has rendered our world a global village. Melissa identifies equally with two houses and two landscapes in two different societies. She doesn't feel that one home is primary to her sense of self while the other is secondary to her sense of self, or even foreign. Rather, she feels that both homes are equally important to her identity, because she can do similar things in either house on either side of the Pacific.

Melissa leads what I call a "transcultural life." She doesn't consider either her Taiwanese or American culture as the primary source of her sense of self. Instead of considering that she is "leaving" or "returning" home when she travels across the Pacific, as one might traditionally think, she has constructed a system of landscapes and social networks that intertwines both of her homes. By letting go of the traditional notion that one needs a single home that is rooted to one unique geographic confinement (both physical and cultural), Melissa readily moves physically from one home to another while remaining psychically attached to both homes through her personal use of twenty-first-century technologies. Her movement across cultures and places is a process that reflects her having let go of traditional definitions that assume cultures, places, and selves are bounded entities that are separate from other cultures, places, and selves.

Melissa and other members of the Taiwanese high-tech diaspora are part of the trans-Pacific commuter jet set. They coexist in multiple geographic locales and nurture a transnational social network. They travel frequently, so while they may take up residence at a particular point in space and time, they are also readily in communication with persons in various places and time zones. The borders between time zones, between cultures, and between persons that existed in the twentieth century and earlier do not apply to Melissa and the growing group of trans-Pacific commuters.

Fax, email, cell phones, teleconferences, and cyber-meetings are the basic tools of this group. Some of them might construct both their company's and their personal home pages on the Internet. Having access to advanced telecommunications technology does not mean that those who lead trans-cultural lives are free from feelings of foreignness or alienation. These days, those of us who have access to a computer and a cable modem, just like the trans-Pacific commuters described above, are able to access the sights, sounds, and texts of foreign cultures in ways that would have seemed impossible to my grandmother. But unlike my grandmother or Joni Mitchell, who took it for granted that the self was a singular, unified entity, Melissa has adopted a self that embraces a shifting home identity—a self that is able to board a jet in San Francisco and land in Taipei twelve hours later without feeling homesick.

Melissa has replaced a traditional singular sense of self with one that is multiple. The construction of a multiple self has enabled her to become attached to both of her Pacific Rim homes at once, through new media and frequent travel that enables her to feel she is virtually in one home when she is at the other. A shifting, multiple self, a self that does not need to be rooted in an actual place, enables Melissa to shift from one home to another, from one landscape or social network to another with ease. A shifting home identity enables her to virtually return to the home that she left just hours earlier and thus avoid the identity crisis that was a way of life for Joni Mitchell and my grandmother.

I find that Melissa is not so different from me, or from many others that I know. As long as we have Internet access, we can virtually experience any time and any place. We can virtually coexist at different places, and interact with the global community. We differ from previous generations in that we have learned how to feel close to an electronic image of a physical place, which our ancestors would have described as an object detached from themselves. My grandmother needed the physical contact of actual local interaction to construct her sense of self, but Melissa has learned to replace interaction with local people and places with image interactions—virtual people and places—as she constructs her sense of self as an inhabitant of a global technological community. This is not to say that Melissa has no contact with actual living, breathing people; she does, certainly. Nevertheless, she is different from Mitchell or my grandmother in that she is just as comfortable with virtual images of faces and bodies as she is with actual faces and bodies. It is important to recognize here that the structure of her new technological way of interacting socially is also the structure that forms a bridge between a new definition of self and a new way of expressing one's self through home and landscape.

Trans-Pacific Commuters' Home Identities

The three patterns described above will soon become useful as I describe how the trans-Pacific commuters I have met have deftly expressed their unique identities through their choice of home, landscape, community, and social network. Although the three patterns have emerged in a sequence over time, I do not want to suggest that they cannot coexist in our current postmodern life.

If we live in different places, have different life paths, or are supported by different technologies, we might experience differing patterns regarding our home return and home identities. If we migrate several times and find that we are attached to more than one home or more than one landscape, we might develop different home return models and home identities associated with our different home places. While the phenomenon of trans-Pacific commuting is very new—developing in just the past decade—it is one that poses a new set of questions about how our views of ourselves, our homes, and our landscapes will evolve as we move into an uncharted future.

Toward the Trans-Pacific Home

Home Beyond the Walls of the House

The economic boom of the 1990s that led to the rapid rise of computer hardware and software companies on both sides of the Pacific Rim also led to the emergence of the new trend of global commuting. Thousands of Taiwanese-born high-tech engineers realized that they could greatly increase their career opportunities by regularly commuting with their families between two homes, one in Silicon Valley and the other in Taiwan (Hsu 1997, 73; Saxenian 1999, 34). "Trans-Pacific home phenomenon" is the term I use to refer to this lifestyle of the tens of thousands of high-tech engineers and their families who not only commute in their cars from their homes to their workplaces, but also commute in planes from their Silicon Valley homes to their Taiwanese homes.

The previous chapter introduces the topic of home identity, or the psychological-physical system of interrelationships in which the home and its surroundings represent one's personal identity. Each of us has a sense of ourselves that we have developed from our personal history (Lowenthal 1985, 197). Our sense of self, of "who we believe we are (our identity)," is something that we express, knowingly or unknowingly, at all times (Castells 1997, 6). The clothes we wear, the music we like or dislike, and our hairstyles are all channels for expressing who we are. The homes that we live in also enable us to express our individual identities (Marcus 1974, 1979, 1995). While a home can be thought of as an object that exists at a particular location, on a particular street in a particular city, I think of a home as more than a mere object. A home and its surroundings provide its residents with a sense of belonging, a sense of community, and a sense of self (Appleyard 1978; Sopher 1979; Marcus 1986).

Home, in other words, is not an object that is separate from its inhabitants. Instead, it is connected to us in very significant ways, allowing us to express who we are and what we are all about. In exploring the connection between home and self (home and identity), it is important to understand the connection between home and its surroundings. In the conversations I had with high-tech families, all of them at one point talked about their homes in the larger context of their surroundings. For some a home was a place that included an adjoining garden. For others the boundaries of their home extended to their neighborhood, community, district, or even region. So when I use the phrase "home place" or "home environment," I am referring to the personal map that people have in mind when they talk about their relationship with their home—a map that extends, to a lesser or greater extent, beyond the actual walls of their house.

Immigrant Transcultural Home Identity

Within the last ten years the issue of home identity, or how homes reflect people's personal identities, has been an emerging topic within contemporary intellectual discourse in fields as diverse as Asian American studies, anthropology, cultural geography, cultural studies, literary criticism, and landscape architecture. But few studies have focused on the immigrants' experience of struggling to reconcile their old identities with their newly forming American identities, as well as the role their old and new homes and landscapes play in that struggle.[1] In the past, when immigrants arrived in the United States, they were severed from their old homeland and either assimilated into the mainstream of American culture or lived isolated from the mainstream culture. The advent of easily accessible air transportation, new methods of telecommunication, and instant global connection through the Internet has expanded options for immigrants of the past decade beyond the either-or choice of assimilating into or living separate from mainstream America.

The Taiwan–to–Silicon Valley commuters I spoke to helped me to understand how those who have immigrated from one culture to another make sense of their home identity, even though they commute between two homes and two very different cultures. I use the phrase "transcultural home identity" to describe the relationship between the psychological reactions of how they relate themselves to their homes and the physical forms and the appearances of their homes. It reflects the additional complexity that trans-Pacific commuters encounter because their sense of self includes the connection across two cultures, and the connections between their old and new homes.

Beginning in 1997 I frequently flew back and forth between Silicon Valley and Hsinchu Science Park because I wanted to understand how high-tech engineers and CEOs who commuted regularly between their homes on both sides of the Pacific constructed the new relationship between their identities and their homes. As it turned out, it was not the overworked male engineers or CEOs but rather the "high-tech housewives" in their forties— the stay-at-home spouses of high-tech professionals—that provided me the insights into how the participants in the trans-Pacific lifestyle construct a relationship between their identities and their landscape. As Melissa (introduced in chapter 1) and other housewives shared their life stories with me, I came to understand how their trans-Pacific lives had led them to invent new, nontraditional relationships between their identities and their homes. The women I spoke with did not think about their homes in traditional terms. For them, home was not a single object rooted in a single location. For them, home existed simultaneously in multiple places. They had constructed new, nontraditional identities in which both the home and the self were embraced as multiple, nonstatic, shifting, and changing.

The Global Home from Women's Perspectives

The stay-at-home housewives I spoke with revealed their sense of a global home that emerged from living lives that called for a constant moving across cultures and places. This sense of global home reflected their having let go of traditional definitions that assume cultures, places, and selves are bordered entities separated from other cultures, places, and selves. At the surface, there was an ease in which they embraced living in multiple homes and communicating across vast distances. But a closer look revealed the intricate connections between identity and place; connections that signified complex sets of relationship between the local and the global (Brah 2003, Lesley Johnson 1999, Martin and Mohanty 1999, Mill 2003).

I want to revisit a topic introduced in the previous chapter, the difference between how Joni Mitchell and Melissa integrated their senses of what home meant to them with the way they created their individual senses of their selves. This difference is a good point of departure for understanding trans-cultural home identity. Both Mitchell and Melissa had experienced leaving a home located in one culture and arriving at another. Mitchell was born in Canada and left for California only as an adult. Melissa was born in Taiwan and then, similarly, left for California. Mitchell's traditional construction of identity as a static, predetermined entity, however, led her to believe that California was the place (and home) that truly reflected who she was. When Mitchell traveled outside her California cultural base, then, she carried her home identity with her.

Melissa, on the other hand, embodies a transcultural home identity. She not only carries her Taiwan *or* California identity with her when she travels between two places, but is able to simultaneously embody both homes when she travels from one to the other. Her sense of self is fluid rather than static, and so instead of getting homesick when she is away from one of her homes, she is able to virtually return.

Many members of the subculture of trans-Pacific commuters whom I spoke with experienced the same kind of transcultural home identity Melissa experienced. They didn't think they had to choose between one home and the other in order to achieve a healthy sense of themselves. Instead, they developed ways of intertwining their old home landscapes in Taiwan with their new ones in Silicon Valley. While they constantly traveled back and forth between two places physically, psychologically, they constantly switched back and forth between their fluid and multiple selves.

In describing the trans-Pacific commuters' relationship between home and self, I have intentionally avoided the use of the term "multicultural" to describe their lifestyles, instead using the term "transcultural." Their trans-cultural lives, their trans-Pacific commuter lifestyles, and their new ways of constructing a relationship between multiple homes and fluid multiple selves challenge the traditional notion that one's selfhood is naturally connected to one's birthplace or homeland.

The term "transcultural lifestyle" is derived from the new concept of transculturalism, a theoretical departure from the long-held notion that there are essential qualities that make cultures distinct from each other and unique in and of themselves. In his essay "Transculturality: The Puzzling Form of Cultures Today," Wolfgang Welsch points out that traditional concepts of cultures—including classic single culture, interculturalism, and multiculturalism—assume that "every culture can be distinguished and remain separated from other folks' cultures" (Welsch 1999, 195). However, transculturalism "sketches a different picture of the relation between cultures, not one of isolation and conflict, but one of entanglement, intermixing, and commonness" (ibid., 205). Welsch argues that we already live in a transcultural context. "Lifestyles no longer end at the borders of national cultures, but go beyond these. . . . There is no longer anything absolutely foreign. . . . Today, in a culture's internal relations—among its different ways of life—there exists as much foreignness as in its external relations with other cultures" (ibid., 197–98). Welsch's conception of transculturalism as an entangled, intermixed relation between cultures is a useful starting point for analyzing the relationship between identity and home.

Place Identity and Home Identity

Welsch's observation that the experience of living a transcultural lifestyle has led to the intermingling of one's domestic culture with many other foreign cultures coincides with the melding and mixing of cultural elements that I observed trans-Pacific commuters use to construct their lifestyles and identities. Those who lead a trans-Pacific commuter lifestyle have begun to blur the traditional distinction between the local and the far-away. Rather than being attached to their homelands and feeling a sense of loss when they travel to their far-away home, trans-Pacific commuters see themselves as simultaneously at home and far-away from home: simultaneously local and global.

Before the recent era of global commuting, the actual physical elements of one's home and local community were the basis for the formation of one's personal identity, but in the 1990s the technological revolution changed all that. The attachment to her home and the local landscape that my grandmother felt is not an attachment that Melissa feels. The map that my grandmother had in her mind—a map of Tienlou that had clear and rigid borders—was the basis of her home identity. Melissa's mental map, on the other hand, was one in which the traditional borders that separated the intimate from the global no longer existed. The traditional self that was bound to one's local home and place did not apply to her because she had integrated a new set of global communications devices, air transportation modes, and multimedia technologies into her nontraditional life. The new set of global tools Melissa used to navigate through her everyday life enabled her to think of herself as simultaneously attached to different homes, different land-scapes, and different cultures.

Yi-Fu Tuan's 1996 book *Cosmos and Hearth* helps frame the new way of constructing the relationship between home and self that members of the trans-Pacific commuter culture have adopted. "At a basic (reflex) level," Tuan writes, "the shift is surprising if only because the life-path of a human being moves naturally from 'home' to 'world,' from 'hearth' to 'cosmos' " (Tuan 1996, 2). Tuan argues that the dramatic change in today's transcultural background and context is foreignness intertwining with folk. Home is seen as the world; hearth extends to the cosmos (ibid., 8–9).

New technologies have enabled Melissa to conceive of her home as the world, an idea that my grandmother could not have understood because she lived at a time when homes were singular objects whose deep roots attached them to a single place. The lifestyles of members of the trans-Pacific commuter culture point to several new ways of conceiving the relationship between home/landscape and personal identity because they take into account the collapse of traditional ways of thinking about the way we live and how we become attached to the places where we live: the collapse of the deep-rooted home, the dissolution of the static identity, the separation between multiple cultures, and the end of one-way migration.

"Bi-gration": The Two-way Transcultural Life

Melissa and the other high-tech housewives I spoke with who frequently traveled back and forth between their original Taiwanese culture and their new American culture experienced a two-way migration, or what I call a "bi-gration." The fact that they were born into Taiwanese culture and later found themselves experiencing an American culture did not lead them to think they had to choose between America and Taiwan as the cultural basis of their identity. Because they didn't think of Taiwan and America as discrete and separate cultures, they were able to give up the old idea that their migration was a one-way journey that led from a homeland to a foreign land (Malkki 1995). Their new transcultural lifestyles, in which the Taiwanese and American components of their homes, their landscapes, and their identities mixed and melded, enabled them to give up the traditional thought that their migration to a new culture would mean that they had no choice but to leave their precious cultural and personal experiences behind.

My close observation of trans-Pacific commuter culture and my many conversations with those commuters have enabled me to differentiate between migration, a one-way finite event, and bi-gration, a two-way ongoing event (David Seamon 1985, 229). In the past, when immigrants entered the United States, they tended to disconnect from their geographic origins (both cultural and physical), and they either assimilated into the mainstream of American culture or lived somewhat isolated from the mainstream culture, often in an ethnic ghetto (Portes and Rumbaut 1990). Chinatown's population is a classic example of immigrants who were alienated from mainstream American culture while re-creating their home culture in a new land (Anderson 1987, 580–98; Kinkead 1992; Him 1992). And, for the most part, those Chinese immigrants who chose not to live in Chinatown adopted an American lifestyle and identity. But since the emergence of the bi-gration phenomenon, having to choose between staying Chinese or becoming American has become a thing of the past.

On the conceptual level, the Taiwanese high-tech families that I spoke with functioned as the carriers of mechanisms that blended the two residential cultures of Silicon Valley and the Hsinchu, Taiwan, regions that they migrated between. Their periodic two-way migration I call bi-gration because that term captures the notion of travel back and forth between two cultures. In contrast to migration, the one-way travel model that demanded that immigrants choose between the old and new cultures, as well as the old and new identities, bi-gration allows for the old and new to readily coexist; both the homeland and new-land cultures are continuously revisited, and so neither is left behind.

The pattern of bi-gration redefines the relationship between the local and the regional, as well as between insiders and outsiders. The following diagrams illustrate the difference between old migration and new bi-gration patterns.

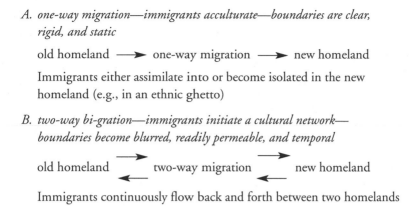

A. *one-way migration—immigrants acculturate—boundaries are clear, rigid, and static*

old homeland ⟶ one-way migration ⟶ new homeland

Immigrants either assimilate into or become isolated in the new homeland (e.g., in an ethnic ghetto)

B. *two-way bi-gration—immigrants initiate a cultural network— boundaries become blurred, readily permeable, and temporal*

old homeland   two-way migration   new homeland

Immigrants continuously flow back and forth between two homelands

Unconventional Identity, Unconventional Women

The conversations that I had with Melissa challenged me to rethink some of my assumptions about the construction of an Asian American home identity, assumptions that were based on thinking about immigrant home identity that was bounded by a conception of immigration as a one-way event (Sørensen and Olwig 2002, 1–2). After my conversations with Melissa I stopped thinking of trans-Pacific commuters as one-way immigrants and started thinking of them in terms of their experience of bi-gration. As I began to view them through the lens of bi-gration rather than migration I started understanding how a person could construct a sense of their home identity even though they commuted between two homes and two very different cultures.

Conventional wisdom suggested that it was natural for immigrants who had arrived in a new land to gradually erase the memories of their homeland and over time render a new picture of themselves that reflected their new social and physical surroundings. Melissa and two other Taiwanese-born women you will encounter in later chapters are unconventional in the sense that despite being great admirers of American culture, they did not feel that moving to the United States necessitated that they adopt an American identity for themselves. Because they didn't regard Taiwan and the United States as discrete, separate cultures, they were not bound by the old notion that their migration was a one-way journey that led from a homeland to a foreign land. Their Taiwanese and American methods of homemaking, their homes' landscapes, and their identities mixed and melded in their new transcultural lifestyles.

Seen in this light, the experiences of the women in this book are un-conventional. They are not torn between their native rural villages and the American homes where they have low-wage jobs, as are Levitt's peasant families from the Dominican Republic living in Boston (Levitt 2001). Nor are they performing the traditional role of Chinese housewives, as Hsu describes in her book *Dreaming of Gold, Dreaming of Home*. They are not required to live widowlike lives in Taishan, China, while their breadwinning husbands slip through the "Golden Gate" to San Francisco to pursue op-portunities that might one day bring wealth back to their Taishan homes (Hsu 2000). The majority of the Taiwanese American women described in this book are highly educated housewives. Some of them are, or have been, engineers, high-level managers, or business owners who were successful in their own careers. They hold degrees from prestigious American universities such as Stanford University, the University of Chicago, Michigan University, the University of Texas at Austin, or the various campuses of the University of California.

Esther Chow (1987) points out that "domination by men is a commonly shared oppression for Asian American women." She argues that "these women have been socialized to accept their devaluation, restricted roles for women, psychological reinforcement of gender stereotypes and a subordi-nate position within Asian communities as well as in the society at large" (ibid., 286). But we cannot simply categorize these Taiwanese American high-tech housewives as traditional Asian American housekeeping, husband-serving women who have been "oppressed" by their male partners. Many of them told me that they enjoyed being a mother and a housewife. And, al-though many previously had professional careers, they decided not to con-tinue working outside the home. Some of them told me that it felt great to be able to stay at home and spend time with their friends while their hus-bands had to work so hard to make the money needed to support their fam-ilies.

Winnie and Julie, two of the many housewives I spoke with, had given up the old notion that an immigrant had no choice but to leave her home-land identity behind and replace it with a foreign identity. Immigration, seen through this old lens, assumed that those who came to America would, in the end, adopt an American identity. But for Winnie, Julie, and others I spoke with identity was a personal choice, not a foregone conclusion. Instead of thinking that they had to adopt an American identity, they viewed identity as a personal choice that emerged from within their very own experiences of bi-gration, of journeying back and forth between cultures. Rather than assuming that she must fight to retain her old identity or adopt a completely new one, each felt that she could create a new identity on her own terms.

Winnie: Transplanting Culture

Situated in the Hsinchu Science Park community in Taiwan, Winnie's Taiwanese-accented Mission Revival–style house could have been in any California suburb, with its red-tile roof and white faux adobe walls. Winnie and her family had lived in this residential area of Hsinchu Science Park known as the Bamboo Village for ten years, and in Palo Alto, California, for one year. She was in her early fifties, and all three of her children attended the local bilingual school. Her husband's extended family had already moved to the United States by the time he and Winnie had moved in the other direction, from Silicon Valley to Taiwan. However, having relatives in the United States enabled Winnie and her husband to relive their earlier bi-gration pattern through regular visits to the United States at least twice a year, with one visit always planned for the Christmas holidays. In addition to their frequent family trips to America, the children attended youth camp in Silicon Valley every summer. As I spoke with Winnie it became clear that the frequent trips back to California served to keep the embers of Winnie's Silicon Valley memories alive.

At one point in our conversation she excitedly told me, "I felt it was great to have a community like that. The life that I and the other wives had was very happy and joyful there in Silicon Valley. We hung out together and chatted, and did nothing. However, our husbands had to work very, very hard. Nevertheless, I often ask my husband if we can go back to Silicon Valley, or if we can migrate there." Winnie went on to tell me that although she and her family only stayed at their Palo Alto house for one year, it was one of the most memorable years of her life. That year started off when her neighbor greeted her with a homemade cake the first day that she moved into her new home. After sharing how that experience "deeply touched" her, she went on to describe the more mundane aspects of her life, but with no less excitement. She took pleasure in telling me about the Silicon Valley public services she appreciated, such as how she enjoyed recycling her garbage.

Winnie's Palo Alto home was a single-family detached house with a swimming pool in the backyard. She recalled how much she loved the house and the adjacent garden, saying, "I loved that garden very much. I liked living in a house with a garden. The garden is so important to me. I never took care of my garden before I lived in America." She observed that Americans were more likely to spend their time maintaining their gardens than their houses, and that it was quite acceptable for an American home to be average looking if the garden was beautiful. Winnie explained, "now I think a garden is even more important than a house. It is just like the face of our house. I should spend my time decorating my garden. It's for the public. I think beautiful public landscapes enhance the quality of life. This is what I learned from my American experiences."

The garden was the face that Winnie's home presented to the public. Her own identity was enmeshed with the garden that she described as her "home's face"; she perceived it as if it were her own face. It was important for her to present a beautiful face that rivaled those that her neighbors' homes presented. The year she lived in Palo Alto was also the first year that she followed her mostly Caucasian neighbors in the annual tradition of decorating her garden and the exterior of her house with Christmas lights. "The whole house becomes very charming and beautiful over the Christmas season," she told me.

Winnie's recollections of the American use of the front yard as a public face became the prelude for a story of victory and defeat. Shortly after she and her family had returned to Bamboo Village after their one-year residence abroad, recalling her late father's ritualistic adorning of the front entry with the national flag on national holidays, she tried to convince her neighbors to join her in decorating their lawns and homes with flags in celebration of National Day, the date of birth of the Republic of China (Taiwan). But, despite her enthusiasm, no one bought into the idea.

Winnie, however, was undeterred by this temporary defeat, and her subsequent Christmas lights campaign resulted in a brilliant victory. Less than eight weeks after she experienced a complete lack of support for the flag installation, her neighbors joined her with enthusiasm in setting up Christmas lights that lit up their Bamboo Village neighborhood. Winnie had succeeded in what she called "transplanting" a piece of her life in America that she valued and felt passionate about.

Winnie's stories about American objects such as the Christmas lights and her garden that she transplanted to her native cultural soil enabled me to better understand how she constructed her transcultural home identity. The transplanting of Taiwanese flags and Christmas lights pointed to Winnie's shifting, entangled, and culturally overlapping sense of her self. By transplanting objects that recall both her childhood and her American experiences, she was able to sustain both sides of her Taiwanese and Asian American dual identity.

Winnie's bi-gration experience enabled her to let go of the set of rules that prescribed either a tenacious retention of one's previous identity and culture or a practical adoption of the identity and cultural framework of one's new location. Her identity was not prescribed or predetermined, but rather it was self-determined. Winnie was just as interested in incorporating the Taiwanese flag decoration that she recalled from her childhood into her contemporary Taiwanese life as she was in importing the use of American Christmas lights. Her cultural references were varied rather than pure: the Taiwanese flag referred to one culture while the American Christmas lights referred to another, and yet both were equally powerful symbols for her. This incorporation of diverse cultural references enabled her to mix and match the two sides of her self, and ultimately gave her control of her personal process of self-creation.

Winnie told me that not only did she transplant the use of Christmas lights, but her children, having experienced an American Halloween and Easter, looked forward to trick-or-treating and hunting for Easter eggs, despite the fact that these two rituals had never been a part of their life in Taiwan. It may sound like Winnie and her family were very Americanized. However, her house in Bamboo Village, although it had an American exterior, had a mix of styles in the interior, with a modernist living room and a very Taiwanese kitchen. Her modern living room was a little bit dark but cozy, but her kitchen and dining room were wonderfully chaotic. Piles of Chinese paintings and books occupied the dining table and chairs, and she had to rearrange those piles to make room for me to sit. Her daily life blended a beautiful outdoor garden (a reflection of her suburban American life), a neat and cozy living room that she transplanted from her Palo Alto home, and a cluttered kitchen that revealed her Taiwanese culinary tendencies.

Inhabiting a home that contained three very different types of spatial experiences didn't suggest any conflicts or contradictions for Winnie. She made no attempt to integrate the spaces, and her description of the spaces did not employ any modernist vocabulary that would have made such integration possible. From a Modernist perspective, a single house could contain lots of different kinds of spaces as long as they shared a common aesthetic thread that served to unify them into a coherent whole. Following a Modernist logic, the absence of a unifying thread compromises a house's unity and coherence. But there was no conflict for Winnie. She enjoyed each of her different and unique spaces without thinking that they had to be knitted into a unified whole. Winnie's transcultural construction of self enabled her to *dissolve* the problem of cultural uniqueness rather than spend time *solving* the Modernist problem of creating coherent wholes. There was no problem with the multiplicity of cultural spaces and references that her home contained. Instead of thinking that she needed to strive for a coherent explanation of how such unique cultures could exist together under one roof, she playfully used her knowledge of those cultures to create an ever-changing story about her house, her garden, and her self. The house, the garden, and the self combined and recombined to tell a never-ending, always-changing story.

Julie: A Collage of Cultural Experiences

The family of Julie, in her late forties, was one of the first to move back from America to live in Hsinchu Science Park. She traveled to the United States with her husband a couple of times a year for business and family trips, as well as for their children's summer camps. Before we talked about her current home, Julie fondly recalled the house where she had grown up. The house no longer existed physically, but it nonetheless seemed as if it would always occupy a space in her memory. Her childhood home had been located in the wealthy Tienmu district, just north of central Taipei. Her beloved house had been a timber-frame Japanese colonial house (Fig. 2.1) with a very large garden that resembled a small orchard, with rows of azaleas and camellias and other ornamental plants that sprang up to her eye level. She said she often cheerfully examined the colors and shapes of the leaves of

FIG. 2.1. A typical single-family detached Japanese house. Many mainlanders who migrated to Taiwan after World War II resided in this type of house in urban areas of Taiwan. Source: Edward S. Morse, *Japanese Homes and Their Surroundings* (New York: Dover Publications, 1961), 56.

various plants. As we chatted, she remembered how she and her father often sat in the garden, sipping tea and telling stories until midnight.

Julie reminisced about her passage from childhood to adulthood and recalled leaving her childhood home for the first time in 1971, when she graduated from National Taiwan University and journeyed overseas to continue her studies in the United States. Although she moved to the United States more than thirty years ago, her childhood home would often resurface in her consciousness. Then, one summer day, her mother called her in New Jersey to tell her that they were going to sell their house in the Tienmu district. "I flew back just for the last chance to stay in it for three months. After my departure, my parents sold it." Our conservation brought up fond memories for her. "I have been attached to this house deeply for my entire life," Julie told me.

> I have many special memories of this house. I enjoyed sitting in the yard alone, immersed within the poetic atmosphere. I learned to play Chinese zither there during my college years. My father got two stone benches with a stone table for me, though I didn't know where and how he got them.

The most memorable feeling for me was when I played my Chinese zither. The sounds of the vibrating strings harmonized as they bounced off the stone table and echoed throughout the garden. It was so peaceful, but lonely. I haven't had the same feeling anywhere later in my life.

As the tide of memory began to ebb, Julie began describing her current home in the Bamboo Village of Hsinchu, Taiwan. She and her family were among the first "foreigners" to move back from the United States. They had lived in the Bamboo Village for nearly sixteen years. Although they rented the house, Julie felt it was hers, saying, "When you live here long enough, you don't quite feel the difference regarding the legal ownership." So even though renters were not technically permitted to modify homes, Julie's sense of ownership motivated her to make changes that she wanted.

Julie described how she and her husband

extended the house and took over half of its front porch and backyard. We tore down the existing outside walls on both sides. At the front entry, we added the acrylic-glass panels to create a foyer out of the leftover porch space, since it's windy and often rainy here. In the back, we added a tatami tearoom, which created a peaceful corner space at the edge of our central public area. The central public area is our living and dining room. We took out the interior wall and connected the two places. It looked more spacious. I like to live in a bigger suburban house in a quiet area. I am not willing to move into an apartment. Luckily enough, I have never lived in an apartment my whole life. (Fig. 2.2)

I was intrigued by Julie's story of having overcome legal restrictions to create the home that she wanted, and by the process by which she had drawn on various types of spaces recalled from her different residential experiences in different cultural settings. At the beginning of our conversation she mentioned that she could not return to her childhood neighborhood because everything that had been so familiar as a child had been much altered. She told me she would rather return to her memories of the place than return to the real place, because in her memory nothing had changed, whereas in reality many things had.

Julie would never return to Tienmu for fear of finding that things had changed, which would lead to an unwanted disruption of the time and space that she had preserved in her memory. But, despite her fear of facing the changes that she would certainly encounter if she returned to Tienmu, she

FIG. 2.2. A typical multistory apartment building in Taiwan. Graphic: Kenya Thompson.

was preoccupied with modifying her Hsinchu home. She controlled the past by keeping her childhood home just the way it was within her memory, and at the same time she controlled the present by changing her current home to suit her needs and tastes.

Because the form of her childhood home would be forever frozen in her memory, the form of her present home was not important for Julie. What really mattered to her was her ability to participate in the home-building process. Her status as a renter did not deter her from modifying her modern American-style duplex home to fit her needs. The physical elements of her home reflected the four residential cultures she had experienced in her life: American, Taiwanese, Chinese, and Japanese. First, she added a fabric-covered porch, a very popular form of wind and rain protection in Hsinchu. Second, the tatami room echoed the tranquil Japanese garden of her childhood. Third, her Chinese dining room, with a large, round Chinese table that could seat about twenty people, served as the house's social hub when friends visited. Finally, her American-style living room was not only spacious but also housed a modern leather sofa set and a fitness machine. A sense of openness was the most important quality to Julie, who recalled how much she had enjoyed the spacious qualities of an American-style detached house and a Japanese house that were her previous homes. These homes provided her with the spacious quality she liked—a quality she sought to replicate in her home despite legal restrictions that prohibited renters from modifying their residence.

The home that Julie created was a collage of sorts, composed of overlapping cultural materials. Although she refused to return to her childhood neighborhood, she had created a mosaic home that integrated her past experiences; she reconstructed certain portions of her life experiences and installed them in a home that did not belong to her from the legal standpoint, but did very much belong to her from the standpoint of her own memories of multiple cultures she had experienced in her life. Unlike many others within the trans-Pacific commuter culture, whose homes existed simultaneously within multiple places, Julie constructed a single home where various memories, multiple places, and an assortment of cultural experiences existed simultaneously.

Bi-gration and Individualization

When cultures mix, as they do in a transcultural lifestyle, there is no single culture left behind when one travels to a "foreign" culture. The trans-Pacific commuters' transcultural lifestyles permit them to think of themselves as belonging to many cultures. The idea that one possesses an everlasting home culture that is opposed to all other "foreign" cultures has been replaced by the experience of embodying a cultural mix in which the foreign and familiar coexist.

Elements of traditional lifestyles that once existed in isolation from one another exist simultaneously in the transcultural lives of trans-Pacific commuters. For trans-Pacific commuters homes, landscapes, and communities are experienced as *physical* realities, but they are also experienced as well as *virtual* realities: they are experienced through the variety of electronic media that have become a familiar part of their lives. There are several shared aspects of their individual constructions of their lifestyle that mark a very uncommon approach to constructing landscape and identity. All three women are part of a growing number of global commuters whose twenty-first-century lifestyles have enabled them to cross the width of an ocean with speed and comfort that their parents could never have imagined. Jets, computers, cell phones, and satellites have made it possible to commute across the Pacific, a once-insurmountable physical boundary. As a result, the vast psychological boundary between one's homeland and one's new home that previous generations of immigrants have had to construct is no longer a reality for trans-Pacific commuters.

It is possible that members of the trans-Pacific commuter culture are the first generation of immigrants whose journey across the width of an ocean has not demanded that they choose between a homeland or new home identity. Bi-gration has enabled global commuters to construct a sense of self and a sense of home that does not require a choice between cultures. The old notion of choosing a single culture, identity, home, and landscape has dissolved and been replaced by a process in which the immigrant's sense of self is constructed by mixing and matching cultures, identities, homes, and landscapes.

Melissa, Winnie, and Julie have been presented here because they embody certain characteristics that reflect the newly emerging trans-Pacific commuter culture. At the same time, each of the women in this chapter has constructed a home and an identity that is unlike the others. This is important because it points to their having freed themselves from an old conception of self and home as essential, an old conception of self and home as static and predetermined. This attempt to *de-essentialize* the definitions of human identity, home, and landscape reflects the emergence of a recent feminist and postmodern critique of the traditional notion of "an essential home that mirrors an essential self."[2] The newly emerging discourse guided by this critique seeks to replace the notion that the purpose of life is to strive for purity and perfection with the understanding that life can be enjoyed by playing with the chaotic, diverse, complicated, and imperfect set of persons and events that is constantly crossing one's path. Seen through the lens of this new discourse, the mixing and matching of cultures in the construction of each of these women's homes can be seen as a process of apprehending and making creative use of the chaos-driven diversity and cultural contingencies one comes in contact with toward one's own ends and individual sense of agency.

People

THREE

Made By Taiwan: The Trans-Pacific Commuters

The previous chapter discusses how trans-Pacific commuters readily live a life of simultaneity. Bi-gration has impacted how we integrate images and bodily experiences with our home identities. In my grandmother's example, memories of the landscape of her home village were the building blocks of her identity. These memories often intertwined with her daily life in Taiwan when she talked to someone who shared similar memories and experiences.

The mothers of both of my parents were from the same village in Shangdong Province. When they were both alive, they chatted daily about the other villagers. They often began a conversation by saying, "So-and-so's children have probably already gotten married by now. When we left home they were just babies. Time flies. Twenty years have already passed." Another familiar chat began "It's the time to harvest the *gaoliang* (sorghum) at home." Then, glancing at me, they would say, "You've never seen the *gaoliang* fields. Their stalks are tall and thick, unlike the rice plant you see in Taiwan; *gaoliang* grows taller than a person. Some people have gotten lost in the *gaoliang* fields. They might have walked for days and nights, but they couldn't find their way out." These memories of people and landscapes remained very vivid in my grandmothers' minds. However, after my father's mother passed away in her early eighties, my mother's mother seldom talked about those memories with others. The language and conversations she had shared with her long-time partner in memory had formed a unique pathway back to their home village. When those conversations were no longer possible, her memories became frozen and isolated; even she herself could not touch them.

Bodily experiences transmute into memories and transform who, what, and where we identify with. We are part of the landscapes we once encountered, while our daily landscapes are part of our self-construction. "If one has been raised at a particular place, its textures and sensations, its smells and sounds, are recalled as they felt to a child's, adolescent's, and adult's body. Even if one's history there is short, a place can still be felt as an extension of the body, especially that walking body, passing through and becoming part of the landscape," writes Lucy Lippard in *The Lure of The Local* (Lippard 1997, 34). In the case of trans-Pacific commuters, their bodily experiences that construct their transcultural home identities have been changed by information technology. With recent advances in transportation and communication, the trans-Pacific commuters' landscape identities have started to blend a tactile and static bodily experience with temporary encounters and visual images with places. Their emerging landscape identities embody their frequent travel from one place to another and the "go-between" pathways that bridge one place with others.

A Floating Community

The length of time one has experienced a particular place is a pertinent criteria for drawing the social boundaries of a community. "In Maine, where you come from is always an issue," writes Lucy Lippard. There are four "fixed" tiers of status that Mainers use to distinguish the relationships among all residents: tourist/out-of-stater, summer person or someone "from away," local, and native (ibid., 33). It is difficult to switch from one tier to another because these tiers are defined by the "rootedness" of the places that people inhabit. One's grandson can be the fifth generation in one's family that visits Maine every summer, but this family might still be considered summer people "from away." For native Mainers, local pride is a product of their long struggle with the harsh climate, both natural and economic. The native Mainers, residents of the second poorest state in the United States, believe that those "from away" may be street-smart or book-smart, "but they lack the knowledge that a true Mainer has of how to survive physically and mentally in a harsh climate," says Douglas Rooks (ibid., 35).

Rather than define trans-Pacific commuter identity in "in-group" and "out-group" (the way that Mainers define themselves and the outsiders they encounter), I define them in terms of their "go-between" life-style; a life-style that calls for constant travels between homes and landscapes located on opposite sides of the Pacific rim. The 2002 report *Local and Global Networks of Immigrant Professionals in Silicon Valley* surveyed two thousand foreign-born engineers (Taiwanese, Indian, mainland Chinese, and others) in Silicon Valley (Saxenian, Motoyama, and Quan, 2002).[1] Its striking finding was that Taiwanese engineers traveled back to their home country more frequently than Indian and mainland Chinese engineers. Of these three foreign-born groups, the report concluded, "the Taiwanese stand out: 20 percent of them report returning home for business two to four times a year compared to 9 percent of Indians and 8 percent of Mainland Chinese" (ibid., 25).

In addition, the report pointed out that, on average, 38 percent of Taiwanese engineers travel to Taiwan from the United States once a year for business reasons (compared to 39 percent of Indian and 31 percent of mainland Chinese engineers). Six percent of the Taiwanese visited more than five times a year, compared with 4 percent of Indians and 5 percent of mainland Chinese. Only 36 percent of the Taiwanese hadn't visited Taiwan in the past three years. In contrast, 56 percent of mainland Chinese and 48 percent of Indians hadn't visited their home country for three years. The survey focused on high-tech engineers, managers, and CEOs and the business trips they took. It did not collect information about other trips that had been taken by other family members, such as spouses, children, and grandparents. Based on my fieldwork, if we include other family members and their family trips, we would discover that fewer than 36 percent of high-tech families had not visited Taiwan in the past three years.

Suddenly, it seems that the sky above the Pacific Ocean must be very busy with all the Taiwanese engineers and their families commuting between Silicon Valley and their Taiwan homes. Among these "made *by* Taiwan"[2] trans-Pacific commuters there are as many as seven types occupying different status tiers: the astronauts, the transplants, the returnees, the wanna-bes, the motherlanders, the travelers, and the green card moms.[3] Remarkably, unlike Maine's fixed tiers of natives and outsiders, the status of trans-Pacific commuters change, and families often shift from one tier to another. Furthermore, they often occupy multiple status tiers simultaneously.

Astronauts are those individuals who have created the Silicon Valley success legacy. Their achievements have been described in many newspapers, magazines, and studies (Hsu 1997; Deng 1998; and Lubman 1999, to name a few). This group consists of those who maintain homes in both the Hsinchu region and Silicon Valley, as well as the 6 percent who live in Silicon Valley but travel to Taiwan more than five times a year. In most cases, these astronauts are the CEOs or senior managers of companies and have jobs that require frequent business trips around the world. Astronauts also often travel because of their transnational family arrangements. Some high-tech engineer husbands have families living in Silicon Valley while they rent a home in Hsinchu Science Park, where they work. Every month or two these husbands shuttle back to Silicon Valley to spend a long weekend with their families.

Although the astronaut phenomenon is well known, there is no solid data on how many belong to this group. Based on the estimated numbers provided by the high-tech engineers I interviewed in Hsinchu, there were approximately 1,200 in 2003.[4] According to them, those that hold PhDs are most likely to be astronauts. The educational data that Hsinchu Science Park released in September 2004 shows the total number of employees working there was 112,877, with 1,291 PhDs (Hsinchu Science Park 2004b).[5] If we include senior-level managers who are not engineers with a PhD, the total number of astronauts is about 3,181 (Hsinchu Science Park 2004c).[6] In other words, only 2.8 percent of all personnel belong to the group of astronauts. Although the number of astronauts is only a small *minority* of the 112,000 people holding jobs within Hsinchu science park, they are the *majority* of those who live in the residential area within the park. Local residents assume that since the astronaut group comprise a majority of the park's residential area population, that they also comprise the majority who are employed within the park. This misconception has led locals to believe that most of Hsinchu's high-tech employees who have families, have two homes and live trans-Pacific commuter lives.

"Green card moms" is a term that Hsinchu residents use to refer to the housewives of CEOs and senior managers. These wives are in the process of obtaining U.S. citizenship, so they must stay in the United States for at least six months per year. Most are unemployed and frequently fly back and forth between Taiwan and Silicon Valley. "No company will hire them, but they don't need to work anyway. Their CEO husbands will take care of them," one Hsinchu resident said about them. It is through their social contact with Hsinchu residents living outside the park that these green card moms have spread the story of their trans-Pacific, jet-set, two home lifestyles. Hsinchu resident's perceptions (as well as misperceptions) of the astronaut group have been highly influenced by the green card wives portraits of their own lives. These women have played a major role in transferring cross-cultural life experiences, but they have been overlooked by most researchers in the past. They frequently travel transnationally, with or without their husbands. While their husbands are occupied primarily with business and career development, the green card moms are responsible for managing family life and the home. They are therefore major consumers in both Silicon Valley and the Hsinchu region. Many of them arrange for their children to live and attend school in Silicon Valley, while they themselves travel back and forth to manage their two homes, one for their husbands and one for their children. Although their husbands are the ones who participate in the high-tech industry, it is the wives who establish the family's transcultural lifestyle.[7]

Returnees and transplants share many American or Silicon Valley experiences with the astronauts and green card moms. The returnees are those who have studied and worked overseas, often in the United States, but have chosen to resettle in Taiwan, most likely to work in Hsinchu Science Park. They make frequent short business trips back to the United States, and they visit their relatives there during the Christmas vacation. Meanwhile, they send their children to summer camps in Silicon Valley or other places in the United States. The transplants, on the other hand, are those who studied overseas, mostly in the United States, and now work in Silicon Valley. They have settled their families in Silicon Valley and don't consider resettling in Taiwan. Their family members or relatives, however, travel back and forth yearly.

The wanna-bes have had experiences of studying, working, and living in America. But because they are at junior level within the high-tech industry, their job status does not call for frequent commuting back and forth between Taiwan and the United States. Their ambition is to start up their own companies and become astronauts themselves someday. There are two types of wanna-bes. One type consists of some of the returnees presently living in Taiwan but contemplating a return to Silicon Valley one day. The other type consists of those transplants presently living in Silicon Valley but looking for an opportunity to return to Taiwan. The families of younger engineers compose the group of wanna-bes. There is no quantitative data for the wanna-bes in Silicon Valley. With respect to those in Hsinchu, according to the fieldwork I conducted, half, or approximately 9,700 in September 2004 (Hsinchu Science Park 2004b), hold Master's degrees conferred by American institutions of higher learning. They consider themselves members of the loosely defined "Silicon Valley club." Generally speaking, most have lived in the United States for one to four years, though some finish their studies in nine months and soon return to Taiwan, while others may take two years to get a degree and then stay in Silicon Valley to gain work experience in the States. They often consider resettling in Silicon Valley, either to provide better educational opportunities for their children or because of the tempting job offers.

The motherlanders are technical workers trained in Taiwan, with educational credentials ranging from a vocational school diploma to a Master's degree in engineering, who work in the Hsinchu region. Although some have traveled to the United States, motherlanders have never lived there. The total number of motherlanders was about 63,300 in September 2004 (ibid.). This motherlander group, which comprises the majority within the park, not only experiences an imported Silicon Valley architecture and landscape, they also experience an American set of office protocols and practices. In daily conversation they often hear co-workers or colleagues (astronauts and returnees) refer to their Silicon Valley or other American experiences.

The last group is the travelers. All high-tech engineers are travelers to some degree, because their companies regularly send them to work in their branch offices or for their overseas clients. These branch offices are located around the globe in many developed and developing nations. Besides the United States, the people I interviewed most often traveled to China, Australia, New Zealand, Germany, the Netherlands, Spain, and Japan.

Accentuating the transnational nature of their work, some astronauts have returned to Silicon Valley, resettled there, and become transplants. At the same time some motherlanders, especially the most senior engineers and managers, have moved their families to Silicon Valley for the first time. Recent joint ventures between companies in Hsinchu and Silicon Valley have bridged all subgroups, allowing high-level managers and senior engineers an opportunity to migrate to Silicon Valley. The motherlanders' arrival in Silicon Valley reinforces the "go-between" Hsinchu Science Park network that functions as the catalyst to nurture transnational family life and trans-Pacific home identities.

Some trans-Pacific commuters revealed that they are often confused about where home is because their two home environments and the people they encounter daily are simultaneously too similar and very different. Meanwhile, within their daily work lives, they tend to form social cliques with other trans-Pacific commuters. Locals may overhear talk about the details of living a transnational life, but they are excluded from these conversations. This scenario often leads to resentment and friction between the locals and the globals. Landscape memories create tensions both during working hours and at informal social occasions. The Taiwan-trained motherlanders often pejoratively call others with more experience in the United States "those Americans." Ken, a motherlander, complained,

> Those "Americans" never talk about neighborhoods like Yan-ji Street [an area where Ken spent many of his teenage years]. They prefer chatting about those places in California. Since we have never been there, we can only remain quiet in those conversations. I find this hard to take. Their collective memory seems to be fixated upon the California landscape. They cannot rewind their memory, skip the California section, and share their youthful Taiwanese past with us.

Steve, a wanna-be, has a different point of view about the professional differences between the U.S.-trained and Taiwan-trained engineers. He told us that "American-trained engineers are more likely to follow all necessary requirements, step by step. They provide higher standards of inspection. Taiwan-trained guys are different. They don't like to follow the rules. They are sneaky, just like the general Taiwanese society, and that can cause a big problem in the final products."

There are also social gaps between the wives of motherlanders and the green card moms. Green card moms have their own exclusive network of friends and acquaintances in both Hsinchu Science Park and Silicon Valley, and they are often members of the Hwei-chu (Gentle Bamboo) Housewives' Club, which is explained further in chapter 7. Lauren was the wife of a motherlander who had recently joined the ranks of the astronauts when he had been transferred to a Silicon Valley company. They decided to move to Silicon Valley because it provided better educational opportunities for their children. She admitted that her green card mom friends led such a luxurious lifestyle that she could barely keep up. Jessie, an astronaut's wife, said, "one can only get acceptably stylish stuff in Silicon Valley. It's my American experiences that nurture my taste in home design."

Although there are various subtle tensions among the subgroups of trans-Pacific commuters, all of them emphasize that their high-tech jobs afford them a higher social status in Taiwan. They prefer to live with people who have a similar social status, and they all insert English phrases into their Chinese speech, regardless of whether they have studied overseas or not.[8] In other words, the Silicon Valley business culture dominates the way that trans-Pacific commuters present themselves in their everyday lives.

All the subgroups play an equally important role in the completion of the *jin-yi-huan-xiang* journey described in chapter 1. This narrative involves one who leaves his or her village while young and poor and returns home years later, after making a name for him- or herself. Those who come back to the village after achieving prestige are the returnees, while those that stay behind and welcome the returnees home are the motherlanders. Returnees have to earn the elevated status that motherlanders respect and aspire to. This status does not mean as much if the returnees do not return to their hometowns.

Only through the motherlanders' eyes does the social status that the returnees have earned become transformed into the prestige that influences the returnees' sense of self. Because intimate bonds link motherlanders and returnees, returnees understand and value their home society. The moment that motherlanders behold a returnee's homecoming is the moment that enables the returnee to reconceive his old identity. Through motherlanders' eyes, returnees are not poor young hatchlings any more; they are handsome eagles soaring high. On the other hand, the homecoming of the poet He described in chapter 1 illustrates the flip side of this story. When He returned to his hometown, the children in the village asked him, "Where do you come from, my guest?" This unexpected question made He realize that the intimate bond between his home village and himself had been broken. Those in his village viewed him as a stranger who was merely passing through. There is no defining moment that enables He to rewrite his identity status.

As in the classic *jin-yi-huan-xiang* narrative, the defining moment of the contemporary trans-Pacific journey is the moment that the astronauts, green card moms, transplants, and returnees meet with motherlanders. Motherlanders respect higher education and U.S. citizenship. Only from the motherlanders' view do the trans-Pacific commuters seem to be dressed in the trendiest fashions. From the mainstream American view, in contrast, Taiwanese Americans are just one subgroup of the Asian American minority. More important, those with PhDs seldom receive as much respect in the United States as they do in Chinese society. Most Americans will only pursue a PhD if they wish to teach at a university. In the culture of college-educated Taiwanese, in contrast, attaining a PhD is expected. If you get only a Master's degree, friends and family are likely to ask, "Why did you drop out?"

Higher Education Overseas

Education means everything for Taiwanese parents. Many green card moms I interviewed had established a transnational family life, their engineer husbands settled in Hsinchu Science Park while they and their children stayed in Silicon Valley. I asked them why they stayed in Silicon Valley while their husbands returned to Taiwan. Why didn't the whole family move together?

"Children's education is the most critical issue for many high-tech families," Careen told me. She explained that most high-tech parents considered the United States to provide a higher-quality education and more economic opportunities than Taiwan. The majority of high-tech parents came to the United States to pursue Master's degrees or PhDs after they finished their college degrees. Many were confronted with a language barrier and many cultural challenges when they first arrived. Therefore, given the choice, they prefer that their children begin their American educations early. Careen went on to say that it was more challenging for returnee families to move back to the United States together if they had already settled back in Taiwan. The most sensible solution was for the husbands to work in Taiwan, even though their wives and children resided in Silicon Valley homes. This solution called for housewives to become the go-betweens who traveled between Taiwan and Silicon Valley on a regular basis.

Clearly, Taiwanese parents are willing to sacrifice their family life for their children's education. But why should higher degrees from American universities be so highly valued? In a way, what the high-tech engineer parents are trying to do is very similar to what Dolores Hayden has described in her *Re-*

designing the American Dream: they are trying to provide their children a home "where they can give their children 'all the things we didn't have' " (Hayden 1984, 18). In the American context, "all the things we didn't have" means a "dream home" with a large backyard, a big family room, a gas-fired barbecue, and a swing set. In the Taiwanese context, a high-quality education from a prestigious American university is the common aspiration.

Studying overseas and returning as a PhD with American citizenship is the contemporary version of the *jin-yi-huan-xiang* experience. Many high-tech engineers who left Taiwan as underprivileged young students have returned years later as high-income professionals. Their degree from a famous university and their American citizenship are the *jin-yi* (beautiful clothes) that the Taiwanese admire. More important, achieving American citizenship is equivalent to reaching the top of the social ladder in Taiwan, and studying overseas is the single most important step toward fulfilling that dream for most Taiwanese families. Studying overseas indeed leads one down the path on the contemporary *jin-yi-huan-xiang* journey. Saxenian's 2002 report reveals that 79 percent of Taiwanese and mainland Chinese engineers attended schools in America before working, while only 54 percent of Indian engineers took a similar migration pathway (Saxenian 2002).

The Taiwanese respect for higher education and admiration of Americanization are the fundamental social values that have fueled the desire to study overseas. Chinese societies, influenced by Confucianism, have bestowed profound respect on those with a higher education for centuries. Following Confucian doctrines and social order, traditional Chinese society was structured into four classes. From the top to the bottom were the *shi* (the literati), the *nong* (farmers), the *gong* (labors), and the *shang* (merchants). Everyone revered the *shi* class, and thus pursuing a higher education, passing the national examinations, and getting a job in the bureaucratic system were the means for people in the lower classes to improve their social status.

Taiwanese society today is still fundamentally influenced by this value. People with a PhD receive more respect than those without, so parents encourage their children to continue their educations, while the government promotes public education, from elementary schools to colleges. According to the 2003 annual report of the Ministry of Education, the percentage of students with a higher education in Taiwan in 2000 (including students at the open university and supplementary junior colleges) was 4.37 percent

(Ministry of Education 2005). This percentage rivaled those of the United States (3.2 percent), Italy (3.14 percent), and France (3.58 percent). Each summer thousands of Taiwanese students pack their luggage and travel to the United States or Europe for postgraduate education.[9]

Why are degrees from the West, and specifically the United States, so highly valued in Taiwanese society? To answer this question, we need to briefly consider contemporary Chinese history. The tradition of study overseas was initiated in the mid-nineteenth century. Technological changes concomitant with political and economic transformations superimposed by foreign interests have fundamentally influenced China. Throughout the twentieth century, Chinese tradition and Western modernization were at odds, and Chinese scholars and government officials believed that only Western technology could help the Chinese address their social conflicts and underdeveloped economy. This consensus shaped the thinking that led to the Chinese preference for study abroad. Yung Wing was the first Chinese student to study in the United States, in 1847. Later, many generations of talented Chinese students followed in his footsteps, studying abroad to fulfill their responsibility to contribute to Chinese modernization (Qian 1997, 27–33).

Taiwan, China's long colonized and marginalized island, shared and carried on this tradition of overseas study. Taiwan has always paid homage to the cultures of powerful outsiders. Prior to 1897, the Taiwanese elite traveled to China for advanced studies. From 1897 to 1949, during the Japanese colonization, most of the Taiwanese elite were educated in Japan or China. After World War II, they began to pursue studies in the United States.

Today, the belief that one has a social responsibility to return home to improve Taiwan is not widely shared by the Taiwanese. Instead, the younger generation study abroad for more self-centered reasons. Fields related to science and technology are still popular areas of study. According to the Taiwanese Ministry of Education's annual report, more than half the students studying abroad from 1955 to 1989 were in science- and technology-related majors. In addition, more than 80 percent of the students who came to the United States to study in 1989 majored in science and technology (Ministry of Education in Taiwan 1999, 58).

Taiwanese students believe that studying in America is necessary to complete their *jin-yi-huan-xiang* journey. Researchers in the fields of sociology and environmental psychology have conducted a few qualitative studies in order to understand the personal and social cultural interactions of the Taiwanese students overseas. For the fifty-three interviewees in Ma's 1998 study, "going abroad" means going to the United States to pursue an advanced degree (Ma 1998). To these interviewees, Chinese and Taiwanese scientists in the United States, as well as to Taiwanese in general, an overseas PhD suggests not only better training, but it also suggests that its recipient is a harder-working employee with greater abilities who is more valuable than an employee with a locally earned PhD (ibid., 8).

Herng-Dar Bih (1992, 107–17), a Taiwanese environmental psychologist, has concluded that there are ten major reasons why Taiwanese students come to the United States. The top three reasons are parental expectation, the desire to seek a romantic relationship or accompany a spouse, and, finally, the wish to use the move as a stepping stone to immigration.

Parental expectation that their children achieve a higher education has been an important motivating factor for students in Taiwan. And, through conversations with the parents, I realized that they have started demanding improvements to the existing Taiwanese educational system. Careen told me that "the education system has not improved at all since my school years. . . . I don't want my kids to go through this creativity-limiting *tien-ya* [duck-feeding] education system." I spoke with many parents who shared Careen's concern.

Certainly, my field observations in Silicon Valley show that Taiwanese parents are very concerned about enrolling their children in the best schools. They hire private tutors; take their children to Chinese school; send their children to organized extracurricular activities, such as painting, piano, or dancing classes, on weekends; and take their children to after-school classes on weekday evenings (Shenglin Chang 1998).

While educational success translates into status in Taiwanese American culture, Taiwanese American parents' desire for educational achievement often creates tensions between Taiwanese immigrant families and their American counterparts. American parents are sometimes outraged by the Taiwanese immigrants who are registered at the best schools, thus creating a highly competitive learning environment that causes their own children to feel academic pressure.[10]

The Symbolic Meaning of Migration to America

It is fair to say that mainstream Taiwanese share a dream of receiving a higher degree and migrating to the United States. According to the most recent annual survey done by *Commonwealth* magazine, in 2001, 32 percent of those interviewed preferred to migrate to the United States or Canada rather than stay in Taiwan (Commonwealth 2001).[11] Estimates by immigrant agencies in Taiwan reveal that more than 500,000 Taiwanese migrated illegally to America in 1993. Taiwanese immigrants composed 12.5 percent of the four million illegal aliens who arrived in the United States that year.[12] Since 1966, more than 10,000 Taiwanese have immigrated legally to the United States each year (Barringer, Gardner, and Levin 1995, 33). Most Taiwanese newcomers settled in the Los Angeles, New York, and San Francisco areas (Portes and Rumbaut, 1990, 34–37). According to Hsiao's study, California had accumulated more than 100,000 Taiwanese immigrants in 1990, the highest number of any state in the United States. Moreover, of immigrants to California in 1989, 42.9 percent were Taiwanese (Hsiao 1994, 69–75).

The pursuit of American citizenship has been one of the most prevalent goals in Taiwanese society since the United States Immigration Reform Act of 1965. According to Chang's 1997 report in *China Times*, more than 11,000 Taiwanese migrated to the United States that year, and nearly 700,000 wished to immigrate. Both domestic and international political issues encouraged the immigrant wave of the 1990s. Since 1987, the year that martial law was lifted, the Taiwanese have grown pessimistic about political stability, environmental quality, and educational opportunities, and the public has little confidence that the government can resolve the political tension between Taiwan and China. Recently, in the wake of the increasing tension between Taiwan and mainland China, American citizenship has become particularly desirable. Taiwanese presume that living in the United States would benefit both a family's security and its children's educational opportunities. On the economic side, upper- and middle-class Taiwanese have already developed personal careers linked to a global economic network. Meanwhile, the high-tech transformations occurring in both Taiwan and Silicon Valley provide high-tech personnel with tempting opportunities to pursue the American dream.

From a theoretical perspective, a home is a shelter, a personal heaven, and a place we feel comfortable inhabiting (Marcus 1986; Bachelard 1958). The United States provides Taiwanese, especially the younger generation and the highly educated, a home that encompasses all three of these dimensions. The Taiwanese people identify America as a shelter from domestic and international hostility. They also consider American suburbs a sort of heaven where they can enjoy a higher quality of life. To the Taiwanese, the United States is a dreamland where one can pursue a far more secure and comfortable life and enjoy greater personal achievement.

As mentioned earlier, study overseas is generally considered the best pathway to the American dreamland. Some talented Taiwanese have embarked on their journey to the United States as early as their twenties. Getting a high score on the TOEFL and GRE tests that are required by most American universities is an important goal for most Taiwanese college students, and many attend TOEFL/GRE programs in their junior or senior years of college. The majority of these programs are located on Nang-yang Street near Taipei Train Station, where every weekend thousands of students are packed into overcrowded classrooms where they take preparatory exams. Indeed, for many young Taiwanese, even the name "Nang-yang Street" suggests the pathway to studying abroad.

I was one of those students who sat in a windowless classroom on Nang-yang Street dreaming about the United States. I remember one late Saturday afternoon when it was time for me and hundreds of other aspiring students to learn our exam results. The school buildings at Nang-yang Street were set back from the sidewalks, and along the street narrow arches 10 to 15 feet wide connected the school buildings. Pedestrians usually walked through the arches because the sidewalks were used as scooter parking lots. However, on this particular Saturday afternoon it was virtually impossible for anyone to walk through the area because hundreds of students were crowding the arcade, trying to check their test results that were coded by ID number and posted outside the front door. On that hot and humid summer afternoon, as I was pushed and pulled by the crowd and heard people yelling about their scores, I wondered if I would finally struggle through the dark tunnel and reach the other side of study overseas.

Huan-xiang and the Reverse Brain Drain

From the time a motherlander student receives her GRE transcripts to the moment she gets the I-20 visa from her dream university, five to ten months might pass. Then it might take her four to six years to complete her PhD study. But what about the *huan-xiang* journey, or return home? Many Taiwanese American high-tech engineers and their families stay in Silicon Valley after they finish their studies, moving back to Hsinchu Science Park for career advancement in their mid-thirties or forties. This results in the so-called "reverse brain drain" that has occurred at Hsinchu Science Park since the 1980s. Scholars have indicated how those who participate in this reverse brain drain have contributed to the high-tech transformation in Taiwan (Saxenian 1997; Hsu 1997; Yang 1998). Data compiled in September 2004 reveals that the reverse brain drain population of high-tech engineers who commute between Silicon Valley and Taiwan invested in 115 of 378 companies operated in the Hsinchu Science Park. Ninety-seven of those 115 companies were registered as Taiwanese companies, while the other eighteen were established by Taiwanese talents in other countries, including the United States (Hsinchu Science Park 2004c).

Obviously, the success of the reverse brain drain is a consequence of the technological and economic transformations that have been going on since the 1960s. The first diffusion of computer technology from the United States instigated an international exchange of computer scientists. Since then, high-tech immigrants from around the world have been drawn to the suburbs of Silicon Valley (Saxenian and Edulbehram 1998). In addition to Silicon Valley's global reputation as the center of technological innovation, the Taiwanese perception that an overseas education secures a higher status serves as the driving force that pushes Taiwanese students to pursue higher education in the United States. These two "push" and "pull" forces have caused the integration of Taiwanese immigrants into the labor forces of high-tech industries worldwide since the 1970s. In her *Silicon Valley's New Immigrant Entrepreneurs*, Saxenian provides statistical data about Taiwanese high-tech engineers: 84 percent of ethnically Chinese high-tech engineers working in Silicon Valley are immigrants, and 71 percent of them arrived in the United States between 1970 and 1989 (Saxenian 1999, 12–18).[13]

In addition to the high-tech policy transformation in Taiwan, the glass ceiling in U.S. workplaces and the excellent Taiwanese engineer networking circles were two factors that contributed to the reverse brain drain (Deng 1998). These two factors correlate to the length of practice and residency in high-tech companies in Silicon Valley. Interestingly, Taiwanese American high-tech engineers became established in Silicon Valley earlier than other foreign-born engineers, such as those from India and mainland China. Therefore, many Taiwanese senior engineers reached the glass ceiling as early as the 1980s.[14]

The glass ceiling in the United States and the industrial transformation in Taiwan created a reversal of geographic attraction for technological talents, causing high-tech professionals to choose to return to their homeland. My fieldwork indicates that many Taiwanese immigrants were confronted by the glass ceiling, their job advancement limited to managerial levels even after holding senior positions in their Silicon Valley companies (Deng 1998; Shenglin Chang 1997). In addition, almost no Chinese entrepreneurs have reached the position of CEO in the past decade in Silicon Valley. Senior-level Chinese managers and engineers often left their companies when those companies merged with another (Deng 1998, 227). Jing, one high-tech housewife I spoke with, emphasized,

> Of course, you don't get promoted to CEO in your American companies. Many of my lawyer and engineer friends have experienced similar glass ceiling scenarios. However, it's different when you work in Taiwan. Your Taiwanese company wants you to participate in all the important meetings and crucial de-cisions. This is why we believe Taiwan is the best place for our career develop-ment. Some people argued that they don't quite feel the existence of the glass ceiling. That is only because they have not achieved that career threshold yet.

Frustrated by career stagnation, many senior Taiwanese American profes-sionals start their own companies in Taiwan while their families remain in the Silicon Valley suburbs. These families have been flying back and forth, both virtually and physically, through the cyber corridor for the past decade.

The social network of the high-tech elite also facilitated the reverse brain drain phenomenon. Silicon Valley immigrants often team up and establish new companies in the Hsinchu Science Park. The successes of Mosel, Vitelic, Macronix, and TSMC are still legendary there (Deng 1998, 237–60).

The college network systems and Silicon Valley working relationships played a crucial role for these entrepreneurial groups (Saxenian 1997; Hsu 1997; Yang 1998).

Following in the footsteps of the pioneering reverse brain drain group of the 1980s, increasing numbers of Taiwanese junior engineers that are currently based in Silicon Valley have made Hsinchu their mid-career location of choice. Professional networks no longer play as critical a role in the decision-making process of the junior engineers group as they did for the pioneer group, because by the 1990s the high-tech industrial career pattern had already been established. Careen, a housewife, explained the situation that led her family to decide to move back to Taiwan. "From 1989 to 1991, there were many Silicon Valley engineers moving back to Taiwan. We didn't even discuss our decision with our friends and relatives. However, we ran into each other in Hsinchu Science Park and realized that many of our acquaintances were here [in Hsinchu] too. Believe it or not, my brother-in-law and my husband moved back almost at the same time, but they never consulted with each other."

In the 1990s a new variation on the reverse brain drain phenomenon began to take place. That's when many technology companies located in the Hsinchu and Silicon Valley regions entered into joint venture partnerships with one another. As a result of these joint ventures, Hsinchu-based entrepreneurs have invested a great quantity of capital in Silicon Valley (Deng 1998, 260). This new reverse flow of capital (i.e., capital investment flowing from Taiwan to the United States) has provided an opportunity for Taiwan-trained engineers and managers to move to Silicon Valley. Through this pathway, many Taiwan-trained engineers (the "motherlanders") have become residents of the Silicon Valley suburbs. They consider this pathway not only a career opportunity, but an opportunity to improve their children's education. Melanie, a CEO's wife, told me her family followed this path. The first couple of years in Silicon Valley were extremely difficult, because her husband had to commute frequently between Taiwan and Silicon Valley. She found herself living in Silicon Valley taking care of three children alone and unable to speak English fluently. However, just like other parents I spoke with, she believed that the arrangement was "in the best interest of our children's education."

In the early 2000s, faced with a global economic downturn, Silicon Valley's tech giants laid off thousands of employees. In order to reduce their costs, many companies have sent jobs overseas in a phenomenon known as "offshore outsourcing" (King 2003). This phenomenon has led to the new wave of reverse brain drain. Many Taiwanese Americans who were laid off by their companies in Silicon Valley have started their own companies with offices in Taiwan, China, and Silicon Valley. Similar to those who returned to Taiwan in the reverse brain drain of the 1980s and the 1990s, the engineer husbands are the ones shuttling among different locations, while the wives and children stay in their Silicon Valley homes.

The United States has historically been a country of diaspora, and this tradition continues. For today's Taiwanese high-tech families, suburban Silicon Valley is the promised land. Whatever it requires, they want their families to move here, to stay here, and to get their education here. The second generation of high-tech Taiwanese American families have unique trans-Pacific experiences. They stress bilingual education and have learned to adapt to the various environmental and social contexts while their families fly back and forth across the Pacific.

FOUR

The Emerging Transnational Family Life

In the previous chapter I discussed how the ancient *jin-yi* ritual has been up-dated in contemporary Taiwanese society; how the beautiful clothes that conferred status in past eras have been replaced today by diplomas from prestigious universities and U.S. citizenship. The trans-Pacific commuters you encountered in the previous chapters sought to improve their status, but in order to do so many of them had to transplant their families across the Pacific. For trans-Pacific commuters, the constant travel between two homes in two countries has engendered new, nontraditional ways of conceiving of the relationship between home and self. Because they are able to shift fluidly from their Taiwanese to their American identities, they feel at home on ei-ther side of the Pacific. But, while they identify equally with their homes on both sides of the Pacific, can they identify equally with their families on ei-ther side of the Pacific?

When exploring this question it is useful to keep in mind three aspects of the lives of trans-Pacific commuters: their *huan-xiang* status-seeking journey, their "re-configured" family life (Lima 2001, 79), and the back-and-forth bi-gration that has become an accepted part of their lives. According to John Liu, "family life" can be defined as "the structure of the family, the func-tional relations between members of the family, and the symbolic meanings of the family as a unit" (Liu 1980, 3). "Transnational family life" refers to the experience of families whose members travel between two homes in two different countries, an experience that is made possible by the ability to easily depart one continent and arrive at another less than twelve hours later.

Transnational family life is not limited to Taiwanese American trans-Pacific commuters but is a global trend. There is a huge body of American scholarship concerning the transnational ties between the United States and, for example, the Dominican Republic (Levitt 2001; Grasmuck and Pessar 1991), Haiti (Catanese 1999), Mexico (Jones 1995), El Salvador (Mahler 1995), greater China (Ong 1999; Ong, Bonacich, and Cheng 1994), and so on. Scholars have also recently started paying more attention to migration patterns in various countries outside the United States. This new scholarship suggests that migration involves not just the United States, but also various countries, ethnic groups, and cultures, such as Croatians in Western Australia (Colic-Peisker 2002), Central and East African–Asians in Canada (Matthews 2002), Turks in the Netherlands (Amersfoort and Doomernik 2002), and Turks in Germany (Jurgens 2001).

Before proceeding further, I should point out that my research on transnational families focuses on the social and physical spaces that permeate international borders (Lima 2001, 77–79). Although economists first used the concept of transnationalism to describe the strategies of market enterprises, in the past decade the concept has "swiftly migrated across disciplinary boundaries" (Smith and Guarnizo 1998). I take transnationalism to mean the set of relationships a family unit has across multiple cultures and international boundaries. But, although families may cross the globe in airplanes, their lives still happen at a down-to-earth, "grassroots" level (Lima 2001, 77). I approach transnational family units from both Taiwanese and American perspectives, because a transnational family lives in more than one country and experiences different cultures. The members of the family maintain the family networks, but they do not necessarily share daily experiences or have face-to-face interactions with each other. Despite the great distances and time differences that separate them, trans-Pacific families remain tied in a primary family relationship. The family ties, however, have been rearranged in a nontraditional configuration. For the trans-Pacific family, the meaning of the family as a whole has been radically reconfigured. This reconfigured family is divided into multicentered units, because family members have more than one home to which they can return. But how have they reconfigured themselves, and how is the change related to the connection between family structure and house forms? Put another way, how does the dynamic relationship between home and landscape relate to the trans-Pacific commuters' new configurations of their family lives? The Taiwanese concept of home, or *jia*, which implies both the location and the physical structure of one's home as well as one's family, can help us understand how home and landscapes relate to a reconfigured transnational family life. Seen from a physical perspective, *jia* is a shelter for a family. From a social perspective, *jia* consists of "kin related by blood, marriage, or adoption, that had a common budget and common property. . . . Popularly translated as 'family'" (Naquin and Rawski 1987, 33–34). Following the dual social and physical aspects embodied in *jia*, both home environments and families embody the home identities that trans-Pacific commuters have developed in the process of their bi-gration. To better elucidate the concept of *jia*, I will explore four related concepts and phenomena: first, the concepts of Taiwanese and American home identities; second, home transformations in modern Taiwanese history; third, transnational family ties and the fluid quality of trans-Pacific living; and, finally, the home memories that trans-Pacific commuters in different age groups experience.

Taiwanese Homes in Transformation

We all think that we know what "home" means, but it actually means different things for people in different cultural contexts. When I lived in Berkeley I shuttled between Taiwan and Berkeley as many as three times a year. I would excitedly tell my American friends, "I am going *home*." These friends appeared confused and amused at the time, although I didn't know exactly why. Later, I discovered that for Americans "home" means the location where one currently lives; it refers to one's current address. In this context "home" refers to a geographic location.

But a home is also a symbol of one's self (Marcus 1995, 1974). When my American friends talk about where they live, the information they convey symbolizes their view of their selves. When I'm introduced to someone and they tell me where they live, they are at the same time letting me know how they see their own individuality. Living in a city neighborhood known for its diversity, for example, implies that one is a different kind of person than one who lives in a suburb known for its status. In most cases they chose to live apart from their parents, away from their childhood homes. When Americans are going to visit the home where they grew up, they say, "I am going *back home*." "Back home," which refers to one's hometown or childhood home, also suggests the linear concept of time that is intertwined with American individualism. Most Americans move away from their parents' home to pursue their career and assert their individualism after they graduate from high school. For them, "back home" is a home in the past, while "my home" refers to where they currently reside.

It is an interesting coincidence that both Americans and Taiwanese use the metaphor of young birds learning to fly to describe the relationship between parents and children. Americans, however, are far less sentimental about an empty nest. American parents believe that they have to push their children out of the nest so that they will learn to fly on their own. Children flying on their own is a sign of a successful family and celebrated by both American parents and children, but Taiwanese parents take far less joy in watching their children take wing.

The two variations on this metaphor of flight represent two distinct identities, one that is based on the individual and another that is based on the family. The American idealization of "learning to fly alone" emphasizes individual identity. It is believed that every child has to learn how to survive on his or her own, and that the parents who end up living in an empty nest must learn to cope with their children's flight.

In contrast to American identity based on individualism, Taiwanese identity is based on the family. The occasion of a child moving out of his or her parents' home is a sad one for the parents. Unlike American children, who typically leave home after high school, Taiwanese children typically stay at their parents' home until they marry. In Ang Lee's movie *Yin-Shi-Nan-Nu* (Eat, Drink, Man, Woman), three adult daughters live with their widower father (Lee 1995). These daughters do not feel it is appropriate or respectful to speak to their father about their desire to leave his home. When the second daughter, a deputy director for an airline, first announces that she has bought a condo and plans to move out, her two sisters and her father feel that she is abandoning them. The other two daughters soon announce their similar intention and quickly move out of their father's home. After his daughters leave home, the father sells the house and starts a new family with a much younger women and her daughter from a previous marriage. Although each of the family members has many memories of the old house, it no longer represents home. The family in essence dissolves as all of its members move on and start anew, leaving the old house behind.

My home identity has always been intertwined with my parents' home in Taiwan. I use the phrase "my home" to refer to my parents' flat that I grew up in, and I still return to it whenever I visit Taiwan. Instead of feeling that I am going *back home*, I consider that I am simply *going home*. Today, even though I am married and live in Maryland, I still feel I am going home when my husband and I take our annual trip to visit my parents in Taiwan. To me, both my Maryland residence and my house in Taiwan (even though it belongs to my parents) are my homes. I make no clear distinction between the two. My Taiwanese friends hold the same view: that there doesn't need to be a distinction between the home where one currently resides and the home one grew up in (where one's parents might still live). Erasing the distinction between one's current home and one's parents' home enables my Taiwanese friends and me to think of ourselves in terms of having two homes simultaneously. I call this the having of double home identity. Many of my Taiwanese friends, especially the unmarried ones, share this double home identity. This tendency to possess a double home identity reflects the Taiwanese inclination to mix and layer people, places, and times in the process of constructing one's Taiwanese home identity.

To understand more about the construction of Taiwanese identity, let us consider the relationships between family members. The extended family structure is fundamental to Chinese society, of which Taiwanese society is a subculture. Today's Taiwanese nuclear family structure is a result of a series of transformations that have occurred within the past fifty years. Before China's modernization, wealthy families typically lived in clusters of houses arranged around a courtyard (Fig. 4.1), "where household becomes an enveloping world in itself" (Naquin and Rawski 1987, 34). Relatives with identical surnames stayed close to each other, whether in a village or an urban ward (ibid., 40).

Figure 4.2 illustrates the four stages in the patterns of everyday family life that have existed in Taiwan in the past century. First, before 1890, traditional extended families were the majority. Up to four generations of family members and other blood relatives or relatives by marriage cohabitated in a traditional Chinese courtyard house (see Fig. 4.1). During the second stage, the

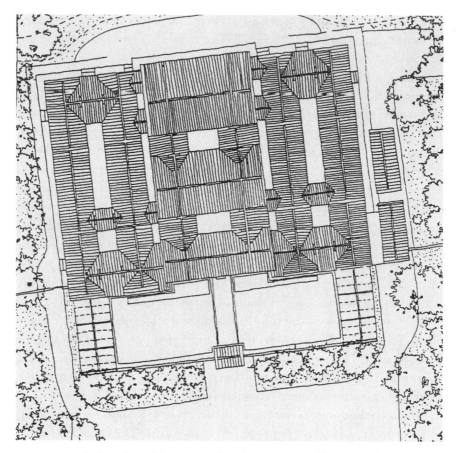

FIG. 4.1. A plan view of a traditional Chinese courtyard house in Taiwan. Source: National Taiwan University Building and Planning Foundation, *Preservation and Reuse of the Lee Family Compound: From Historical Preservation to Cultural Regeneration* (Taipei: National Taiwan University Building and Planning Foundation, 1997), 171.

period of Japanese colonization from 1895 to 1945, "adapt stem families" lived in either Japanese houses (see Fig. 2.1) or Chinese courtyard houses ("stem family" refers to a family unit that includes grandparents, parents, and children; "adapt stem family" refers to three generations of primary family members living together, and it may also include other relatives, such as uncles, aunts, or unmarried siblings).

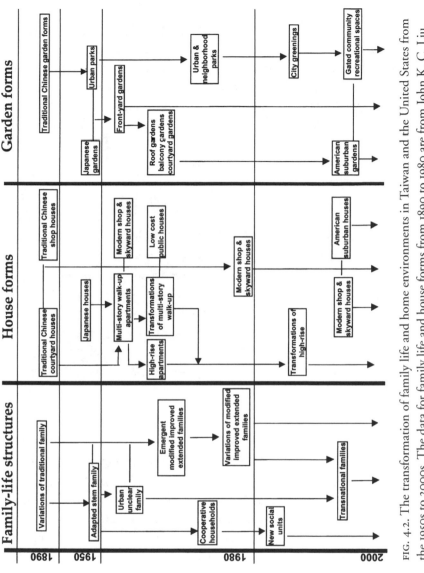

FIG. 4.2. The transformation of family life and home environments in Taiwan and the United States from the 1950s to 2000s. The data for family life and house forms from 1890 to 1980 are from John K. C. Liu, Housing Transformation: A Study of Family Life and Built Form in Taiwan. Ph.D. diss., Department of Architecture, University of California, Berkeley.

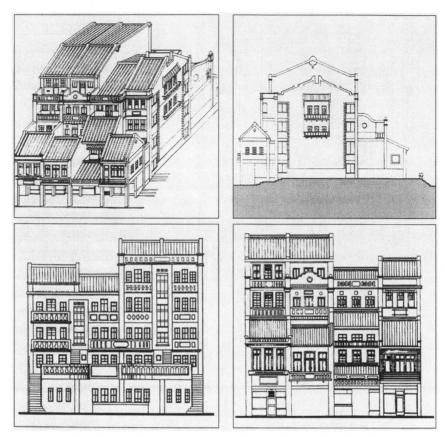

FIG. 4.3 Traditional Chinese shophouse. Source: Chao-ching Yu, Place Making: from Cities to Communities, Urban Design Studio CYCU, 1999.

Third, between the 1950s and 1970s, an era of rapid urbanization and industrialization, multicentered family units became the common form of residence for the "modified improved extended family," which, according to Liu, refers to a family pattern in which relatives of a stem family or a nuclear family live in close proximity in order to assist one another in their daily lives. Similar to a co-housing situation, in which neighbors help each other by providing childcare or running errands, the Taiwanese modified improved extended family entails relatives belonging to a family-based network dwelling within adjacent residential units. The residential units can consist of any type of housing, and in some cases relatives live close by rather than

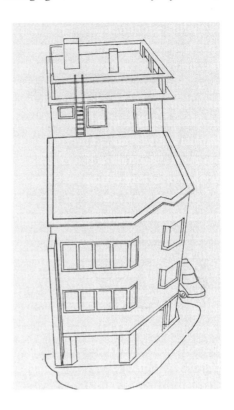

FIG. 4.4. Skyward houses are identified as modernized shophouses in Taiwan. A skyward house is a multistory walk-up building constructed of reinforced concrete. Its unique characteristics are its narrow but deep shape and the uncut rebar tails on its flat rooftop. The square footage of these houses varies depending upon the size of the property, but in some cases the lots on which the houses stand are extremely narrow. Graphic: Kenya Thompson.

in the same building (Liu 1980). Constrained by economic and real estate considerations, relatives and primary family numbers would become neighbors, living in traditional courtyard houses (see Fig. 4.1), apartments (see Fig. 2.2), shop houses (Fig. 4.3), or narrow multi-level residences called "skyward houses" (Fig. 4.4). Grandparents, for example, might live in the same building as their daughter's family, but in a different apartment unit, or they might live in the community nearby and provide domestic support, such as childcare and meal preparation.

The fourth and most recent phase in Chinese family life patterns was initiated by some trans-Pacific commuters in the 1980s when they moved into their suburban American houses. Parents and their children, spouses, and siblings now operate daily in separate spheres, and they no longer share the same life experiences and cultural identities. Some family members even have difficulty communicating with others in the family. In many cases children who have grown up in the United States can barely speak Chinese, while their parents and especially their grandparents do not understand English very well or at all.

Along with these revolutions in housing forms and family structures, the forms of gardens and the meanings of gardening have also been transformed over time. Interestingly, cultivating a garden in one's yard is generally considered unimportant in Taiwan. However, from the Song dynasty (late tenth century to the twelfth century) through the end of the Ming dynasty (the seventeenth century), wealthy Chinese families in Jiangnan, a region south of the Yangtze River, popularized private gardens (Ebrey 2001). But in those times it was the elite, not the middle or lower classes, who owned private gardens. Most of the Chinese populace who had yards preferred to plant vegetable gardens rather than traditional Chinese gardens. Today, senior citizens who can't afford to own a private yard often illegally plant vegetables in neighborhood parks in many metropolitan areas in Taiwan.

High-density land use and apartment residences have also shaped Taiwanese lifestyles since the 1950s (Fig. 4.2). Generally speaking, 82 percent of households in Taiwan were located in urbanized areas (as defined by the 2000 U.S. census) at the end of 2003.[1] Currently, more than 63 percent of Taiwanese households (60 percent of the population) are situated in urban areas where the population density is higher than five people per acre, while more than 33 percent of households (30 percent of the population) are located in seven major cities with an average density of 26.5 people per acre (Ministry of the Interior 2003).[2] It is therefore clear that urban parks, neighborhood parks, and other green spaces in cities have played an important role in Taiwanese life throughout the twentieth century. Due to space limitations, Taiwanese people typically have at most a balcony garden in their high-rise apartment homes, and they consider a yard or a garden as a symbol of luxury.

It is fair to say that in modern Taiwan there are few home gardens compared to the vast number of gardens and lawns available to suburban American families. However, this should not suggest that green spaces or plants are not important in Taiwanese culture. Most families maintain beautiful indoor plants in their apartments, and many prefer to live close to public parks and other open spaces. The Taiwanese affinity for gardens and plants is also reflected in the way that the Taiwanese use public parks and open spaces as their outdoor living rooms for social gatherings, karaoke performances, ballroom dancing, tai chi practice, and so on.

FIG. 4.5. Seniors practicing tai chi and qigong in the early morning at Dr. Sun Yat-sen Memorial Park in Taipei City. Photo by author, 2004.

Many self-organized group activities take place daily in neighborhood parks, while local residents coordinate their schedules to share these spaces. For example, at Dr. Sun Yat-sen Memorial Park, adjacent to my apartment in Taipei City, seniors can be seen practicing their tai chi and qigong as others walk their dogs early in the morning (Fig. 4.5). Just as the seniors finish up their morning exercises around 8 or 9 A.M., housewives show up to start their karaoke, ballroom dancing, and yoga groups. When they rush off to prepare lunch around 10 A.M., schoolchildren's picnics or other outdoor activities take over. In the late afternoon the arrival of dog owners and their pets signals the start of the park's evening activities. Starting at dusk groups who prefer to practice tai chi, qigong, yoga, ballroom dancing, and karaoke at night arrive. And finally, around midnight, the park transforms into one of Taipei's most popular spots for young couples on dates.

The sharing of neighborhood open spaces by diverse user groups is the norm for the majority of Taiwanese urban residents. However, at the end of the twentieth century, open spaces located within newly developed gated communities significantly challenged this norm. In the case of the Hsinchu region, while trans-Pacific high-tech families happily moved into beautiful

American-style homes in Hsinchu Science Park and other newly developed gated communities; other residents of the area have been angered by the gate that bars them from access to well-maintained open spaces. The wall that excludes local residents has become a source of great hostility between the Hsinchu old-timers and the trans-Pacific newcomers that reside there. These issues will be further addressed in chapters 7 and 8, while in this chapter I will continue to focus on the ways in which reconfigured family life reflects the transformation of Taiwanese homes.

Multicentered Homes for Contemporary Taiwanese

The family-based home transformations described above provide a backdrop for understanding the contemporary Taiwanese perception of multicentered homes. Over the course of many conversations I realized that, for the most part, Taiwanese don't distinguish between their parents' residence and their own, whether those homes are rented or owned. This is especially true for unmarried Taiwanese. They consider their parents' homes as much their home as their current residence, and moving from their parents' home is accompanied by a sense of guilt.

This sense of guilt can be better apprehended by understanding *cheng-jia*, which literally means "family completion" or "home building" but also means "marriage." The American concept that comes closest to the multiple meanings of *cheng-jia* is the newlywed's process of "setting up house." But, in contrast to the newlyweds' break from their parents that is celebrated in American culture, Chinese and Taiwanese newlyweds stay attached to their parents' and in-laws' homes.

Before industrialization accelerated after the 1950s, a newly married son and his bride would become the new addition to the family configuration that included the son's parents, grandparents, and great grandparents. Today, some married couples still live with their parents in apartment homes, which the young couple is likely to inherit some day. Daughters, however, rather than *cheng-jia* experience *chu-jia*, which means "marrying out." On her wedding day, a daughter moves out of her parents' home to become a member of her husband's (and his parents') family. Seen from a traditional Chinese perspective, daughters are raised by parents for the express purpose of one day being "married out." For the daughter, marriage entails leaving her biological family to become a member of her husband's family. The old Chinese folk saying "A married-out daughter is like the water poured out" reflects this process, in which the daughter is "poured out" of her biological family at the same time that she is "poured into" her husband's family.

Strong family ties profoundly influence Taiwanese home identity. In contrast to the individualism that drives the physical and social form of the American house, Taiwanese identity, which is based on family ties and ancestral history, results in multicentered forms of homes and family configurations within homes. As I pointed out earlier, when a Taiwanese says "my home," it implies one's own home *in addition to* one's parents' home. When you ask a Taiwanese "Where is your home?" you are most likely to hear where his or her parents live. One needs to ask "Where are you living?" to learn about a current address.

Trans-Pacific Commuters' Fluid Family Arrangements

Because the Taiwanese conception of family is relational rather than based on the individual, the physical nature of the Taiwanese home is determined by the multiple family ties within the home. The key mechanism shared by all families for tying the family together is the fluid family arrangement. As Peggy Levitt argues in *The Transnational Villagers*, even when family members live an ocean apart, they put into place fluid arrangements to maintain their connection. In Levitt's study, the transnational villagers that traveled between Miraflores, in the Dominican Republic, and Boston were mostly peasant families. "These fluid family arrangements mean that children in Miraflores have always been raised by multiple mothers. Grandmothers and aunts, along with parents, play a central role in their daily lives," writes Levitt (2001, 76). The parents, and especially the mothers, of these transnational families work in Boston and send their salaries back to Miraflores to support their families. They can only visit their children once a year, so their children grow up with relatives in the extended family network. Many emotional gaps affect intimate family ties. For example, Nancy left her son when he was only two months old because the U.S. consular officer refused to issue him a visa. Her sister and mother agreed on a fluid arrangement for taking care of her son whenever she had to work in Boston. Every time she returned home to visit her son she felt "that there was always something missing, like I had missed so many important parts of his childhood. We couldn't make it up" (ibid., 77).

Although there are class differences between Taiwanese high-tech families and the Miraflores peasant families, the families that I interviewed, which Paul Stubbs would call the "global professional middle class" (quoted in Colic-Peisker 2002, 29–40), also develop fluid family arrangements for their children. They also miss part of their children's childhood, as their children grow up with "part-time parents" or live with other relatives.

Men and women have been shuttling between Silicon Valley and the Hsinchu region to improve their career opportunities and their children's educational opportunities since the 1980s. Parents might change their children's residence depending upon their age. Many of the wives I interviewed said that they wanted to send their children to Silicon Valley when they began the eighth or ninth grade. These children would be uprooted from their Taiwanese classrooms and dropped into American classrooms in Silicon Valley.

Based on my field observations and interviews, I identified three primary fluid family arrangements established by Taiwanese trans-Pacific commuters: the real but virtual marriage, the parachute children arrangement, and the multiple family tie extended family structure (or out-of-place grandparents). Next I examine how different families participate in, and emotionally respond to, these newly reconfigured family patterns.

The Real but Virtual Marriage

Within the world of transnational commuters, a real but virtual marriage is one in which spouses are separated by a large distance. Spouses in transnational families, especially the middle-aged astronauts and green card moms, must frequently maintain their marriage ties through high-technology forms of communication and transportation. Either the husband or wife, or sometimes both, must travel frequently between two homes in two societies. This marriage pattern creates a unique family culture that is distinct from the traditional face-to-face family culture. In each case of a real but virtual marriage the individuals struggle with complicated psychological factors. One interviewee, Melanie, for example, stated that "it is extremely difficult to pull a family together in our situation. Only those who have gone through the process can understand my painful experiences." She and her husband decided to migrate to Silicon Valley from Hsinchu a few years ago. At first they had a long-distance marriage, but they finally settled down together two years ago.

Many of the Taiwanese American high-tech wives have chosen to pursue the role of a housewife, which has led to the interesting phenomenon of many real but virtual marriages existing by choice, because the wives have opted to live an independent life in Silicon Valley. "Being independent," however, means something different to Taiwanese American high-tech housewives than it did to American first-wave feminists (Lerner 1993). On the one hand, this particular group of Taiwanese American wives, most of whom came to the United States between the late 1970s and the early 1990s, did not participate in the feminist movement that was led by black and Hispanic women in the mid-1960s and the 1970s in the United States (Chow 1987, 287; Hayden 1991, 291), because most of them were still in Taiwan during that period. On the other hand, they were also absent from the Taiwanese feminist movement that occurred in the late 1980s.

Uninfluenced by the "women's consciousness" that emerged from both the American and Taiwanese feminist movements, the wives I spoke with talked about being "independent women" in terms that were not related to being financially independent or pursuing a professional career for themselves. Instead, they relied on their husbands' incomes and performed the traditional roles of caring for children and managing domestic affairs, often with much pride and a sense of accomplishment. However, these wives believed that they had the right to decide where they would live, just as their husbands had the right to choose to work in Hsinchu Science Park to advance their careers. They made the choice not to return to Taiwan with their husbands. They saw their independence, therefore, in terms of their freedom to experience the higher quality of life in Silicon Valley in the company of their children and without their spouses.

Marital problems, infidelity, and divorces, however, frequently occur in these marriages. Most of my interviewees were very sensitive about this topic. None revealed much about their intimate lives. They enjoyed gossiping about each other's private affairs, but they did not talk about themselves. One of my interviewees, Kelly, explained to me that these issues were social taboos. She repeatedly remarked, "There is too much gossip about the green card moms. I really enjoy the environmental quality here [in Silicon Valley], but I am worried about my marriage." Ideally, she would have liked a life that included *both* a close marriage relationship with her husband (in Taiwan) *and* the wonderful qualities she enjoyed living in Silicon Valley. But being realistic she concluded, "life is tough; you cannot have both."

Parachute Children

Another popular fluid family arrangement among the trans-Pacific commuters that I spoke with was the "parachute children" arrangement. This refers to a common phenomenon whereby Taiwanese parents send teenage children to the United States so that they will receive a high-quality education. These children might live with relatives or with close friends of their parents who have already immigrated to the United States while their parents (or one of their parents) continue working in Taiwan. In many cases one of the parents, usually the mother, will stay with the children for a few months during the year but spend the rest of her time in Taiwan.

In most cases parachute children struggle to adapt to their new sociocultural environments. They often feel abandoned by their parents and develop a closer relationship with their siblings, with the eldest sibling often assuming the role of parent to the younger ones. The parents, who might visit only every other month, often generously support their children's lavish lifestyles out a sense of guilt. This leads to social tensions and misunderstandings at a community level, as some of these children, in the company of others in their exclusive social network, form gangs that instigate racial conflict. In Cupertino, California, one reporter investigated the tensions between parachute children and local community members in a March 5, 1997, report (Tien Hwei Chang, 1997). The city of Cupertino was the first local government in Silicon Valley to hold multicultural community meetings to resolve the racial tensions among Caucasians and the Asian newcomers.

In general, many parachute children experience an identity crisis. Unlike their parents, who consider both their native and new homelands home, parachute children identify with neither of them. When asked "Who are you?" they might reply "I don't consider myself either Asian American or Taiwanese. I didn't grow up in either place. I grew up in-between." Jenny is a high-tech engineer who grew up as a parachute child. She confessed that the parachute children are not comfortable being friends with American-born Chinese (ABC's) because they find that "ABC's are too banana [Chinese on the outside but white inside]. These ABC's are very discriminating. They only like to participate in teams with Caucasian students, because they identify themselves as Americans. The only exception is when they can use us." Recalling her teenage years, Jenny said,

> I sat in front of my new suburban home and cried every afternoon after I came back from school for the first six months. I was in my high school years. I had to face the American teenagers. I didn't even know how to speak English when I got here, so the kids treated me badly. I became a very shy person and was afraid of going any place other than home. It indeed affected my personality and the way I pursue friendship.

The Multiple Family Tie Extended Family Structure

After they finish their Master's degrees or PhDs, many Taiwanese studying in the United States get professional jobs and qualify for U.S. H-1 immigration status. These mostly younger transplants rely on their own parents to provide full-time daycare for their children. However, for these three generations to live together, many daily interactions must be modified. Grandparents typically undergo culture shock in these transnational families. They often find it very difficult to confront unfamiliar languages and lifestyles so late in their lives, and many find it challenging to adjust their thinking and behaviors.

The authority and veneration reserved for grandparents in a traditional Chinese family has also weakened as the families have relocated to America. In Guan-Chien Lee's report in *Sinorama*, he pointed out that these differences in values often cause conflicts in Taiwanese American immigrant families. For example,

> Mr. Lee, who works for a computer firm in Silicon Valley, found himself repeating the words "Come on, this is America, so don't bother bringing up the ways things are done in Taiwan" several times a day when his 70-year-old father came to the US. He takes a self-mocking tone as he describes how "America" practically became a cure-all for handling situations with his father. "My father constantly called me about small matters, sometimes even phoning me at the office to complain when he had a minor squabble with my wife— it was enough to drive me crazy!"

Indeed, grandparents no longer enjoy the authority that they did in traditional family life. They often do not understand or speak English, and

FIG. 4.6. Tom, a retired medical doctor, stays with his son's family in Cupertino and provides full-time daycare for his two grandchildren. Photo by author, 1998.

thus they must rely heavily on their children. Their fear of driving causes inconvenience and isolation in their daily life. Many grandparents are also segregated in their suburban homes because they are providing full-time daycare for their grandchildren (Fig. 4.6).

When I spoke with grandparents Tom and Lily they complained that they lost their sense of control over their own lives when they stayed with their son's family in Cupertino. Lily repeatedly emphasized her frustration during our conversation. Her home identity fluctuated with her emotions. She said, "When I am in good mood, I feel this is my home. If I am in a bad mood, I miss my home in Taiwan a lot." Tom explained that car-oriented suburban life was very isolating. "In Taiwan, we go anywhere we want, but here we have to ask our children to drive us to places." Tom was depressed because he didn't have the opportunity to visit his old friends who lived fifty to sixty miles away. He prepared a gift for his friend last year when he discovered that his friend's family was also in Silicon Valley. A year later, the gift is still in his drawer. Neither he nor his friend could visit each other's house, because neither of them drove. He told me another story about reading about his college alumni reunion in the newspaper. "I really wanted to join their party. However, I was afraid my son was too busy to drive me there, so I ended up not going."

Tom and Lily believe that easily accessible public transportation would be the best way to remedy the isolation of their suburban lives. They told me it would be much better if they could take a bus to visit other places. Lily said, "I sometimes feel we have to beg them [their son and daughter-in-law] for whatever we want to do. I really dislike this feeling. We've just lost control of our lives. More importantly, we have to maintain our health. If we need to see doctors, they have to take a day off and drive us to the hospital."

In addition, there are conflicts between grandparents and their grandchildren. Their grandchildren often ask, "Grandpa, how long are you going to stay? Why don't you go back to your home?" (Lee 1998). Their grandchildren assume that they are temporary guests because they keep flying back and forth from the United States to Taiwan. This causes the seniors, who are used to the idea of stem or extended families, to feel very unwelcome.

As mentioned earlier, family ties form the foundation of Taiwanese society and identity. It is crucial to investigate the reconfiguration of family patterns and how these reconfigurations impact house and family transformations for contemporary Taiwanese across the Pacific. On the one hand, these emerging transnational family lives radically challenge the traditional extended family pattern in which all members reside in a big courtyard house cluster. The new transnational patterns geographically separate children, parents, and other relatives and divide them into different locations in different societies. On the other hand, in contrast to the American home identity, which is driven by a strong sense of individuality, Taiwanese experience a multicentered home identity. While in American society the nuclear family is a symbol of individualism, Taiwanese nuclear families are parts of larger family networks and maintain ties with members of their extended families, such as their parents-in-law, siblings, or other relatives by blood or marriage. The Taiwanese American trans-Pacific commuters blend individual home identities with family-based home identities. Astronauts, transplants, and green card moms, for example, might live either with their nuclear families or with their extended families at either of their two homes. If a green card mom stays with her husband in Taiwan while her children remain in Silicon Valley, she will not be perceived as neglecting her children, or as submissive to her husband's demands. Rather, the fact that she is taking care of her husband, her parents, or other relatives who live in Taiwan will be viewed with appreciation. She will be seen as acting honorably and dutifully on behalf of the *entire* family network, rather than as neglecting one member of the network for the benefit of another. Home consists of multicentered units woven together by family ties. Each unit is unique and independent, while all the units, no matter where they are, interlink as one.

The Experiences of Shifting Homes

In the previous section I discussed how the tradition of the multicentered home has helped trans-Pacific commuters construct new, fluid family arrangements that suit their new lifestyles. Their fluid social arrangements and their comfortable view of themselves as residing within many homes simultaneously are very different from my grandmother's static home identity. My grandmother felt trapped in Taiwan because she was unable to return to her home village in China. She often told my mother that she wanted to return to *lou-jia*, her old home. Her *lou-jia* was a traditional courtyard house with a dirt floor and no electricity. She missed her eldest son and his extended family, who had remained in China. She never entirely enjoyed her modern life in our apartment in Taipei. Worse, she often got lost whenever she went outside since she was unable to identify which door was ours. To her, "every door looks the same. I cannot find my home!"

In contrast to my grandmother, frustrated at having to adapt to a new home, trans-Pacific commuters can take advantage of modern transportation and communication technology to adapt more easily to different residential environments, while they simultaneously adjust to newly developed fluid family arrangements. For the remainder of this chapter, I want to examine the fluid family lives within the context of Taiwanese home transformations, because different generations embody different home and landscape memories. It is important to understand how these memories relate to the various phases of child rearing and career development within trans-Pacific commuters' family lives. For example, the arrangements made to accommodate the phase of raising infants is quite different from arrangements made during that phase when children reach high-school age. Understanding how these family-life phases relate to memory of home and landscape is important. To achieve this understanding, I identified three age groups that confront family arrangements differently: the senior generation (fifty years of age and older), the middle-age generation (from forty to fifty years of age), and the younger generation (under forty years of age).

First, the senior generation interviewees possess a more stable transnational family life compared to the other groups. Because their children are in high school or college, they do not have an urgent need to fly between Taiwan and the United States every month, unlike the middle-aged group. Their children often work or study in the United States, and they visit them during American holidays such as Thanksgiving or Christmas, or at Chinese New Year. Family gatherings at these holidays symbolize that, although they are separated by physical distance, they are a united group as family members.

My interviewees in the senior group were born in mainland China near the end of World War II. Their family histories were similar to my own. During the years following World War II, from 1945 to 1949, the Chinese Civil War between the Chinese Communist Party and Chiang Kai-shek's Kuomintang (KMT) government took place. Many families fled to Taiwan with the KMT regime around 1949 to avoid war atrocities and poverty. When these newcomers arrived in Taiwan, instead of building and living in traditional Chinese rural courtyard houses, they moved into urban Japanese houses.[3] Most of my interviewees told me that they had loved the spaciousness of their Japanese home and went on to describe the house's physical form: most were duplexes or detached homes with private gardens. These were the only types of houses they had lived in before they studied overseas. To them, the American single-family detached house was reminiscent of the spacious homes they had enjoyed during their childhoods.

The interviewees of the middle-age generation told me that they experienced an unstable transnational family life. Some maintained two homes, one in Silicon Valley and the other in Hsinchu region. Their children were mostly in junior high or elementary school, and many of them traveled between the two areas each month.[4] Some sent their children to summer camp for stays with their relatives or friends every year.

These interviewees had grown up in urbanized Taiwan environments. Their memories of their home environments were more diverse than those of senior and younger generation interviewees. They had been born in the 1950s and grew up against the backdrop of urbanization that occurred from 1960 to 1970. Most of them had studied overseas in the mid-1970s or the beginning of the 1980s. They had experienced four major housing forms before their transnational migration: (1) Japanese houses, (2) traditional Chinese courtyard houses, (3) modern shop/skyward houses, and (4) multistory walk-up apartment buildings.

Some of them had moved from a Japanese house or traditional courtyard house to a skyward house or apartment. Others had only lived in apartments. Those who had lived in Japanese houses or Chinese courtyard houses during their youth preferred the spaciousness of the single-family detached house. In this respect, they were similar to the senior group. Among those who had only experienced apartment living, the majority declared their dissatisfaction with Taiwanese residential life. They were surprised by the quality of life when they arrived in the United States to study. Both subgroups appreciated having a garden with their home and fantasized about having a garden such as those featured in magazines or about establishing vegetable gardens in their yards.

In my conversations with younger generation interviewees, I found that they had remained connected to their parents. Some of my interviewees were single, while others had young children of their own. Their parents, the out-of-place grandparents that I described above, had shared their experience of transnational life with them. These grandparents often cared for their grandchildren, jetting back and forth while experiencing many transcultural differences and pains.

My interviewees in the younger generation had memories of two types of home environment: (1) skyward houses and (2) walk-up or high-rise apartments. Before studying overseas in the 1980s, many had never had the chance to live in a detached house with a garden. They enjoyed living in American single-family detached houses, but they did not care for their gardens; they either hired professional gardeners to manage their yards or paved their yards, which enabled them to use the paved areas as a sort of outdoor attic space, a space for storing items like unused furniture, children's toys, bicycles, and so on. However, when asked about their dream homes, most said they would prefer a house with a nice garden or one surrounded by nature.

The three generations of trans-Pacific commuters thus experienced dif-

ferent memories of the home environments they had grown up in. The senior group remembered the courtyard houses and Japanese houses against
the backdrop of rural Taiwan. The middle-age group experienced the transition from a rural to an urban environment. They were the most diverse
group, and their residential memories included courtyard houses, Japanese
houses, skyward houses, and apartments. The younger group was born during the period of urbanization. High-rise apartments dominated their residential experiences.

Although the three generations had diverse home memories, they shared
the same romantic notion of a beautiful house standing against an open field
of grass. This idealized home was a product of landscape photos, country
music songs, and Hollywood movies. At the same time that John Denver's
"Take Me Home, Country Roads" became popular in the United States in
the 1970s, songwriter Liu Jia-chang's "My Home Is There" was a big hit in
Taiwan. Although I don't know whether John Denver inspired Liu, Liu's
lyrics depicted a romantic picture of a rural home and landscape that most
young Taiwanese dreamed about.

My friends from dance school loved to sing "My Home Is There" after
our evening rehearsal. As the school van drove us through urban streets,
crowded neighborhoods, and busy night markets, inside we twelve or so
adolescent girls sang the song that evoked for us a romantic rural image:
"Southern wind's blowing again, blowing the meadowland. . . . Sun is setting and washing the land. The meadow is washed in golden light. Meadow
is waving. Sunset is shining. The landscape is enchanting. . . . We follow the
stream to a little bungalow. It is my warm home. And there I live."

FIVE

Transcultural Lifestyles Across the Pacific Rim

On a cold winter night in December 1978, the dancers of Cloud Gate Dance Theatre performed a dance entitled "Legacy" in the southern Taiwan city of Chiayi, which is known for its many historical buildings and neighborhoods. "Legacy" was based on the well-known migration story of mainland pioneers who braved the treacherous journey from China to Formosa Island more than three hundred years ago. Dancers wearing traditional blue cotton robes and loose pants performed with bare feet. Suddenly, a huge white scarf symbolizing ocean waves caught the attention of everyone in the audience. The chief choreographer, Lin Huai-Min, a graduate of Martha Graham's School of Contemporary Dance, adopted this symbol from traditional Chinese opera.[1] A few dancers held the four edges of the scarf and shook it to form ocean-like ripples. One wave came after another; some were strong and fast, others gentle and slow. At one point dancers increased the height of the ripples, symbolizing the arrival of the storm. All the dancers sitting on the "boat" started to jump and tumble, performing fierce spiral turns that could only be performed by dancers trained in Martha Graham's techniques.

On the same day that "Legacy" premiered, the United States withdrew its recognition of Taiwan as a country, ending its direct and formal diplomatic relationship with the Kuomintang government in order to establish state-to-state diplomatic relations with the People's Republic of China. Meanwhile, the Taiwanese government in Taipei announced that Taiwan would leave the

United Nations. Since then, Taiwan's status as a country has gone unrecognized by the United States, as well as many other countries.

Because of this unexpected political catastrophe, the dancers and the audience at this performance of "Legacy" that night shared feelings of shock and disappointment. As the dancers desperately struggled with the white scarf symbolizing the ocean storm, they broke into tears. The audience also cried over Taiwan's new predicament: it had become an isolated little island tossed about in the wind and waves.

As it turned out, however, the cultural, economic, and technological ties between the United States and Taiwan only grew stronger after that day. Instead of formal diplomatic relationships, Taiwan's mass media has played a significant role in bridging the East and the West. The introduction of televisions into every Taiwanese household has resulted in significant cultural developments. According to a survey in *Commonwealth* magazine, 77 percent of households in Taiwan had TV sets in 1972, while 90 percent of households had color TV by 1985. Popular American sitcoms and Hollywood movies influenced every Taiwanese household. *Flipper, Mission Impossible, The Bill Cosby Show*, and Warner Brothers and Disney cartoons were favorites among Taiwanese families. Teens were crazy about George Lucas's *Star Wars*. High school students updated one another about new songs that they heard on the latest *Osmond Family Show*. Young people read *Rolling Stone* and learned disco steps from John Travolta in *Saturday Night Fever*. They chatted about American sitcoms like *Cheers, Who's the Boss?* and *Murphy Brown* during their lunch breaks and when they were waiting for the bus after school. More important, McDonald's opened its first Taiwan restaurant in 1984, at a location a few minutes walk from my parents' flat. Since then, dining out at McDonald's has been trendy for middle-class urban families. Shortly after McDonald's arrived, Kentucky Fried Chicken and Wendy's began colonizing Taipei's urban landscape. Children born after the late 1960s became "McDonald's babies." For better or worse, my younger brother was one of them. His generation and those after him adored McDonald's. They ate there, dated there, hung out there, and got a job there. My younger brother finally overcame his love affair with McDonald's after he arrived in America to study and found out that many members of the American middle class loathe the fast-food chain.

At the same time that Hollywood entertainment and American fast food were becoming popular, Hsinchu Science Park staged its grand opening on December 15, 1980. Suddenly, everyone in Taiwan wanted to learn about computer technology. Classes on Fortran 77 became the most popular courses on every Taiwan university campus, and there was a long waiting list to get in every semester. Then, as soon as personal computers became available (IBM introduced their first PCs in 1981), they became the focus of attention. During this era of the rise of computer technology, Morris Chang left his position as CEO of GM, moved to Taiwan, and founded Taiwan Semiconductor (TSMC). By 1985 he had become the father of semiconductor industry in Taiwan (Chung-Mou Chang 1998, 192).[2] A decade later TSMC became one of the largest semiconductor companies in the world.

Chang and others who launched the first wave of successful high-tech companies were also the first wave of trans-Pacific commuters to establish their start-up companies in Hsinchu Science Park. Their pattern of traveling between Taiwan and Silicon Valley became a model emulated by many Taiwanese families who wanted to immigrate to other countries, such as the United States, Canada, and Australia. Migration from Taiwan was an extremely hot trend in the 1980s and 1990s. I remember that one or two of my elementary school classmates moved away every semester, becoming the parachute children described in chapter 4.

Several scholars have examined the transnational economic connections established between the Asian immigrants' homeland and their new land since the beginning of the 1990s (i.e., Ong 1992, 1993; Ong, Bonacich, and Cheng 1994). During the 1980s and 1990s many middle-class Taiwanese families migrated to suburban neighborhoods in the United States. One result of this mass migration to the United States was the emergence of Monterey Park, a suburb of Los Angeles, as "Little Taipei." In the 1970s, Monterey Park had become a gateway for Asian immigrants arriving in the United States, especially those from Taiwan. Then, the Asian population in Monterey Park increased from 15.3 percent in 1970 to 56.4 percent in 1990 (Horton 1995, 12). Facing this rapid growth of the Asian immigrant population, Monterey Park's Caucasian old-timers became very cautious and frustrated. In John Horton's book *The Politics of Diversity*, a white senior citizen and long-time resident of Monterey Park is quoted as saying, "Before, immigrants were poor. They lived in their own neighborhoods (Chinatown) and moved into ours (suburbs) after they learned English, got a good job, and became accustomed to our ways. Today, the Chinese come right in with their money and their ways. We are the aliens" (ibid., 20).

While Monterey Park gained fame as the home of the first suburban Chinatown, Little Taipei, many other "mini-Taipei" communities were cropping up along the Pacific coastline, in Cupertino (in the San Francisco Bay Area), Seattle, and Vancouver, Canada. Why were these middle- to upper-middle-class suburban Taiwanese communities suddenly mushrooming up and down the coast? What the elderly woman in Monterey Park did not know was that Chinese American real estate agents had already established a trans-Pacific market for potential Taiwanese and Chinese newcomers. Properties of all sorts along the West Coast were "all vigorously marketed in Taiwan and Hong Kong by enterprising Chinese real estate and interests who saw a future in a convenient, pleasant, and affordable suburb" (ibid., 15).

By the mid-1980s, real estate companies on both sides of the Pacific had realized that there was a growing market of Taiwanese looking for homes. In the United States, ambitious Chinese American realtors promoted their suburban properties not only to the middle-class Chinese newcomers, but also to their relatives and friends back in Taiwan or Hong Kong. In Taiwan, investing in American real estate, especially on the West Coast, had become fashionable. Residents of my Taipei neighborhood frequently found flyers in their mailboxes promoting beautiful suburban properties in San Francisco and Los Angeles (Fig. 5.1). Taiwanese bought these homes and dreamed about the new lives they might lead in the United States. Some invested in U.S. real estate to meet migration requirements. Others were in it simply with the goal of investing their money in a secure place. The United States was considered much safer than Taiwan, primarily because of the belief that Communist China would never attack the United States.

Real estate companies provided potential buyers with comprehensive packages, including mortgage payment plans, rental agency services, and rental management, which made investing in an American home convenient for overseas buyers. Buyers no longer had to leave Taiwan to buy an American property. Many Taiwanese buyers first visited the homes they purchased many years after the original sale.

I would not have paid attention to the trans-Pacific real estate network if my parents had not bought a property across the ocean. Most Taiwanese who invested in suburban American properties did not base their decisions

FIG. 5.1. A real estate advertisement that attempts to attract investors to buy single-family detached houses in Los Angeles, California. Source: CinTi Leghorn Building, No. 47.

on flyers they received in their mailboxes, but rather on the advice of relatives or friends who had already emigrated to the United States. In my family's case, my mother's best friend had decided to send her two sons to Seattle. Her husband stayed in Taiwan while she shuttled back and forth between Seattle and Taipei. It was she who convinced my mother to buy a house in Seattle.

My father showed me a picture of the house when he first received it. It was a three-bedroom single-family detached house with a huge tree in the backyard. The real estate company provided my parents with an annual update on the house each year that they owned it, including a special report on how they had removed the tree after a thunderstorm. My parents never visited the house until ten years after they bought it. On their way back to Taiwan after visiting me in California, they stopped in Seattle and took a walk in "their neighborhood" and finally saw the house from the outside. A year after my parents sold the house, I was in Seattle. A friend asked me if I wanted to visit the house. "No," I replied. For me, the memory of the house conjured up my ambivalence about my parents' purchase of a house so that they could feel some sort of connection to the dream of an American life.

"Identity is people's sources of meaning and experiences," writes Manuel Castells (1997, 6). My ambivalence about the Seattle house intertwined with the ambiguity of my Taiwanese identity within a global sociopolitical context. Taiwan's diplomatic relationship with the global community was dramatically impacted by the U.S. withdrawal of diplomatic recognition for Taiwan. The day on which Taiwan entered its post–United Nations era marked the dramatic transformation of Taiwanese identity, of how Taiwanese view themselves collectively and individually. While Taiwan is not a country recognized by the world, Section 4 of the Taiwan Relations Act adopted by the U.S. Congress in 1979 declares that "the absence of diplomatic relations or recognition shall not affect the application of the laws of the United States with respect to Taiwan; . . . whenever the laws of the United States refer or relate to foreign countries, nations, states, governments, or similar entities, such terms shall include and such laws shall apply with such respect to Taiwan" (Chang 1999).

The diplomatic action that resulted in Taiwan existing as a de facto but not an actual country has caused the Taiwanese to struggle with both the questions "Who am I?" and "What is Taiwan?" My own answers to these questions shift from one situation to the next, just like my Taiwanese identity. Because Taiwan is a de facto state, we Taiwanese have no fixed rules by which to construct our identities. As a Taiwanese embodying a shifting identity, I have learned to live comfortably with the constellation of contradictory meanings and fragmented experiences that blend Eastern and Western cultures and politics in my everyday life. Just as the Cloud Gate dancers wore traditional long blue robes, I wear an orthodox Chinese costume on the outside. But the Cloud Gate dancers challenged the orthodoxy of Chinese opera by juxtaposing it with Martha Graham's modern choreographic concepts and movements. The message that I took away from their performance was that I didn't have to choose between traditional and modern identities; that instead I could make the choice to juxtapose, mix, and meld the traditional with the modern, the urban with the suburban, and the Taiwanese with the American. Instead of constantly trying to define exactly who I was, I could begin to think of my ambiguous identity as an opportunity. As a result I have come to think of myself as a Taiwanese in Taiwan in one situation and a Taiwanese American in the United States in another. The ambiguity I feel about who I am enables me to flow comfortably between different cultures.

Transcultural Thanksgiving Dinner

In my own experience of living in post–United Nations Taiwan, the traditional "rule" that one thinks of culture as a fixed and coherent entity was constantly and easily broken. My culture was not singular but instead a blend of many cultures. I first became aware of the process of the blending of cultures at a Thanksgiving dinner in California at which the American turkey was seasoned with Chinese ingredients and the entertainment was karaoke with Taiwanese rock-and-roll songs.

Before further describing my first California Thanksgiving dinner in 1998, I should step back and describe my experience of eating American meals in Taiwan. During my elementary and middle school years, from 1969 to 1978, only those with the highest income could afford to eat Western- or American-style meals in Taiwan. Those of the lower middle class, like my family, went to Western-style restaurants only for very special events, like my parents' ten-year wedding anniversary. My brother and I were always very excited for this special occasion, when everyone in the family dressed in their best clothes.

Our excitement was tempered by the challenge of having to learn how to eat in a formal Western style. Although for Chinese meals we used only a pair of chopsticks from beginning to the end, to eat at Western restaurants we were required to learn complicated processes, such as how to spoon soup from a bowl and how to use the proper knives and forks for each course. The day before our first American meal, at the Shanghai Lou-da-chuang Restaurant in Taipei City, my mother patiently trained my brother and me in the important skill of eating soup. She repeatedly emphasized that only well-educated people ate at American restaurants and that we must behave ourselves. Otherwise, those sitting close to our table would laugh at us and belittle our family. I also remember watching a short public education television series that taught us the proper manners for dining the Western way and thinking that American culture must be very "civilized" because of the procedures we were expected to follow.

The American restaurant meals we ate would include bread and butter, salad, soup, and a main course. Then came a choice of dessert and coffee or tea. I always chose coffee because having tea seemed too Chinese. Before 1984, the year that McDonald's arrived in Taipei, most Taiwanese did not know what a hamburger was, and many had the impression that all Americans ate those formal meals every day. I was also impressed by the difference in how meals were served at Chinese and American restaurants. At Chinese restaurants food was typically placed in the center of the table for the family to share, while at American restaurants individual choice was emphasized as each plate was served separately. I was amused that when eating an American meal I was required to ask permission if I wanted to try something on someone else's plate.

Despite having learned the graceful Western manners required to eat American meals in Taiwan, I never used any of these skills when I came to the United States twenty years later. Like many Taiwanese trans-Pacific commuters, I have created a transcultural lifestyle that blends Taiwanese, American, and other cultural practices together at the dinner table. One such transcultural meal stands out in my memory. In the fall of 1998, I was invited to Thanksgiving dinner by a family in Cupertino, California. The husband was a manager of a high-tech company, and the wife had her own career. The young couple had two children, a boy about five years old and another that was two. The husband's parents lived with them and shared the responsibility of taking care of the children. In this regard, the grandparents were trans-Pacific commuters, spending a couple of months each year in Taiwan and the rest of the year in Cupertino.

With the exception of the grandparents' global commuting, the family, composed of grandparents, parents, and children living together, was very like the typical modern extended family that you would find in Taiwan.[3] As was common in Taiwan, the grandparents provided free day care for the young couple. The only major difference I noticed between this family and a typical family in Taiwan was that the grandparents spoke Taiwanese and Chinese while the grandchildren replied in English, Chinese, and Taiwanese.

Their house was located within a ten-minute drive of the Ranch 99 supermarket where they did most of their grocery shopping and dining out. In addition to their single-family detached house they enjoyed a beautiful garden. When I complimented them on their well-maintained garden, they told me that they hired a professional landscaper to take care of it. They had both grown up in urban apartments in Taiwan and lacked the time and knowledge to tend the lawn and ornamental plants.

The interior of the house was modern, with elegant furnishings in the living room and a thirty-inch stereo TV in the family room. Each child had his own computer in his bedroom. Everything displayed in the living room could have been in a typical middle-class American home. However, at the center of their dining room was a big, round Chinese dining table. About twenty of us—including their relatives living in Fremont and Los Angeles—gathered around that table for Thanksgiving dinner. We spoke Chinese, Taiwanese, and English as we drank wine from Napa Valley and ate homemade Chinese dishes, a salad made from California produce, and an American roast turkey stuffed with Chinese ingredients. We used chopsticks for every dish. Although serving spoon and forks were available, we did not always use them to serve ourselves. People served themselves whatever they liked, whether soup, salad, or rice, in no particular order.

Following the feast, we all moved to the basement family room and sat around the big TV. They had a very large collection of karaoke video compact discs, from very old Chinese songs that the grandparents were familiar with to trendy Taiwanese rock-and-roll that was very popular among the younger generation at the time. While the young couple was singing, Lily, the grandmother of the family, asked us all to follow her in ballroom dance steps that she practiced every morning in her neighborhood park in Taiwan.

There was nothing purely Taiwanese or Californian, Chinese or American, at this Thanksgiving dinner in Cupertino, as different cultural practices intertwined with each other randomly. I can easily identify the mosaic cultural components, from family life to food, language, furnishings, interior design, and gardening. For example, following mainstream American preferences, they lived in a typical American single-family house with a nice garden. However, they did not enjoy taking care of their garden themselves. Although gardening is part of American suburban life for many American families, this young couple had never had the experience of taking care of a garden by themselves and preferred spending their free time catching up on sleep. When choosing the location of the house, the young couple had considered moving to a good school district the top priority. The husband emphasized that they wanted their children to receive the best education. In addition, they wanted to live in a suburb because they felt that it represented their achievements: "A nice suburban house represents that we have made our immigrant lives successful. It is very important to us," the husband told me. In terms of furniture, the big round table in the dining room serves as the center of activity for family events during important holidays such as Thanksgiving, Christmas, New Year's Day, Chinese Moon Festival, and Chinese New Year. In terms of the food, the "traditional" Thanksgiving turkey that we had eaten was prepared by the Ranch 99 supermarket with Chinese ingredients. In addition to this "transcultural turkey," we had Chinese dishes, American salad, Mexican guacamole, and California rice.

The intertwining of cultural practices in this family's Thanksgiving dinner expressed their ambiguity about who they were and which culture they belonged to. As mentioned earlier, the ambiguity of Taiwanese identity contributes to the ease with which the Taiwanese accept transcultural experiences. In the following sections, I elaborate on how bi-gration movements accelerate this transcultural phenomenon, how this phenomenon relates to the thirdspace theory, and how the transcultural phenomenon intertwines with the *jin-yi-huan-xiang* narrative and influences lifestyles and landscapes on both sides of the Pacific.

Bi-gration in Thirdspace

While shifting Taiwanese identities function as the catalyst for transcultural changes in Taiwanese daily life, bi-gration constructs a new type of fluid space, the "thirdspace," where meanings, events, and experiences change and transform. I will first address the relationship between bi-gration and thirdspace, then follow up with a discussion on transcultural lifestyles.

As I described in chapter 1, bi-gration accelerates the adoption of transcultural lifestyles, because trans-Pacific commuters can simultaneously experience the cultures of both their old and new homelands. The simultaneous experience of both homelands profoundly influences their relationships with their homes and their home identities, that is, where their homes are and what types of home express their view of themselves. What I learned from my interviewees was that some of them felt that both their old and new homelands were their homes. As they fly frequently between their two homes and two cultures, they discover that both express parts of their personal and cultural identities. They cannot distinguish their American selves from their Taiwanese selves. They feel a sense of ease at both homes, and this suggested to me a paradigm shift that was driven by the trans-Pacific commuters' transnational bi-gration.

From a theoretical point of view, the bi-gration phenomenon, which has been emerging since the late 1980s, signals a paradigm shift in how we perceive the migration cycle. It challenges the traditional presumption that migration is a one-way voyage, and that immigrants seldom return to their old homelands (Seamon 1985). Recently, a few researchers have observed the paradigm shift in other transnational migration scenarios. For example, in her book *The Transnational Villagers*, Peggy Levitt investigates how immigrants from the Dominican Republic intertwine their political and economic participation in both Boston and Miraflores. She argues:

> Many Americans . . . assume that migrants will eventually transfer their loyalty and community membership from countries they leave to the ones that receive them. But increasing numbers of migrants continue to participate in the political and economic lives of their homeland, even as they are incorporated into their host societies. Instead of loosening their connections and trading one membership for another, some individuals are keeping their feet in both worlds. They use political, religious, and civic arenas to forge social relations, earn their livelihood, and exercise their rights across borders. (Levitt 2001, 4)

The new bi-gration paradigm that I want to bring into focus is much less about political and economic connections and more about the links between landscapes and the lifestyles of the homeland and the host societies. By viewing immigration through the lens of two-way bi-gration rather than one-way migration, we can see that immigrants not only carry their homeland cultural practices to their new homes, but they also transplant cultural practices from their new homes back to their homeland. In other words, seeing immigration through the bi-gration lens enables a new view of the relationship between home identities, lifestyles, and physical forms of buildings and landscapes, and it demonstrates how economic transformations impact cultural transformations and consequent landscape transformations.

From the formation of their home identities to the arrangement of their family lives, the lives of Taiwanese American trans-Pacific commuters are played out in their travels between two homes separated by great distances. Their way of thinking about their homes, families, and communities as fluid processes rather than static objects enables them to think about their two homes in terms of the fluid experiential self that they construct during their daily routines and practices. The homes they choose for themselves, and the landscapes upon which the homes are situated become material reflections of their process of identity formation.

Indeed, trans-Pacific commuters no longer think of the self as a reflection of home and community, but rather as a process that enables the ever-changing construction of the meanings of home. For them, the self does not match up to the home in a one-to-one correspondence; their conception of self is not framed as an object whose fixity enables it to mirror another fixed object. Rather than being fixed and static, the trans-Pacific commuter's self is subject to a fluid process of construction, and its resilience enables an easy transition between a set of everyday transcultural experiences. The changing self enables the trans-Pacific commuter to live a life in which he or she becomes adroit at shifting between different sets of cultural practices. This adaptive self enables trans-Pacific commuters to bounce from location to location, from culture to culture, and to randomly bump into multiple cultural artifacts (foods, books, landscapes, homes, movies) and many types of people without thinking that they have to view these "other" cultures or peoples through a stable or consistent lens.

I found that I began to understand how trans-Pacific commuters make meaning of their multiple homes when I gave up the old notion that home was an object that mirrored the self and instead began to think of home as one of many locations experienced within a process of constructing a self. Edward Soja's concept of "thirdspace" helped me put a conceptual frame around the trans-Pacific commuters' individual and collective lives. Soja developed the thirdspace concept as a way of convincing his readers to stop thinking about Los Angeles as a stable place and start thinking about it as a fluid place, one that is ever-changing in physical form and, therefore, in meaning. He wanted his readers to question old and familiar ways of thinking about physical and geographic space in favor of new ways that aim "at opening up and expanding the scope and critical sensibility of . . . already established spatial or geographical imaginations" (Soja 1996, 1). Soja elaborates on this concept, writing that thirdspace is "a purposefully tentative and flexible term that attempts to capture what is actually a constantly shifting and changing milieu of ideas, events, appearances, and meanings . . . there is a growing awareness of simultaneity and interwoven complexity of the social, the historical, and the spatial, their inseparability and interdependence" (ibid., 2, 3).

The thirdspace concept helped me to understand how Melissa thought about her life as a member of a transnational community whose geographic boundaries and social rules seemed so strange to me at first. As I began to understand thirdspace, I was able to think about Los Angeles not so much as an object made up of a collection of buildings and streets, but as an ever-changing series of physical and spatial events. It became possible for me to understand that Los Angeles's inhabitants could make individually valid statements about what their city meant to them—statements that did not have to be judged in terms of which was the truest or best or most universal—because singular, static meanings no longer applied within a thirdspace framework of change and multiplicity. I realized that I had to abandon my perspective that spaces, places, and communities were singular and static so that I could describe the changing and multiple aspects of the trans-Pacific commuter lifestyle and how landscape reflected the commuters' sense of their selves.

As the trans-Pacific commuters experience a shifting set of psychic meanings as they move physically from one location to another, they construct their homes, their landscapes, and their identities by intertwining the place that they are experiencing in the present and the place that they have temporarily left behind. Their flights back and forth across national boundaries, their psychic experience of being in multiple places at once, and their way of sustaining a coherent identity by thinking of themselves as simultaneously attached to different homes, different landscapes, and different cultures are all aspects of these trans-Pacific commuters' daily lives. A more detailed view of that life lies ahead.

Members of the trans-Pacific commuter community embody a new way of thinking of and constructing home identity. They understand the self as a process rather than an object, and this reframing of self suggests a reframing of the approach to analyzing the role one's home plays in the process of constructing a sense of self. The trans-Pacific commuter's reconception of the self as a process, rather than an object, reflects a new understanding of identity that feminist and postmoderninist theorists have recently developed (Rorty 1989; Butler 1990; Belenky et al. 1997).

Reconceiving the self as an ongoing event rather than a static object enabled the trans-Pacific commuters I spoke with to continuously encounter lots of unfamiliar sorts of people and cultural situations with pleasure rather than with the sense they were in danger of losing their connection to their roots. They took pleasure in identifying with and moving across diverse cultures and blending in with the culture they were experiencing. The energy they employed in this process was the starting point from which there emerged a new set of transcultural home identities.

Emerging Transcultural Lifestyles

As trans-Pacific commuters have reconceived themselves and their fluid homes, they have also assigned new meanings to the *jin-yi-huan-xiang* (beautiful clothes returning home) narrative. *Huan-xiang*, or returning home, to them means returning to either of their homes on opposite sides of the ocean. This is not only because they have multicentered family networks that span the Pacific. They have also developed transcultural lifestyles in both homes. When I interviewed them in Hsinchu, they told me they enjoyed Hsinchu Science Park because it allowed them to feel as if they were in the United States. Then, when I interviewed those same trans-Pacific commuters in Silicon Valley, they said that they really enjoyed life in Silicon Valley because they felt as if they were in Taiwan.

Transcultural lifestyles express a new set of transcultural home identities across the Pacific Ocean, and embody a postmodern interpretation of the *jin-yi-huan-xiang* journey. The thirdspace constructed by the action of bigration sets up the stage for the postmodern journey. The postmodern journey allows trans-Pacific commuters to feel quite comfortable about crossing back and forth between personal, social, and political borders. For example, Taiwanese television and print media constantly present their public with a

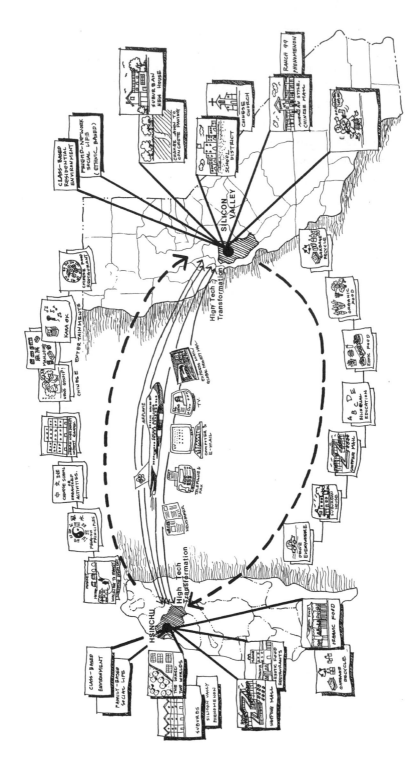

FIG. 5.2. Transcultural lifestyles flow across the Pacific Ocean. Graphic: Kimmy Y. C. Chen, 1999.

rhetoric that states that on the one hand "Taiwan is its own country," while on the other "it is part of China." Seen from a modern perspective, this rhetoric poses a paradox filled with contradiction, and results in a sense of identity that is equally contradictory and paradoxical. But from a postmodern perspective, where media rhetoric is viewed as a political stage for theatrical performance, and identity is also seen as a performance, the contradictions of the past are taken less seriously, and the borders between nations are taken less literally.

Under these circumstances, trans-Pacific commuters pursue two different sets of *jin-yi* (beautiful clothes) in an attempt to achieve status in both Hsinchu and Silicon Valley. The *jin-yi* that confer status in Taiwan are different from those that are highly valued in the United States. In Hsinchu the trans-Pacific commuters want to be perceived as returnees from the United States and constantly remind local residents of their American status. In Silicon Valley, on the other hand, they want to be perceived as middle-class Taiwanese Americans who have achieved mainstream American status. In the meantime, they want to enjoy their Taiwanese way of life in the American suburbs. Depending on whether they are in Hsinchu or in Silicon Valley, they dress in the proper "beautiful clothes" specific to their geographic context. Their beautiful clothes, therefore, are fluid and always changing. All the contradictory meanings, activities, and events they experience become intertwined with their fluid self-identities within the thirdspace that they create through their bi-gration.

Figure 5.2 shows the relationship of transcultural lifestyles flowing between Hsinchu and Silicon Valley, the exchange of physical environments and daily habits, and the striking exchange and merging of Taiwanese and American lifestyles. Technological advances such as television, cell phones, telecommunication devices, and advanced air transportation enable the exchange across the two regions.

Trans-Pacific Life in Silicon Valley

Regularly jetting back and forth between one's place of birth and one's adopted place has enabled global commuters to freely flow between cultural practices, to mix and meld cultural practices or choose between the two as they see fit. However, the free flow of cultures is complicated by their need to be acknowledged for the *jin-yi* status that they have acquired.

After many hours of conversation with and observation of these trans-Pacific commuters, I realized that they considered living a Taiwanese life in an American suburban environment—enjoying *both* their Taiwanese way of life *and* Silicon Valley's ranch houses, good schools, and thriving computer industry—the ultimate sign of having achieved the status they prized. They felt they had achieved the best of both worlds when they lived an American suburban life while simultaneously experiencing aspects of their Taiwanese way of life.

Many high-tech Taiwanese immigrants had moved into nice suburban houses located in good school districts in Silicon Valley. They preferred new houses to ones built before the 1980s. It was a plus for them if their house were located close to shopping centers, especially those carrying Chinese groceries. In Taiwan, on the other hand, convenience was typically rooted in mixed-use environments. Most did their daily shopping at morning or afternoon markets adjacent to their neighborhoods, and public and private services were within walking distance.

In Silicon Valley, taking care of their lawns and gardens was generally considered a big headache. Some of them converted their grass lawns to Astro Turf. Others who considered a large yard a waste simply decreased the size of their yards by attaching storage structures to their garages. However, no matter what they did to their homes and gardens, they tended to dutifully respect conventional principles of feng shui.

During the weekday, they worked at high-tech companies and collaborated with colleagues with multiethnic backgrounds (English-Lueck 2002). Some of their cohorts were immigrants from other countries, which provided a certain degree of cultural diversity.

However, many Taiwanese engineers admitted that they still paid more attention to issues in Taiwan than news of events in California or the United States. They confessed to checking Taiwanese news web sites whenever they had a break. One engineer revealed, "I have to make an effort to listen to local news when I drive to work every day. Otherwise, I just check Taiwan news and hang out with my Taiwanese engineer friends."

They spent most of their leisure time with family and Taiwanese friends. Their parents might stay at their suburban houses and take care of their children. On Saturday mornings they would drop their children off at Chinese school or other educational programs before they went shopping with their parents at Chinese markets. Around noon they would pick up their children from their classes, and then the entire family, grandparents, parents, and children, ate at one of the many Chinese restaurants at the Ranch 99 market.

Sunday morning some of them attended a Chinese church. Those who were not churchgoers invited their Taiwanese friends to their houses and had a potluck meal before playing mah-jongg together. During the mah-jongg game they updated each other on the gossip gleaned from other Taiwanese friends or chatted about the recent news from Taiwan. They sang karaoke at home or at popular karaoke bars.

They liked to participate in outdoor activities as much as most Californians do. Hiking, biking, and skiing were popular activities. Golf, tennis, and working out were also trendy, especially with single male engineers. Those who had small children and dogs enjoyed strolling in parks close to their homes. Watching their children play at playgrounds with other children from different ethnic backgrounds was one of the very few multiethnic interactions they might have.

The sum of their Silicon Valley activities—their lifestyle choices, homes, landscapes, and living and working environments—described above added up to the trans-Pacific commuters' perception that they had acquired the status of *jin-yi*, but enjoying that status required the acknowledgment of those they had left behind in Taiwan.

Trans-Pacific Life in Hsinchu

Upon their return to Hsinchu Science Park, they liked showing local residents the physical manifestation of their beautiful clothes—their Hsinchu California-style suburban homes—which represented their PhDs and American citizenship. In addition, they wanted to live an Americanized lifestyle, as that was a way of drawing a line between themselves and the motherlanders. That line distinguished them as a group that embodied highbrow American culture.

It was primarily the astronauts, green card moms, and returnees who subscribed to this double cultural standard, living a Taiwanese way of life in Silicon Valley and an American way of life in Hsinchu. The motherlanders and local residents formed the audience that simultaneously loved and hated the trans-Pacific commuters' show of their "beautiful clothes." Although the

F I G . 5 . 3 . Carrefour displays their merchandise very similarly to Kmart or Target in the United States. Photo by author, 1998.

locals were upset that their lives and landscapes had been impacted by the suburban houses and Americanized way of life of others, they were simultaneously jealous and wanted to obtain the same American "beautiful clothes." The motherlanders and local residents, however, did not understand that they only got to watch half of the show, the part performed in Hsinchu.

In Hsinchu, the high-tech Taiwanese families had moved into newly developed homes on the hillsides outside the city. Local real estate developers had started promoting the homes in these gated communities after discovering the trans-Pacific commuters' desire to lead a California lifestyle that would distinguish them from their neighbors. These gated communities of townhouses and single-family detached houses became popular not only with trans-Pacific commuters, but also with the wanna-bes, the motherlanders, and local Hsinchu residents. Meanwhile, Carrefour Shopping Center, a multistory shopping center that provided indoor parking, became the most popular place for global commuters to shop. The layout and displays at Carrefour were very similar to those at Kmart, Target, and other large chain stores that these commuters frequented in the United States (Fig. 5.3).

Driving to stores was commonplace in Hsinchu, as in the United States. Hannah told me that she enjoyed the convenience of having a freeway entrance close to her home, which meant that she could drive to Carrefour in less than ten minutes to buy "fresh vegetables and exotic food items," and then drive to Taipei for other goods. Hannah then realized that, despite having lived in Hsinchu for six years, she still retained the shopping habits she had acquired in America.

In addition to their fondness for shopping in supermarkets that they reach by car, the trans-Pacific commuters also adopted trendy new eating habits, developing a taste for the healthful and exotic foods they first experienced overseas. They liked to dine out at upscale ethnic restaurants, a symbol of their highbrow status, but they also complained that the food at Hsinchu restaurants could not compare with that in Silicon Valley. In addition to enjoying ethnic foods, they preferred eating organic vegetables and shopping at health food stores. Organic grocery stores became a center for their daily social interaction, and they also organized shopping networks to obtain special items like organic produce and meats and unusual varieties of tofu. They believed they could get higher-quality ingredients through their networks of various ingredient providers than others were able to get from local markets or Carrefour Shopping Centers. Their network shopping system was also an extension of their experience of studying overseas. Most Taiwanese students, especially those living in small college towns, could only buy certain types of food, like tofu and handmade dumplings, through local Taiwanese student networks. Finally, they were also very serious about recycling garbage. The Hwei-chu Housewife Club adopted recycling garbage as their most important goal when the club was first established.

In terms of education, bilingual education was considered essential for the children of trans-Pacific commuter families. Advertisements for new bilingual kindergartens and daycare facilities were posted everywhere in Hsinchu. The experimental bilingual school located inside Hsinchu Science Park was their top choice, but only families who lived inside the park were allowed to send their children there. Some who worked inside the park but lived outside preferred placing their children in good Silicon Valley schools to enrolling them in Hsinchu public schools.

When it came to their recreation, engineer families expressed a strong desire to be close to nature. For management-level personnel, tennis and golf, associated with upper-middle-class status, were their two favorite sports.

Their participation in tennis and golf not only suggested their elevated social status, but it also provided them with business networking opportunities. Some parents in fact enrolled their teenage children in golf programs to
prepare them for a higher-status life. Single men preferred working out or at-
tending picnics, since both activities provided them with opportunities for
meeting potential dates. Otherwise, they had few opportunities to meet potential partners in their male-dominated working environments.

Three hundred years ago the ancestors of today's Taiwanese left their
homes in mainland China and traveled across the stormy Taiwan Strait to
settle on the little island of Taiwan. Fast-forwarding to the 1970s, many up-
per- and middle-class Taiwanese embarked on a second wave of mass migration, traveling across the Pacific Ocean and settling in the United States.
Today, as the Taiwanese American trans-Pacific commuters bi-grate between
Taiwan and the United States, they keep alive the traditional *jin-yi-huan-xiang* narrative. For their ancestors, *jin-yi-huan-xiang* meant a return to their
homeland, a reunion with family, and a reception conferring honor upon
them. For today's trans-Pacific commuters, *jin-yi-huan-xiang* is played out
through an actively maintained go-between status and its outcome of a
transcultural lifestyle, because, in today's Taiwanese society, motherlanders
respect the go-between status.

The ambiguity and confusion that trans-Pacific commuters have experienced since the United States withdrew its recognition of Taiwan as a country can be seen as an asset rather than a liability. The result of living as trans-
Pacific commuters in the post-UN era is that they constantly shift their
Taiwanese identity between the either-or choice that politicians and the media present to them—a choice between "Taiwan is a country" or "Taiwan is
not a country." But the experience of shifting Taiwanese identity has become
so much a part of their lives, so natural, that it has enabled the breakdown
of traditional cultural boundaries. Their capacity for fluid family arrangements and for dealing with fragmented experiences and seemingly contradictory values has enabled them to arrive at a "thirdspace." Within this
thirdspace, depending on which home they are returning to, they put on the
beautiful clothes that tell the story of the faraway place that they come from.
In Hsinchu, they prefer the American landscape. In Silicon Valley, they love
Taiwanese spaces, places, and amenities. Their *homes* may be located in two
different countries and cultures, but their sense of *home identity* depends on
being in both places at once.

Communities

SIX

Ranch 99: A Virtual Chinatown

When I first visited Hsinchu Science Park in 1997, I was immediately surprised by the contrast between the area and the far more crowded urban landscapes that surrounded it. Inside the park were suburban American–style corporate campuses typified by glass-enclosed offices and low-density housing. Everything was neat, green, and clean. Outside the park, the streets were congested day and night, with scooters zigzagging through traffic and vehicles parked illegally. Even the pedestrians had to weave their way along the sidewalks, which were packed with people and the colorful commodities that merchants displayed outside their shops.

The contrast between the two worlds was very disoriented because they were separated by only a three-minute drive. Local residents living in Hsinchu City outside the park also felt the sharp contrast between these two worlds daily. Although they admired the "highbrow" American suburban landscape, they also harshly criticized their trans-Pacific commuter neighbors for importing too much of America into the local community. In a conversation I had with two Hsinchu residents, Pat, a community activist, told me, "The Bamboo Village in Hsinchu Science Park looks just like an American colonial town on Halloween and Christmas. It is fine if they [the trans-Pacific commuter families] are Americans, like Chinese in Chinatown." "But look, they are Taiwanese," Marie, a congresswoman in the district that included Hsinchu, added quickly. "Why don't they pay more attention to the local religious and cultural festivals that we try to promote?"

To Marie and Pat, trans-Pacific commuters seemed highly Americanized: they celebrated American holidays, lived in California-style houses, and routinely appeared and disappeared, flying back and forth between Taiwan and the United States. For the most part, trans-Pacific commuters in Hsinchu were not bothered by the attitudes of locals like Marie and Pat. They made no effort to blend in with the local social and physical landscape. Quite the contrary, they viewed the fact that they stuck out as a sign that they had risen above the local Hsinchu community. They regarded their "go-between" lives and their Americanized homes and habits as signs of their elite status.

However, as explained in the previous chapter, this same group of global commuters had a very different relationship with their local context when they were living in America. Instead of wanting to distinguish themselves from the local landscape, as they did in Taiwan, in the United States they preferred to blend into their environment. But, although their relocation from Hsinchu to Silicon Valley entailed a change from *contrasting with* to *integrating with* the local scenery, their melding in with their physical surroundings in the United States did not equate to adopting an American identity (Portes and Rumbaut 1990, 50). Their way of melding into the surroundings while simultaneously retaining their Asian American identities is what made members of the trans-Pacific commuter culture quite different from members of previous Asian immigrant groups.

That same year I first visited Hsinchu Science Park, I flew back from Taiwan to the United States. Shortly after I arrived in California I attended an event in which I was one of hundreds of Asian Americans witnessing the colorful sights and sounds of a Chinese dragon dance. But the occasion was not the Chinese New Year, nor was the location San Francisco's Chinatown. The dance was performed at the grand opening of the Ranch 99 market (Tawa 99, in Chinese) in Milpitas, a town of 62,000 in the southeast of Silicon Valley.

The celebration in Milpitas in April 1997 marked the opening of the fourth Ranch 99 in the San Francisco–Silicon Valley region. More than 95 percent of the crowd that came to shop at Ranch 99 that day was Asian Americans. As I listened to the dialect they spoke, it became clear to me that Taiwanese dominated the crowd that had gathered for the event.

The dominance of Taiwanese Americans was not surprising. The Ranch 99 markets specialize in Chinese food and home supplies, attracting Asian

Americans with roots in Taiwan, Hong Kong, and mainland China. In most locations a large Ranch 99 market functioned as the anchor store in a shopping center that also included dozens of Chinese restaurants, bookstores, and grocery outlets. In an ad that invited potential customers to this particular grand opening event, Ranch 99 claimed that its Milpitas store covered the largest area of any Asian American shopping center in North America.

What surprised me was not the area that the store covered, nor the incredible variety of Asian products I saw as I pushed my cart up and down the aisles. What surprised me was what I learned in conversations I had with shoppers who were members of the trans-Pacific commuter culture. I discovered that shopping had a very significant impact on Taiwanese American identity. As Sharon Zukin wrote in her book *Point of Purchase* (2004), "We dream of shopping for beauty, truth and perfection, and if we do not shop for a perfect society, at least we shop for a perfect self." I was surprised to find that for those persons who had chosen a life of commuting between their high-tech jobs in Silicon Valley and Hsinchu, shopping at Ranch 99 was an important part of the process that enabled them to sustain both their Taiwanese and Asian American home identities (Fig. 6.1). Their process of constructing a shifting, multilayered identity pointed to the difference between the trans-Pacific commuters' process of retaining a dual identity and the previous immigrant population's process of giving up one side of their Asian-American identities.

Peter, a high-tech engineer in his mid-thirties who commuted between his Silicon Valley and Taiwan homes, told me that every time he walked into Ranch 99 he felt that he was back in Taiwan. "In Ranch 99 I don't feel I am a minority at all," he reflected. "I can buy all the things I need there. Although JCPenney is built in a similar American style, everything they sell in Ranch 99 and the other stores in Milpitas Square is so familiar to me, and related to Taiwan. . . . I claim the Ranch 99 can represent my culture."

Although Peter used "culture" in its singular form, I found in talking with him and other trans-Pacific commuters that the Ranch 99 experience represented their sense of belonging to multiple cultures rather than a single culture. The Taiwanese families I spoke with experienced a sense of homecoming whenever they arrived at their local Ranch 99. And just as their suburban homes symbolized their individual identities (discussed further in chapter 9), the Ranch 99 market represented their collective Taiwanese

FIG. 6.1. Ranch 99, a shared Taiwanese American symbol, combines modern American architecture outside with Taiwanese merchandise inside. Photo by author, 2000.

American identity in Silicon Valley. Their process of identity formation through the experience of shopping is what I call the "Ranch 99 experience." For Taiwanese trans-Pacific commuters who lived a portion of their lives in Silicon Valley, the Ranch 99 experience supported them in sustaining a dual identity; it enabled them to present an exterior self that reflected the standard markings of an American identity while simultaneously helping them to preserve their dual Taiwanese–Asian American identity. For the trans-Pacific jet set, the Ranch 99 experience allowed them to not only bring home the groceries, but also participate in a process by which they could hold onto both their old and new selves rather than give one up in order to adopt the other (Miller et al. 1998).

The Emergence of a Taiwanese Population Outside Chinatown

To understand the complex identity formation process used by trans-Pacific commuters to intertwine the *presentation* of an American exterior with the *preservation* of a dual-identity interior, it is useful to compare their bi-gration pattern with the traditional migration pattern of early Chinese immigrants who have settled in Chinatown since the mid-nineteenth century (Chinese Historical Society of America 1991). Taiwanese immigrants actively segregate themselves from the Chinese American culture of Chinatown. Of course, it makes sense that trans-Pacific commuters settled in Silicon Valley communities such as Palo Alto, Cupertino, and Milpitas, because that's where their workplaces in the computer industry were located. But it's also a fact that the mixed-use, high-density environment of San Francisco's Chinatown has enabled a convenient urban lifestyle that is similar to that in most cities in Taiwan. The Silicon Valley Taiwanese commuters, however, have attached their identities to a form that is not related to Chinatown. Instead, Ranch 99, with its American megastore appearance, is the form that speaks to most high-tech families.

Because the history of the Taiwanese trans-Pacific commuter phenomenon is based on a two-way immigration pattern, it cannot be investigated based on the classical Chinatown one-way immigration pattern that Western scholars have previously developed and often apply to examine immigrants who carry on the Chinese cultural heritage (Lyman 1974; Starr 1985, 172; Takaki 1989 and 1993, 191–221). Chinatown is a traditional immigrant community that has been shaped by the one-way migration pattern. Although I use the term "one-way migration" to describe the traditional immigrant pattern, I do not wish to imply that the early Chinese immigrants did not have transnational connections with their hometowns and their families back home. Indeed, many of the early Chinese immigrants who settled in Chinatown maintained connections with their families through the mail, and some sent their savings back to their families in China. In addition, similar to those who participated in the fluid family arrangement that I described in chapter 4, the early Chinese immigrants also struggled with their experiences of "split household families," as Madeline Hsu explains in her book *Dreaming of Gold, Dreaming of Home* (2000). However, the majority of the early Chinese immigrants seldom returned to their hometowns in

FIG. 6.2. Taiwanese American high-tech engineer families prefer Cupertino to San Francisco's Chinatown. They identify Cupertino as their suburban Chinatown in Silicon Valley. Photo by author, 2000.

China; instead, they restructured their hometowns within the physical boundaries of San Francisco's Chinatown. Chinatown was thus transformed into a socio-spatial prototype symbolizing Chinese Americans' collective identity, because the majority of traditional Chinese American networks have been intertwined with the history of San Francisco's Chinatown since the nineteenth century (Yip 1985; Anderson 1987, 1991; Zhou 1992; and Zia 2000).

From the trans-Pacific commuters' perspective, the socioeconomic networks in Chinatown have nothing to do with their lives. Their bi-gration patterns and the technological advances in telecommunications and transportation connect Silicon Valley Taiwanese immigrants with Taiwan directly. They do not need to go shopping in Chinatown for everyday goods because they can go back to Taiwan easily, and the suburban Ranch 99 also fulfills their needs.[1] Neither do they need to establish a social network within Chinatown communities, because they have established their own transnational networks with other Taiwanese professional families.

Cupertino is a good example of how some areas function as a suburban Chinatown. According to the 2000 U.S. Census, its population was 50,546, of which 44 percent were Asian American and 24 percent were Chinese. Six of my interviewees living in Cupertino said that they felt that Cupertino is their Chinatown (Fig. 6.2).

When I asked my interviewees about their Chinatown experiences, a young female engineer, Annie, replied,

> Which Chinatown do you refer to, the San Francisco one, or here [Cupertino]? I think here is our Chinatown. I don't need to speak English, and Chinese commercial signs are everywhere. More importantly, it is very convenient to buy Chinese stuff and Chinese food. I hang out with my Taiwanese friends, plus I browse Taiwanese news on the Internet daily. There is no point for me to go to the one in San Francisco. Though Cupertino is suburban, it's pretty much a Chinatown for me.

The ubiquity of those who speak their language in the suburbs, the presence of social networks, the ease of obtaining information from Taiwan, and the availability of Taiwanese products at Ranch 99 have all caused the creation of a new type of Taiwanese American community in Silicon Valley. The physical forms this community takes consist of modern, Americanized wrappings that have nothing to do with ornate Chinese eaves or pagodas; instead, it is the social networks, information networks, and lifestyles of the trans-Pacific community that create the feeling of being in Taiwan.

Asian American Newcomers in Suburban Silicon Valley

The Ranch 99 experience is linked to the transnational family lives and the transcultural lifestyles described in the previous chapters. The astronauts, returnees, and transplants all live what I have been calling a transcultural lifestyle. Unlike Asian immigrants of the past who have segregated themselves from mainstream American life by settling in Chinatowns, this new Taiwanese immigrant population has chosen to merge right into an American life-style by settling into American suburbia. Most of them bypass settling in Chinatown when they first arrive, as immigrants traditionally do, and instead move directly to a suburban neighborhood when they move to the United States.

Historically there have been two types of Chinese Americans in Silicon Valley. The first type consists of the earlier generations of immigrants who moved to Silicon Valley at the beginning of this century or earlier—when the area was primarily agricultural (Sachs 1999)—and were mainly farmers who grew flowers (Michale S. Chang 1997).[2] The second type consists of middle-class professional immigrants, including the trans-Pacific commuters, the earliest of whom arrived in Silicon Valley after World War II. Most of the latter group have been highly educated and originated from Taiwan or Hong Kong.[3] According to Chang's research on immigrants from the 1960s to the 1990s (ibid.), the new wave of high-tech immigrants started arriving in the 1960s, when the Civil Rights Act of 1964 and the Immigration Reform Act of 1965 facilitated their immigration. Since then, the population of Chinese immigrants in Silicon Valley has soared dramatically.

According to the 2000 U.S. Census (Figs. 6.3 and 6.4), the Chinese American high-tech population in Silicon Valley is concentrated within five municipalities: Cupertino (23.8 percent), Saratoga (18.2 percent), Fremont (14.4 percent), Milpitas (12.9 percent), and Los Altos Hills (12.7 percent). In addition, Palo Alto (9.3 percent) is favored by Chinese high-tech families because of its good schools. The surge in the Chinese-American population corresponded with the high-tech industrial development that began in the area in 1971. From 1965 to 1979, more than 50 percent of Chinese immigrants to Silicon Valley held a bachelor's degree. Many of those holding bachelor's degrees come to the United States on F-1 student visas, to pursue a graduate degree. By Michael Chang's estimation, between 1965 and 1979 one-third of Chinese immigrants who held college degrees began their high-tech entrepreneurial careers there after completing their graduate education.[4] The high-tech engineer identity and the Silicon Valley industrial culture permeate their daily lives.

From Monterey Park to Silicon Valley

What happened in Silicon Valley is very similar to what happened in Monterey Park, the first suburban Chinatown, located outside Los Angeles, in the 1980s. Many Taiwanese businessmen and their families flew back and forth between Los Angeles and their Taiwanese homes, creating the so-called Little Taipei in suburban Monterey Park. Many Caucasian old-timers sold their houses to the new Asian immigrants, especially those from Taiwan, and left town between the late 1970s and the 1980s. The new Taiwanese population became the majority and dramatically transformed the local culture. For example, many Chinese grocery stores, including Ranch 99, were introduced during this period. Signs written in Chinese suddenly took over the traditional landscape in Monterey Park. Residents who did not understand Chinese were extremely upset by the changes, because they felt they had become outsiders in their homeland. It led to ethnic tensions among Chinese, Latino, Caucasian, and African American groups, while it simultaneously created a new matrix for cultural diversity on a regional scale. Sociologists identify this phenomenon as the "Monterey Park syndrome" (Horton 1995; Fong 1994).

From Monterey Park to Cupertino and Fremont, the confrontation between old-timers and newcomers has always been sparked by foreign-language signs. Based on my survey, the high-tech groups in California produce suburban commercial enterprises that spatially resemble other suburban malls but use Chinese-language signs and sell Chinese items and services almost exclusively. In addition, their high-end homes are laid out according to the principles of feng shui, with lucky door numbers, symbols, and Asian-style gardens. Some streets in the suburbs are also named after cities in Taiwan (Mark 1999). Although these changes have minimal impact on the overall development of suburbs in California, these unfamiliar forms of "Asian signage" have set off racial and class tensions between Asians and non-Asians.

Racial prejudices are not always set off by conflicts between Asians and non-Asians. Sometimes stereotypes and prejudgments occur entirely within groups of Chinese immigrants. For example, when I discussed with Henry, a single man in his late twenties, the issue of ethnic diversity, his comments stunned me. He said that although he is Taiwanese, he feels threatened living in a neighborhood dominated by the Chinese. "They are noisy, because they like to speak loudly. Then, it is dangerous to be neighbors with them because they do not follow the traffic rules when they drive. If you hear your Mexican neighbor finally bought car insurance, it means there must be some Chinese moving into your neighborhood." He was also very annoyed that his Chinese neighbors liked to save parking spaces by illegally leaving planters at their curbsides, and that they littered. These are common practices, it should be noted, in Taiwanese cities.

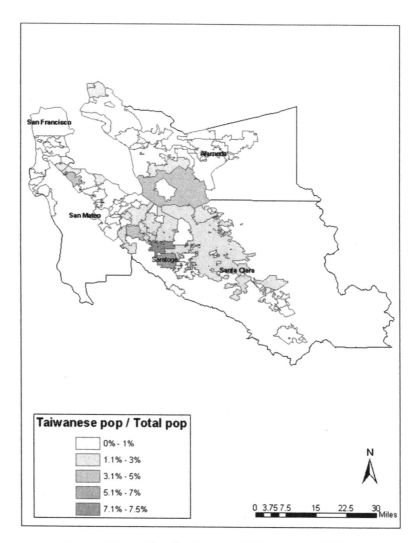

Taiwanese pop / Total pop

- 0% - 1%
- 1.1% - 3%
- 3.1% - 5%
- 5.1% - 7%
- 7.1% - 7.5%

N

0 3.75 7.5 15 22.5 30 Miles

FIGS. 6.3 and 6.4. The distribution of Taiwanese and Chinese American populations in the San Francisco Bay Area. Numbers in both figures represent foreign-born Taiwanese and Chinese populations. "Chinese" in Fig. 6.4 refers to people from China, including Hong Kong and Taiwan. For total Chinese American population in the San Francisco Bay Area, refer to Table 9.2. Source: 2000 U.S. Census; data converted by Ping Sung.

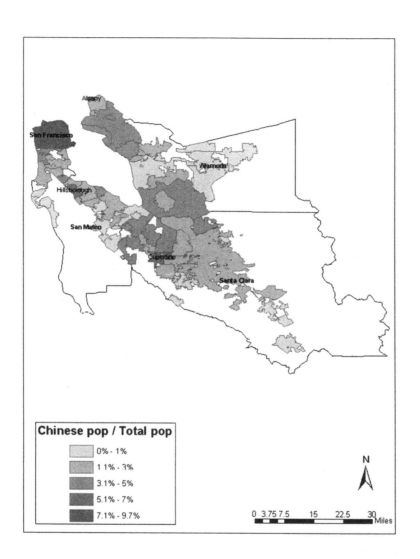

Chinese pop / Total pop	
	0% - 1%
	1.1% - 3%
	3.1% - 5%
	5.1% - 7%
	7.1% - 9.7%

0 3.75 7.5   15   22.5   30
                                    Miles

Ranch 99 Inside and Out

The suburban Ranch 99 has become the social and cultural hub for Taiwanese American immigrants in Silicon Valley. The supermarket chain is a symbol of collective identity for the high-tech Taiwanese in Silicon Valley. Most Americans, however, do not even notice that the Ranch 99 stores are the single most important shopping and entertainment centers for Asian Americans in Silicon Valley.[5] The landscapes of Ranch 99 malls are no different than those of typical American shopping malls. There are no pagoda-like roofs or temple gates on the facades, as you would see in San Francisco's Chinatown. Nor can you see the Chinese merchandise, as you would on Main Street in Monterey Park, where the shop owners display their wares. The exterior of the Ranch 99, which looks like any American megastore, embodies the American image that my trans-Pacific commuter interviewees want to project. It is an example of the beautiful clothes they want to dress in.

Inside the Ranch 99, however, Asian Americans can purchase virtually anything they want from Taiwan, Hong Kong, or other Asian countries (Brown 2003). The majority of my interviewees (thirty-six out of thirty-seven) said that they very much liked to shop at Ranch 99 because they were comfortable and felt at home there. The remarks of one interviewee, Jack, represent the feelings of many engineers I interviewed. For him, Ranch 99 represented his identity much more than Chinatown. Comparing the new Ranch 99 with San Francisco's Chinatown, Jack said:

> Well, eating and drinking are really important activities in Chinese culture. Ranch 99 may represent some collective identity for us under certain circumstances. . . . Chinatown is way too crowded and chaotic. Because of traffic, I seldom go there. I do not like it. It looks like an enclave. The people who live there can hardly become members of mainstream American society. However, I do agree that it has cultivated many excellent second-generation Chinese Americans. Well, the problem is that they do not want to stay in Chinatown, either. To me, Chinatown is like a mother who never gets nurturing from her kids. Her blood has been drained out while feeding her kids.

For trans-Pacific commuters, Ranch 99 symbolizes their shifting home identities, the intertwining of their Taiwanese way of life with their American aspirations. My interviewees pointed out that they do not feel they are in the United States during their stays in Silicon Valley. One reason for this is that Ranch 99 provides everything that they are accustomed to having in Taiwan. In chapter 1 I told the story of Melissa, who flew with her husband five times a year between Silicon Valley and Taiwan. She did not sense any difference between her two homes because she could do everything she might do in Taiwan in Fremont, including driving her mother to visit local friends, shopping at Ranch 99, getting her hair styled at the salon at the Ranch 99 mall, buying Taiwanese groceries, and eating at Taiwanese restaurants. All these opportunities made her feel that "I can enjoy my perfect Taiwanese life in Silicon Valley these days." Although the majority of the Taiwanese American high-tech engineers and their families embraced shifting home identities, a few had different feelings. Jenny, who was a parachute child when she arrived in the United States, mentioned that she did not feel like she was back home when she went shopping at Ranch 99. She said, "I don't feel Ranch 99 represents my sense of home in Taiwan, because those supermarkets in Taiwan, from my memory, were pretty different than Ranch 99s. They were small, dark, and more like mom-and-pop grocery stores. However, when I go back to Taiwan these days, I can't find those, either. I lost my past. There is no way for me to find the Taiwan I remember anymore." Like the return of the stranger in He's poem that I describe in chapter 1, Jenny's return to Taiwan causes something of a cultural shock because the market landscapes and grocery shopping experiences of her childhood now exist only in her memory.

Jenny's story made me aware that when trans-Pacific commuters think about Taiwan, they think about a version that they have reconstructed in their minds rather than what is actually there. Why? The Ranch 99 markets are typical of suburban malls, so much so that most Americans do not even distinguish between them and other American malls. What do the trans-Pacific commuters mean, then, when they say they "feel at home" at Ranch 99? Why do they feel that Ranch 99 is very similar to Taiwan? Which Taiwan are they referring to?

The Taiwan they refer to is the restructured Taiwan of Hsinchu Science Park, and not the chaotic urban landscape of Hsinchu City that is similar to the high-density Chinatown in San Francisco. In my survey, trans-Pacific commuters described the Ranch 99 environment with the following terms: modern, clean, well managed, spacious, and luxurious. In contrast, they de-

F I G .   6 . 5 . Items sold by street vendors in Taiwan are nicely wrapped and beautifully displayed in Ranch 99. Photo by author, 1997.

scribed the Hsinchu urban landscape as dirty, chaotic, and overcrowded. For
these respondents, Ranch 99 markets were not at all similar to traditional
Taiwanese commercial streets, neighborhood markets, or even supermarkets.
Ranch 99 still reminds them of home, however, because of the predominantly Chinese environment and the familiar goods from Taiwan that are
sold there. Not only can they buy their groceries at Ranch 99, but they can
also purchase authentic Chinese food, videotapes, music, and books, as well
as engage in conversations with friends.

The experience of shopping at a Ranch 99 is very different from the typical experience of shopping at street vendors or night markets in Taiwan.
There are no food peddlers outside the Ranch 99 malls. Everything that
would be sold by street vendors in Taiwan is instead neatly wrapped and
beautifully displayed on racks in the mall (Fig. 6.5). One of the most obvious contrasts between the two shopping experiences is in the way that the
popular Taiwanese pearl tea drink is sold. In Taiwan, street vendors usually
sell the beverage for less than $1. In contrast, shops the size of an ice cream
parlor or bakery sell the same drink at Ranch 99 for $2.50 or more. Some

FIG. 6.6. A typical street market in Taiwan. Photo by author, 2002.

stores have periodic buy-one-get-one-free promotions, while others give out coupons such as ones that can be redeemed for a free cup after eleven are purchased. These promotions are very typical of the United States, as is the modern shopping mall environment where the drinks are purchased.

When my interviewees enjoyed their pearl tea drink in Ranch 99 markets, they would say, "We are in Taiwan!" or "This is so similar to Taiwan." However, most interviewees also complained about the dirty street environment in Taiwan. "I never visit street vendors in Taiwan," they claimed (Fig. 6.6). The question, then, is what is the "Taiwan" they are referring to when they have their pearl tea drink in Ranch 99? It is a Taiwan that is constructed by intertwining certain real and imaginary experiences in their minds.

Returning to Taiwan Though Ranch 99

We are beginning to get a sense that the Ranch 99 markets have successfully created a shopping experience that allows trans-Pacific commuters to virtually return to Taiwan. Shopping at Ranch 99 intertwines the imagined experience of returning home with access to Taiwanese goods that consumers can touch, grasp, and buy. Most of the time, the food eaten there recalls meals eaten in Taiwan, even though the physical environment is like a suburban American shopping mall. And, because the customers encountered at Ranch 99 are predominantly Asian American, the shopping center serves as a sort of community center that ties suburban Taiwanese Americans together.

Collective Identity in a Suburban Space

How does Ranch 99 physically construct an imaginary Taiwan for the suburban Taiwanese families in Silicon Valley? Jeff is a Taiwanese American architect involved in the Ranch 99 development in Milpitas. He explained the development strategies that Ranch 99 has applied in Silicon Valley. He emphasized that the primary concerns that drive their decision making are the store's accessibility to Chinese-Americans, the development patterns in the area where the store is located, and maintaining a Chinese American character.

Accessibility. Jeff pointed out that the following three criteria were considered essential for a new Ranch 99 location: (1) a large Chinese population, (2) accessibility by car, and (3) a large lot of fifteen to twenty acres. These large lots are usually either empty or declining American malls. Jeff claimed that, according to these three criteria, Silicon Valley was ideal for the development of Ranch 99s, but Berkeley and Oakland, nearby cities in the San Francisco Bay Area, were not suitable locations. Accessibility by car is difficult to achieve in Berkeley, and Oakland is predominantly African American. San Mateo fulfills the first two criteria, but the Ranch 99 developers could not find an available site of a suitable size.

Ranch 99 development patterns. Ranch 99 complexes contain various retail outlets, but no other commercial spaces or residential development. Bookstores, jewelry shops, watch stores, beauty salons, and a few Asian restaurants typically inhabit the complex. Some of these shops are chains and follow Ranch 99 wherever it opens its next facility. They firmly believe that following Ranch 99, which conducts comprehensive marketing surveys before making its investments, will result in improved business opportunities. So far, this has been the case. The San Jose Starlite Court, however, differs from other Ranch 99 complexes in the way that it combines residential and commercial development. Ranch 99 complexes are typically developed without any residential units, because the Taiwanese investors are primarily interested in building supermarket branches. In the case of the San Jose Starlite Court, however, the local land developer had decided to reserve half of his land for residential development. He built the Pacific Rim Plaza and Ranch 99 first, and then watched business take off. Consequently, the surrounding land prices began to soar. He then began to develop town houses and condos on the other half of his land. "Adjacent to Ranch 99" was the slogan used to market these residences, even though those developing Ranch 99 never intended this.

Kicking out McDonald's: Creating the Ranch 99 identity. Most Ranch 99s in the Bay Area essentially consist of newly constructed, generic American commercial buildings inhabited predominantly by Chinese franchises. The creation of a multicultural shopping space is not the goal of Ranch 99 developers. Instead, they attempt to attract two types of consumers: (1) Chinese Americans, whom they hope will consider Ranch 99 a weekend destination, and (2) high-tech engineers who work in the nearby business parks, whom they expect to visit for lunch and dinner on weekdays. However, since there are few residential areas close to the Milpitas Ranch 99, compared to the one with residential development on Lundy Street in San Jose, it is somewhat empty on weekdays. Ranch 99 developers want to create a shopping mall composed entirely of Chinese stores. When they planned the Ranch 99 in Milpitas, they required all the restaurants and shops to have a different content, so no store would duplicate what another store offered its customers. For example, only one restaurant (Hot Pot City) was allowed to serve Chinese fondue in the shopping center, even though the managers cannot completely enforce this rule. They think that American fast-food chains such as McDonald's would spoil the Chinese atmosphere, so they raised their rental rates to discourage them from moving in. For example, the rate in the neighboring American shopping mall on McCarthy Boulevard is $2 per square foot, but the rate in the Milpitas Ranch 99, just across the freeway, is $2.50 per square foot. Given this difference, McDonald's would probably not be interested in opening a branch in Ranch 99.

Ranch 99 as an Immigrant Cultural Center. The physical appearances and development patterns of Ranch 99 markets have provided a new symbol of identity for suburban Taiwanese Americans. At the same time Ranch 99 markets have provided this same Taiwanese American group with a place to develop and sustain their social networks. Ranch 99 markets serve as community centers for suburban Taiwanese immigrants. They function as places for friends and families to congregate on weekends, as places for young Taiwanese on dates to visit, as the family kitchen for housewives, and as a place for seniors to reunite.

A weekend gathering place. During lunchtime on weekdays, the food plaza at the Ranch 99 is always occupied by groups of high-tech engineers, most of them men.[6] If you visit on a weekend, you will see three generations of Taiwanese families (grandparents, parents, and children) shopping and dining there as part of their weekend routine. On Saturday mornings most Taiwanese parents drop their children off at Chinese-language school while they and the grandparents go shopping at Ranch 99. When the children are finished with school, their grandparents will stay at Ranch 99 while their parents pick the children up. Next they all meet at their favorite Chinese restaurant at Ranch 99 and eat together. This routine is shared by many suburban Taiwanese families. Ranch 99 may not be the only place for them to shop in Silicon Valley, but it is the location that connects them to their Taiwanese lifestyles and culture. All of my Silicon Valley interviewees claimed that convenience was the most important factor when they decided where to do their daily grocery shopping and run other errands. If there were no Ranch 99 near their homes, they would go shopping at Kmart, Target, or another American chain store. However, when they wanted to get together with their friends, they went to Ranch 99, where they were able to virtually return to Taiwan.

The grocery-shopping date. Grocery shopping is a very important activity for young Taiwanese forming romantic relationships, and visiting the Ranch 99 market together is often considered a public statement that two people are involved. Men and women have very different feelings about this fact. Jenny, a young female engineer, declared, "I don't like to go to Ranch 99 with a male friend. If I run into other acquaintances, which is very likely to happen, it would turn out to be a big subject of gossip." Since most of the young high-tech singles are churchgoers, gossip spreads quickly through their church networks.[7] My male interviewees agreed that being seen with a woman at Ranch 99 would inspire gossip, but, unlike the women, they seemed not to mind. Andy, for example, an engineer in his mid-twenties, claimed, "If I am going to date some girl, I would like to help her do grocery shopping. It's the easiest way to date girls, because it is natural for us to give them a ride to Ranch 99. Then, other people might think we are in a relationship. It is a subtle way for us to declare our intentions." That being seen grocery shopping with a member of the opposite sex might be interpreted as a sign that the couple is dating steadily, and that young people might choose to shop together as a form of recreation while dating, are both concepts that are unique to young Taiwanese professionals in Silicon Valley. To them, shopping together is an intimate yet subtle way to learn what kind of food their potential partner prefers and which brands they favor. And, in some cases, the date to go grocery shopping takes a romantic turn, as the young women might invite their partners to their places and make meals with the groceries they just bought. On the other hand, going shopping together at a time when one's friends are likely to be roaming the aisles is equivalent to announcing a committed relationship. Shopping for groceries together is a common dating ritual of Taiwanese students in the United States, although it does not take place in Taiwan.[8] The students' courtship culture extends to that of young high-tech engineers in Silicon Valley. Meanwhile, other Taiwanese immigrants who were students in the United States perfectly understand the underlying meaning of the grocery-shopping date.

Ranch 99 as a home refrigerator and family kitchen. Most of my Silicon Valley interviewees pointed out that a desire for convenience is one of the most important cultural characteristics of the Taiwanese. Jenny in fact argued that she did not think there was anything uniquely Taiwanese about Taiwanese residential culture, claiming, "If you really want me to say there is anything special about Taiwanese residential culture, I think 'convenience' is the only thing I can come up with." High-tech housewives enjoy shopping at Ranch 99 markets because it is convenient. Many women in Silicon Valley gather at a friend's house and chat for a while before they go to a nearby Ranch 99 for lunch. After lunch, they may go back to one of their homes and have tea, or they might go to another friend's house to play mah-jongg. During this period some of them may run out to pick up their children from school or run other errands. Finally, all of them will return to their homes to prepare dinner in the late afternoon, before their husbands return home from work. The distance between their homes and Chinese markets and restaurants is crucial to these women. Shopping and dining out are popular daily activities in Taiwan, and they are similarly popular in the United States. One of my interviewees, Melanie, was the wife of a CEO. She explained during our interview how much she liked the suburban home she and her husband had recently purchased. After our interview she invited me to have lunch with her. As we drove to the restaurant and back home, she was extremely excited. She repeatedly said, "Look! It only takes me five minutes to drive to Chinese restaurants and the supermarket. The Chinese supermarket is just like my refrigerator at home, and the restaurants are like my kitchen. I can walk with my husband to this place every day. We can buy fresh vegetables and the Chinese newspaper." This convenience is similar to what she would experience in the inner city in Taiwan.

A reunion location for trans-Pacific grandparents. As I discussed in chapter 4, grandparents who travel back and forth from Silicon Valley to Taiwan are often isolated in their suburban homes while in California. Dining at Chinese restaurants in the Ranch 99 malls affords them the opportunity to run into their old friends. The grandparents in Cupertino that we met in chapter 4 are a good example. They are both well educated; the grandfather is a retired doctor, his wife a retired government official. When I interviewed them, they mentioned that Ranch 99 is the only place where they might meet their friends spontaneously. They did not need to know where their friends lived, because they could not travel to visit them anyway. After our interview, I spent some time with them in a park and then went with them to a Chinese restaurant at the local Ranch 99. As we sat down the grandfather realized that someone at the table adjacent to ours was his former colleague from the Chinese Military Hospital. They left us sitting at the table and talked for a while, even though our meals were served while they were chatting. Neither of them asked the other where he lived. Ranch 99 is their common address.

SEVEN

Heaven and Hell:
Silicon Valley in Hsinchu Science Park

In the preceding chapter we explored the transnational family lives of trans-Pacific commuters as they were played out in Ranch 99 markets, the popular Asian shopping malls in suburban Silicon Valley. These Ranch 99 markets became Chinatowns where transplants could search for merchandise that reminded them of their childhood in Taiwan. Here Taiwanese could run errands as if they were in Taiwan. Green card moms spent time socializing at Ranch 99 with their friends, and uprooted grandparents could count on casual encounters with their old friends while strolling through the shops.

All the people that I spoke to described the pleasure they felt in visiting Ranch 99. They enjoyed shopping there not only because its modern landscape represented their *jin-yi* (beautiful clothes), the symbol of their success as immigrants in America, but also because they felt that going to Ranch 99 was like virtually visiting their homeland. Everything they encountered there reminded them of Taiwan, from the hot pot fondue to the pearl tea drink, the Vietnamese food, the Korean, Japanese, and Chinese soap opera videos that are popular in Taiwan, and the latest Taiwanese pop music and concert posters printed in Chinese. Even the way that roasted ducks were hung in the windows and live seafood was displayed recalled Taiwan. In other words, the trans-Pacific commuters I spoke with saw Ranch 99 as the psychic and physical symbol of Taiwanese American community in Silicon Valley. Rather than simply being a "home away from home," Ranch 99 fulfilled their need to feel *at home* while *away from home*. Being *away from home* but *at home* simultaneously is the essential quality that trans-Pacific commuters pursue on both sides of the Pacific. Their home identities shift between their local and their distant homes. When they are at one home, they wish to be at the other. Their local social network—friends, business associates, and family members—view their distant homes, landscapes, and culture with envy. The status they gain from having a distant home is one they relish, and it becomes an important part of each of their identities. And because they regularly travel between two homes and have two sets of local social networks their psychic sense of who they are, what their homes and landscapes mean to them, is complex. Their complex, shifting psychic reactions to their homes and landscapes have dramatically impacted the physical landscapes they travel between. In the previous chapter I described how the Taiwanese high-tech immigrants enjoy the Ranch 99 markets that provide them everything they could want from Taiwan. In this chapter and the next I will focus on how they form their transnational communities and how they reshape their Hsinchu communities into the form of American suburbs.

It should come as no surprise that Taiwanese American high-tech families seek to replicate their homeland experiences in Ranch 99 markets. There is a huge body of scholarly work that examines how people try to re-create their experience of home when they migrate to a new country, and how their identities shift between their homelands and new homes (see, for example, Bhabha 1994, 1996; Akhtar 1999; Kurien 1998, 37–70; Wellmeier 1998, 97–122). Immigrants from all cultures and ethnic backgrounds have a fundamental need to reconnect with their homeland experiences, which are felt deeply within the body and reflected in their daily lives.

Shifting between their homelands and new homes is a process whereby bodily feelings, associated with significant memories of the past, are united with current situations to form new "mosaic identities" that enable immigrants to experience their homelands within their new host countries. Shay, an Iranian-born Palestinian American student of mine in her twenties, received her high school education in England, then migrated to the United States two years ago. She told me, "I doubt I will ever want to be truly an American, because then I know I would lose my identity—an identity that I was born with and grew up in." She said that she does not mind being a part of American culture "and contributing to its future while standing aside and upholding the very reason I am who I am." Shay's shifting identities are played out in the way she longs for the touch of a Persian carpet. Her early memories inspired her to choose a redwood floor instead of a more common oak one when she redid the floor at her home in Maryland. She said, "I made sure it was a dark mahogany color with a vibrant wood grain pattern, because it reminded me of a Persian carpet I once crawled on."

Immigrants always long for the smells, the tastes, and the landscapes that alleviate their homesickness (Marcus 1978, 1992, 89; Matless 1995, 93–122; Rapport and Dawson 1998). The memories seduced by familiar sensations return the immigrant home virtually. However, what makes the Taiwanese American trans-Pacific commuters' shifting home identities unique is that when they return to their Taiwan homes, they would prefer not to be experiencing those sensations that they had originally left behind. After talking to many trans-Pacific high-tech engineers and their families, I realized that no matter how much they appreciated Ranch 99 bringing their Taiwanese life to Silicon Valley, they had no intention of being associated with the local Taiwanese communities and lifestyles in Hsinchu, Taiwan.

The families I studied wanted to be Americans. And instead of returning to the Taiwan of their childhoods, they re-created their American experiences in Taiwan. They valued car-oriented suburban lifestyles, shopped at American-style markets, and socialized with people who shared the same American experiences as their own. The experience of bi-gration that they shared with other trans-Pacific commuters fostered a unique transnational community network. They feared *being localized* by their old homes. They want to stand out from the Taiwanese landscapes where they grew up and that were familiar to them before they migrated to the United States.

Hsinchu Science Park is the single most important landscape that enables trans-Pacific commuters to simultaneously experience being *at home* and *away from home*. The epicenter of the high-tech transformation in Taiwan, Hsinchu Science Park is located in the Hsinchu region, southeast of metropolitan Taipei. The region covers fifteen hundred square kilometers (579 square miles) and has a population of 830,000.[1] Several of my interviewees told me that when the park was first established in 1979, there were only a couple of "ugly and lonely concrete boxes" within. At that time no locals would have imagined how the landscape would be divided into "heaven" and "hell" within twenty years. Nor could they have imagined just how many trans-Pacific commuters, whom Hsinchu-area locals have come to call "Americans," would resettle within the park.

Before I describe the physical landscape of the park, it is useful to remember an important aspect of its residents' identities: they consider themselves middle-class Taiwanese Americans when in Silicon Valley and middle-class American Taiwanese when in Hsinchu. Their shifting identities are a part of a system in which their detachment from their local context is a sign of gained status. As I argued in previous chapters, trans-Pacific commuters' community lives are not much different than those of other immigrants. Like immigrants living in a Chinatown, high-tech Taiwanese-Americans prefer staying within their Taiwanese networks during their leisure time. They rarely get involved in neighborhood activities in Silicon Valley. Andy, an immigrant with a Master's degree in electrical engineering from Stanford University, told me that he felt "totally disconnected from American society," except for the few minutes he listened to American news on the radio during his commute to and from work.

This disconnection from American culture was an emblem of pride for Andy and others, who perceived themselves as members of an exclusive social network that jetted back and forth between Silicon Valley and Hsinchu Science Park. Both the engineers and their wives who formed this exclusive network spent time with the same group of friends at both places. When I spoke with Sandy, a housewife, about learning English, she became excited and stated, "I went to an ESL [English as a Second Language] course for a couple of months when I first arrived here, but I quit! I realized I don't even need to speak English daily, because I always hang out with my housewife club friends in Ranch 99s."

We can gain insight into this transnational community by investigating the network of the Hwei-chu (Gentle Bamboo) Housewife Club, active in both Silicon Valley and Hsinchu Science Park. The core members of the club, which functioned to connect high-tech wives, numbered more than two hundred. The club originated in the face-to-face conversations of women who wanted to support each other in the education of their children, daily chores, and recreation. They exchanged information about their American experiences and updated each other on the details of their children's educations during both formal and informal gatherings in Hsinchu Science Park and Silicon Valley (Tseng 1995; Chang 2000).

Ingrid, the founding member, explained how the club was established in 1990. At that time Ingrid had already been living in a high-rise apartment inside the park for eleven years. She and a few other housewives of the same age always waited together every afternoon for the school bus to drop off their children, who attended a bilingual school. While they were waiting, they chatted, usually about the education of their children. As a result, they became very good friends and realized that they faced similar family and personal issues.

Ingrid volunteered to organize the club, since she had experience organizing student clubs during her college years. They invited a professional consultant to help them at first. With her help, they developed a set of club guidelines. According to the club's inclusive policies, every member had the opportunity to be a committee or board member. After the club was established, members began to organize educational programs (such as instruction in Japanese and choral music and a book club) not only for the mothers, but also for their children (classes included those in English, painting, dancing, and calligraphy). Every year they organized seasonal picnics, flea markets, and holiday festivals. Every month they coordinated community recycling and published a newsletter. They also developed an informal support network for daily chores. They helped each other with child care, grocery shopping, and garbage recycling. Members also attended lectures, museum exhibits, and performances together. Ingrid concluded her description of her experiences with the club by expressing her appreciation, saying, "Our club not only extends my life in the community, but also nurtures me with new knowledge. More important, I should say my two daughters grew up with our club. They have participated in all the courses provided by our club."

Currently, all the members of the club are high-tech housewives whose husbands are employed in Hsinchu Science Park.[2] It is not a cyber-club; it does not meet online. Interestingly, most club members seldom use the Internet or email.[3] They treasure group activities that involve face-to-face interaction, and they spend time together in both Hsinchu Science Park and Silicon Valley (Tseng 1995, 41–54). All the members I spoke to seemed to appreciate the club as much as the founding members. Club members had no interest in establishing relationships with other housewives in the Hsinchu region. They did, however, expand their club to an international network when members who had once lived in the Hsinchu region and Silicon Valley moved to various places around the globe.

Ingrid explained that she had "suffered from separation" when her good friends came and went, many flying back and forth between the park and Silicon Valley. Last summer, when she visited Silicon Valley, she found out that others in the Hwei-chu Housewife Club had similarly "suffered from separation," and as a result had relocated to California so that they could "hold parties in Silicon Valley" and regain the sense of community that they had established with one another. But Silicon Valley was not the only place to which club members migrated. In Ingrid's personal experience, twenty-three of her twenty-seven neighbors had migrated to other countries, most to the United States, Canada, Australia, New Zealand, and mainland China.

It should come as no surprise that the club disturbed Hsinchu locals. Pat, the community activist introduced earlier, explained, "It's a very exclusive club. They have their upper-middle-class activities—very Americanized." Marie, the former congresswoman in Hsinchu, described the impression that local residents had of the club:

> There are many green card moms inside the park. They don't need to work, but just fly back and forth between Hsinchu and Silicon Valley for two reasons. First, their husbands can support them. Second, their children are studying in America and they are currently applying for their PR [U.S. permanent resident] status. Since they regularly fly back and forth between countries, no company will hire them anyway. It's okay for them. They have their housewives club.

Today, most Hsinchu residents consider the park a colonized territory. Standing on a crowded street adjacent to Hsinchu Science Park, John, an old-timer and a block leader of the Jin-shan-mian district, looked at illegally parked cars and recently opened restaurants that served various exotic foods from overseas. He was very frustrated by the wall that divided the park and the city into two worlds. "Inside the park is heaven. All the best facilities and the highest quality of life are available to the high-techers that meet the American standard. Outside the park is hell."

Heaven and Hell in My Backyard

While the park's upper-middle-class residents eagerly engaged in not-in-my-back-yard campaigns to bar dangerous facilities from their community and avoid other negative impacts (Hester 1996), local residents of Jin-shan-mian seemed to be powerless and silent. They were not allowed to participate in the decision-making process when Hsinchu Science Park was first planned in 1979 by the Taiwanese government, nor were they part of the developer's decision-making process. No one asked them if the park should be a research campus or a manufacturing center for semiconductors; it was the Taiwanese government that decided to transform its traditional industry into high-tech industries (Castells and Hall 1994, 105–6). The global spatial division of labor and the transnational technological network fostered outstanding technological improvements (Hsu 1997; Saxenian 1997). Within the past two decades the park has expanded rapidly, generating billions in revenue for the Taiwanese economy. Today it covers 770 hectares (1,900 acres) and provides the region with more than 100,000 jobs. It influences the local culture, and it challenges the community identities of those in the area in ways that cannot be measured in terms of economic growth or GNP (Leu 1997; Yang 1998).

Indeed, Hsinchu Science Park represents the United States to both local residents and the high-tech employees and their families, the latter nicknamed "parkers" or "high-techers."[4] Parkers have achieved the highest socioeconomic status in Taiwan society today.[5] In particular, those who live in duplex houses in the Bamboo Village inside Hsinchu Science Park are considered the most prestigious of the trans-Pacific commuters.

From Golden Mountain to Golden Child

Hsinchu Science Park is located in Jin-shan-mian,[6] which has been a traditional Chinese religious locale, organized around the Jin-shan Temple, since the late Qing dynasty. Before Hsinchu Science Park was established, most of the population of Jin-shan-mian had been Hakkanese, a subgroup of Han Chinese.[7] Though the literal meaning of *jin-shan* is "golden mountain,"[8] the agricultural productivity of Jin-shan-mian has always been the lowest in the Hsinchu region because of the poor soil.

Hsinchu Science Park has dramatically changed Jin-shan-mian since 1979

FIGS. 7.1 and 7.2. The photo above represents "heaven." Residents of the park enjoy suburban houses and quiet pedestrian paths shaded by beautiful trees. There is also a large open lawn area behind these houses. The photo on the left represents "hell." Residents living outside the park have to endure traffic jams, scooters, illegally parked cars, and commercial signs everywhere. Photos by author, 2002.

(Chen 1988). The park transformed Jin-shan-mian from a backward village of tea farms into a "global golden child" (Lee et al. 1997; Wu 1998). As mentioned earlier, the transition not only generated billions in revenue, but it was also responsible for the creation of approximately 100,000 high-tech jobs as of October 2004 (Hsinchu Science Park 2004b). The transition also caused rapid changes in land use patterns and population, as native Hakkanese residents were relocated to the territory outside the park.

The relocation not only segregated local Hakkas from the high-techers, but it also changed the relationship of Hsinchu Science Park to the surrounding Jin-shan-mian area. Newcomers, the high-tech families attracted by the booming economy, moved into the park without forming any connection to existing Hsinchu society. As a result, the Hakkas, who felt a bond with the old Jin-shan-mian district and had historically been the insiders, became the outsiders when the new Hsinchu Science Park was built. The development of the park led to the demolition of traditional Hakka communities and their subsequent relocation to high-density urban communities. Bill, a local architect who supported Hakkanese culture, claimed that Hsinchu Science Park has become Taiwan's "American colonial town." Not only is the land upon which Hsinchu Science Park is built the original location of Hakkanese homes, but even more frustrating, there is now a long concrete wall about eight feet high that divides the park and the rest of Jin-shan-mian into two worlds. As John, the community activist, claimed, "Inside the wall is heaven, outside is hell" (Figs. 7.1 and 7.2).

John recalled that formerly none of the high-tech newcomers wanted to live here. Most had homes in Taipei and merely rented a room in Hsinchu. They were called the "three-five group" because they commuted between Hsinchu and Taipei every Wednesday (the third day of a week in the Taiwanese calendar) and Friday (the fifth day). "Can you believe that?" he asked. He recalled that ten years ago the park looked like a ghost town on weekends and during the Chinese New Year. "People just did not believe that the high-tech transformation would work in Taiwan. No one wanted to invest their money and time in this area."

With an emotional tone, he said, "All the neighbors of the park get nothing from it but traffic jams and skyrocketing housing prices and living expenses, as well as garbage and lots of toxic air and water pollution." He added, "For example, the government and high-tech companies never respected local cultural landscapes and feng shui. They proposed an express train system that would cut through the most important harmonious relationship between mountain and valley (a relationship known as "dragon feng shui") that existed in Feng-cong, the historical valley of Jin-shan-mian. Meanwhile, the second-phase Winbond development has already destroyed the other important feng shui spot in Jin-shan-mian. So when Winbond caught fire in 1998, local Jin-shan-mian residents all felt they were *huo-gai* [that they deserved their bad luck]."

The new park dramatically changed the community landscape that Jin-shan-mian residents had been familiar with for generations. Historic temples were uprooted and relocated, and the pilgrimages to them were disrupted. According to John, the Hsinchu Science Park administration moved six earth god shrines into one new temple in the relocation process. Historically, every earth god had been worshiped by different local villages in its own shrine, so relocation disrupted traditional religious networks. Moreover, agricultural land use patterns were significantly disrupted. Rice fields, tea terraces, and sugar farms were wiped out, and all of the existing irrigation ponds were drained and filled.[9] Local agriculture and the pottery industry declined (Lee et al. 1997, 75–85) as roads and highways that met American standards were established, cutting-edge high-tech companies moved in, and American-style housing was built.

There were four serious issues that deeply divided the Jin-shan-mian community and Hsinchu Science Park into two worlds in the late 1990s (Shenglin Chang 1998; Ching-Jie Wu 1997). First, the water pollution created by the high-tech industry had always been poorly managed by the Hsinchu Science Park Administration Office. Local residents had protested many times, but the office never took their petitions seriously. Second, the heavy traffic congestion became a nightmare for the residents living adjacent to the park. Third, the cost of living became very high. Fourth, the new developments and the proposed express train system destroyed Jin-shan-mian's "dragon" feng shui. The traditional feng shui of Jin-shan-mian and its agricultural landscape never concerned the policy makers, planners, and high-tech companies.[10]

By 2004 ecological and occupational health crises had come into the spotlight. According to an investigation conducted by the Taiwan Environmental Action Network from 2000 to 2004, local residents and workers have slowly come to recognize the pressing environmental and occupational health issues that have been caused by the park (Chang et al. 2001; Chang, Chiu, and Tu forthcoming). The high-tech corporations within the park have been marketing themselves as clean and pollution-free, as "industry without smoke stacks." In the past two decades, however, old-time Hsinchu residents whose homes are close to the park's wastewater discharge systems have questioned how the high-tech industry might have impacted the environment. They did not know that it also took residents of Silicon Valley twenty years to realize the extent of the damage done by toxic pollutants from the high-tech industries in that region (Byster and Smith, forthcoming).[11]

In our forthcoming article "Breaking Silicon Silence," I and my colleagues Chiu and Tu argue that the dominance of the information technology (IT) industry has penetrated the sociopolitical culture in Taiwan. This dominance, caused by the success of Hsinchu Science Park, has silenced the voices of both local residents and IT workers with concerns about the adverse effects of IT development and manufacturing. Community criticism and environmental activism have largely been absent from the political and academic debates on IT industrial development, and government officials often ignore the few oppositional voices that can be heard because they consider them threatening to the IT economic boom. More important, the public widely shares the belief that attachment to the IT industry will result in economic betterment.

It is easy to see how the dominance of IT has influenced the relationship among different government bureaucracies if one follows local and national news in Taiwan. Investigative reporting and other research have revealed that the Taiwanese central government and the Science Park Administration (SPA) attempted to cover up the documented pollutants produced by the high-tech companies during the last three decades (Chang et al. 2001; Tu 2003). The Hsinchu municipality has been extremely frustrated by the socio-environmental impact that the park has had on the city (Castells and Hall 1994, 109; Tu 2003). The municipality, however, could not participate in any of the park development decision-making processes because the park is under the control of the central government, not the Hsinchu municipality.

When the municipality issued the press release "The Sorrow of the High-

Tech Colony" in April 2000, the mayor of Hsinchu explained how the local residents had been adversely affected by the socio-environmental impact of rapid high-tech industrial development. The press release explained how the municipality would no longer attempt to address the problems of heavy traffic, the overcrowded school districts, water pollution, and public health crises without the help of the global high-tech companies that were responsible for the problems. The mayor went on to outline steps that high-tech companies could take to improve public facilities and reduce negative environmental impacts. However, because of political tensions between the municipality and the Hsinchu Science Park administration, and because of endless legal battles among grassroots activists, local government, and the high-tech companies, very little progress on the environmental future of the park has been made (Chang et al. 2001, 32–38).

The Love-Hate Relationship

Approximately 30 percent of employees in Hsinchu Science Park, or about 30,000, are high-tech newcomers. The remaining workers are local laborers from the Hsinchu region. Although the park benefits most local residents economically, both the indigenous population and local high-tech families, those that work in the high-tech profession but are originally from the area, feel excluded by the wall that separates the city from the park.[12] Charles, a community designer and grassroots activist, explained, "There is a love-hate relationship between the park and us [local residents]. Many local Hsinchu residents actually work inside the park." In 1998, Charles estimated that the park employed about 40 percent of local residents between the ages of twenty and thirty-five.[13] He objected to the "ignorant attitudes" of the Hsinchu Science Park administration. However, at the same time that he protested the negative influence the park had exerted on the local residents, he also admitted that he appreciated the job opportunities that had been created by the high tech industry. He described himself, his younger brother, and his sister-in-law as examples of locals who lived outside but worked inside the park. They received great salaries and benefits from their companies, and their family lives had improved because of the high-tech industrial development. If it were not for Hsinchu Science Park, he and his family members would have had to move to Taipei or elsewhere to establish their careers.

Many others shared Charles's contradictory opinions. Charles told me about Marie, the congresswoman we met earlier, who had vociferously protested the water pollution caused by the park. At the same time she was protesting, however, her husband worked in the park as a highly reputed senior staff member at the Industrial Technology Research Institute.

Copying Silicon Valley in Hsinchu Science Park

The stories above reveal the extent of the influence that Hsinchu Science Park exerts upon the psychic and physical identities of its community residents. Many trans-Pacific high-tech engineers who live in the park seem to forget any negative experiences from their Silicon Valley lives when they arrive in Hsinchu (Chang and Hester 1998, 118). "Hsinchu region is nothing like Silicon Valley at all. The whole city has been growing without any plan," one engineer remarked. Many of them contrast the park with Jin-shan-mian village and the Hsinchu region. Another told me, "Every time I drive into our park, I take a deep breath, then feel so relaxed. To me, our park is more like a place in America."

However, as mentioned previously, when the park was first built, the high-techers who worked there preferred living in Taipei to living in the park, despite the long commute. They talked about the park as "a deserted place," "very isolated"; they claimed there was "nowhere to go shopping," and described it as "a ghost town on weekends or holidays, because people fled to Taipei or their hometowns." But by the year 2004 much had changed. In the Bamboo Village neighborhood within the park, residents could enjoy the highest quality of life of anywhere in Taiwan, based on the standards of Taiwanese who were familiar with the United States. That consensus was shared by all the subgroups of the trans-Pacific commuters, including the astronauts, returnees, motherlanders, and green card moms. This fact is particularly startling in the case of the motherlanders, who commute between the Hsinchu Science Park and their urban homes daily. Though they have never been to Silicon Valley, they are aware of the stunning contrast between the green landscapes of the park and the crowded urban area outside. Ken and Carol, who had never visited the United States, expressed their feelings about Hsinchu Science Park by simply saying, "Our park is America."

FIGS. 7.3 and 7.4. Well-maintained lawns and colorful shrubs are characteristic of Stanford Research Park in Palo Alto, California, the prototype landscape for high-tech industrial parks around the world. The top photo shows the entrance to the headquarters of Hewlett-Packard. The photo below overlooks the hilly landscape and park-like corporate campus within the Stanford research park. Photos by author, 2003.

The physical wall that separates the park from the surrounding environment plays a significant role in the process of shaping the physical and psychic community identities. Earlier I described the effect of the wall from the perspective of the local Jin-shan-mian residents. Now I want to focus on the transformation inside the wall and tell the story from the point of view of the trans-Pacific commuters.

Just as the suburban corporate campus and the office park development were transplanted from the New York–Boston area to California in the United States (Mozingo 2003, 255), Hsinchu Science Park is a modified Stanford Research Park (Findlay 1992, 118; Briggs and Watt 2001) and the result of corporate planning principles of the 1960s and 1970s (Figs. 7.3 and 7.4). Not only is the park separated from Hsinchu municipality by a wall, but it also forms its own political jurisdiction. It is a mix of a small-town community and industrial development and consists of three major land use zones: office and industrial, residential, and commercial. Although the majority of the approximately 100,000 employees commute to the park, there is a group of about 2,000 employees who live within the park. This prestigious minority consists mainly of high-level managers, CEOs, and senior engineers. The residential areas within the park include 701 units for families and 957 units for individuals (Hsinchu Science Park 2004a). The family units are of various types, including duplex, townhouse, single-level apartments, and multiple level apartments. The individual units include one-bedroom and two-bedroom apartments. The most famous residential area, Bamboo Village, consists of forty duplex houses. In addition, Lakeside Community contains thirty town houses, each with a view of an artificial pond. There is also a bilingual experimental school reserved exclusively for the children living inside the park.

According to Jan, a former park planner, many American planning ideas were applied in the development of Hsinchu Science Park. Jan served as chief planner for the park from 1983 to 1990, after her husband decided to relocate from Silicon Valley to Hsinchu Science Park.[14] She recalled that when she first came to the park it was deserted; only the administration building and a few other very ugly buildings stood there. Based on her experience developing industrial park projects in Palo Alto, California, she revised the master plan for the park. Her boss, the former chair of the Hsinchu Science Park Administration, was also an American-trained returnee. He was very concerned about the quality of the park environment and fully supported Jan's ideas. "I thoroughly established and enforced the planning and building codes that I learned from my Silicon Valley experiences," Jan told me.

Although the general public in Taiwan did not understand the American concepts of urban design and landscape design, Jan did all the things that she believed were important for the park's future. "I didn't care about other people's complaints. . . . I relocated the local residents because their original relocation site was too close to the park." With respect to the very controversial wall, Jan recalled that during that period a couple of companies had been burglarized. The equipment they lost cost more than a hundred million Taiwanese dollars. Jan said, "I decided to add the wall that separated the park from the local community because of security."

Today, its well-maintained green spaces have come to represent the park for many. The landscape of Hsinchu Science Park, dominated by American-style lawns, is indeed different from any other urban landscape in Taiwan (Teyssot 1999; Mozingo 2003). In addition, it has wide boulevards lined with trees and buildings surrounded by parking lots. Jan explained to me with pride that she was the first designer to introduce many design ideas from the United States to the park. She was the one who prevented them from adding more duplex homes to Bamboo Village, because she believed that having more green space was crucial. The artificial pond inside the park she thought was very unattractive, as well. To improve it, she designed a pavilion for a sculpture donated by Chu Ming, Taiwan's most famous sculptor. The area is now well used. "It is important to add some cultural characteristics to the park," she told me with great confidence. "This is the first sculpture in Taiwan standing in the middle of an industrial park. People just didn't have these ideas in earlier days."

Nowadays, many families living and working in the park show Jan their appreciation. They say that without her efforts, the park wouldn't be as enjoyable as it is. In turn, Jan revealed her appreciation for her boss, saying, "Without the support of the former chair of the park, I don't think I could possibly have implemented so many progressive American concepts."

Bamboo Village Re-creates the Silicon Valley Dream

Almost everyone I spoke to emphasized that living in Hsinchu Science Park felt like living in the United States, and that their homes in Bamboo Village reminded them of their Silicon Valley houses. The similarities between their two homes can be categorized in terms of four physical and two social characteristics. The physical characteristics are: (1) low residential density, (2) a secure living environment, (3) luxurious lawns and green spaces, and (4) the proximity of high-quality educational facilities, while the social characteristics are: (1) the similarity of social class and (2) shared transnational residential experiences.

Bamboo Village Physical Characteristics

Despite the fact that everyone emphasized that they felt as if they were in the United States when they were in the park, the housing and land use patterns of Bamboo Village were not at all typical of Silicon Valley suburbs. First, none of the homes in the park were single-family detached houses. Instead, there were 701 family units and 956 single units (Hsinchu Science Park 2004a). The family units consisted of duplex houses (Fig. 7.5), town houses, and high-rise apartments, the latter either a single-floor or double-

FIG. 7.5. An open lawn area is shared by the duplex houses in Bamboo Village. Photo by author, 2003.

floor unit. Single units consisted of either one-bedroom or two-bedroom apartments.

The residents I spoke with perceived the Science Park as reflective of an American suburb. But the lack of any single-family detached homes within the park tells a different story. In 1998, 30 of the 645 family units were town houses, and forty were duplex houses (Chang 2000). All the other units were apartments. By American standards (the number of apartments and lack of any single family homes), Science Park would not be characterized as sub-urban. When I talked to returnees and astronauts, however, most of them seemed to ignore these high-rise apartment buildings. Leo, a high-tech engineer living outside the park who had studied at Georgetown University and often traveled to New York City, was one of the few residents that I spoke with who attested to its urban (not suburban) character. When I asked him about the high-rise apartments, he commented that they were like "public housing projects in New York City."

Another major difference between the park and the Silicon Valley suburbs has to do with the land use concepts that guided the planning of Hsinchu Science Park. Compared to the car-oriented suburbs in Silicon Valley, Bamboo Village is a self-sustaining community. The village consists of: work-places, a small supermarket, a post office, a bank, a gas station, a clinic, a garage, a bilingual school, parks and other open spaces, and a recreational area combining a swimming pool and tennis courts (Castells and Hall 1994, 108). Everything is within walking distance.

Just as those who drank pearl tea drink in a Ranch 99 in Silicon Valley told me that they felt they were in Taiwan, almost everyone in Hsinchu Science Park told me they felt they were in the United States. This surprised me, because the land use patterns in the two places are so different. I began wondering what the residents meant when they said that Bamboo Village was similar to the United States. What role does physical form play in re-structuring high-tech families' American community experiences? Why did almost everyone I talked to want to *be home* but *away from home*?

Importing American Experiences

How was the United States imported into the park? How could the trans-Pacific commuters feel *at home* but *away from home* at the same time? On the one hand, according to the Hsinchu Science Park planning documents and the professional planners responsible for its design, American city planning concepts were applied in the physical design of the park. On the other hand, the land use patterns, housing density, and building forms were not identical to those of Silicon Valley suburbs.

The feeling that residents have of being in America while in the park has developed over time. Over its twenty-year history, Hsinchu Science Park has been transformed from a deserted place into a symbol of the United States in Taiwan. Today the luxurious green spaces, low density, and duplex houses with gardens in the front yard distinguish it from ordinary urban environments in Hsinchu and other places in Taiwan.

When these physical features were first planned and built as early as 1979, high-tech families disliked living inside the park and did not consider it to resemble the United States at all. Many apartments and houses in Bamboo Village were vacant, and many who worked in Hsinchu Science Park chose to maintain homes in both Taipei and the park, commuting between their homes on shuttles provided by the Hsinchu Science Park Administration.

Jan remarked that at the time there weren't many places for the high-tech newcomers to live in the park, and at any rate the quality of local housing was very poor. Even worse, there was no place to go shopping around the park, especially on weekends, when it became a ghost town. If Jane wanted to buy something she had to go to the central business district of Hsinchu City, or she would simply go back to Taipei, where her mother lived.

By the end of the 1980s, however, dramatic changes had taken place in the park. Many more companies had moved in, while the landscape had become much greener. Trees had grown, creating shade that made the hot summers more pleasant. Grassy lawns overcame poor soil conditions. Shrubs and flowers began to blossom year-round. The Hsinchu Science Park actually became a park. More important, as jobs were created in Hsinchu Science Park the surrounding neighborhoods and Hsinchu City grew rapidly. Both motherlanders who had been living elsewhere in the Hsinchu region and astronauts and returnees who had been living far away decided to work and live in Hsinchu Science Park. The astronauts moved into Bamboo Village around the early 1980s, helping to establish the foundation for the park's improved economic performance.

The second wave of returnees contributed to the trend toward returning home in the early 1990s.[15] Settling in Bamboo Village was considered superior to moving to the crowded residential developments in surrounding areas or to densely populated metropolitan Taipei. In addition to the luxury landscape features, there were other advantages only park residents could enjoy, such as access to a prestigious bilingual school and a short commute that allowed residents to avoid the daily traffic jams that occurred outside the park.[16]

The park had become sought-after real estate, and the demand for housing there could not be met. This shortage of housing, increased traffic jams, the high cost of living, and air and water pollution issues paralleled issues that were plaguing Silicon Valley at the same time. However, none of trans-Pacific commuters related these issues in Hsinchu with their Silicon Valley residential experiences. When I spoke with park residents, many of whom had homes in Silicon Valley, they could not seem to recall experiencing any problems in Silicon Valley at all.

Acting Globally, Disengaging Locally

For the trans-Pacific commuter, individual identity was formed through "acting globally," that is, through cultivating a global set of friendships, networking with global business colleagues, and living in multiple geographic locations. As a result, the need to relate to a local landscape or to local peoples reminiscent of their homeland, which may have characterized the needs of previous immigrant groups, was not a central aspect in their lives. In Silicon Valley the Taiwanese high-tech families, as a marginalized group, preferred to disperse into the suburbs and become as Americanized as possible; the Chinatown environment was entirely alien to them. None of the trans-Pacific commuters I spoke to cared to become neighbors with other Taiwanese people. Some of them even mentioned that they were afraid of living in a predominantly Asian, especially Chinese, neighborhood. Predominantly white, suburban neighborhoods came to embody a sense of home to them for several reasons. The suburban habitat provided them with a single-family home, a good school district, a middle-class status. These were the values of mainstream American culture that they preferred, and that suburbia could provide much more than inner-city residency.

Like other socially marginalized groups, the Taiwanese employed in the high-tech sector felt strongly that a favorable suburban home location would advance their position on the social ladder. Significantly, good school districts were generally associated with these desirable suburban communities. Good school districts provided the high-quality education that promised prosperous futures for their children, and this fulfilled a fundamental Chinese value. The problem with this "good school district" scenario was that the more Asians that moved into a suburban neighborhood for the good schools, the less desirable the neighborhood became for Asians themselves. Asians, in other words, preferred that other Asians *not* move into their Caucasian neighborhoods. A Caucasian neighborhood meant status, and that status would be compromised if it became predominantly Asian.

In Hsinchu, the trans-Pacific commuters did not want to be "localized" by the communities on the other side of the wall. They had developed their own culture and habits influenced by their American experiences, and they continued to participate in certain types of activities they had become accustomed to in Silicon Valley, such as: (1) recycling and gardening, (2) shopping for contemporary fashions, (3) shuttling their children to various activities, and (4) participating in sports and recreation events. All of these activities took place on both sides of their cross-Pacific commute.

Winnie, a core member of the housewife club that we met earlier, declared that she learned to enjoy recycling and gardening during her year in Palo Alto. She thought it was important for those in Bamboo Village to participate in similar activities. However, she complained that those outside the park never paid attention to public landscape and recycling issues. Even worse, she complained that these neighbors dumped their garbage bags in the park's trash cans.

Shopping for clothes that suited their international taste and shuttling their children around were two other highly visible activities of the high-tech wives, who told me they seldom shopped in Hsinchu City. Their shopping habits were still very American. For daily groceries, they preferred going to recently opened megastores near freeway exits. However, despite the effort of local developers to make the shopping centers look Californian, the high-tech housewives were not satisfied. For their interior decorations and home furniture they preferred shopping in Silicon Valley or Taipei. Jessie told me, "There are not many good stores to get the stuff I really want . . . so I go shopping in the Bay Area every summer, while I bring my kids to attend summer camp there."

For status-conscious high-tech families, participating in sports and other forms of recreation was important. High-level managers and CEOs tended to play golf in both the Hsinchu region and Silicon Valley. Playing golf not only displayed their class identity, but it also satisfied their desire to flaunt their success. Mike told me, "When I play golf in Silicon Valley with those Americans, I like to speak Chinese. They are the ones who want to do business with me. Why should I speak English?" He also brought his children to practice golf with him. His wife, Kathy, said, "My son is only a teenager, but he enjoys playing golf with his father. They play golf together every two weeks. It only costs NT$6,000 to NT$8,000 every time (US$180 to US$250). It's a long-term investment for him, so I don't think it's expensive."

For many high-tech families, traveling was sometimes combined with "global-shuttling" for the sake of their children's education. I use "global-shuttling" to refer to a system that aligned the Pacific-commuters' summer vacation plans with their children's summer camp stays in the United States. High-tech families generally preferred taking vacations in foreign countries. Many of them had friends and relatives living in other countries. According to my interviewees, high-tech housewives would often bring their children to the United States to attend American summer camps. During this period they might stay with friends or relatives. The husbands would then generally take about two weeks of vacation time to meet with their wives and children and travel to other places. Kelly explained her summer plan: "Every summer, my sister's home [in Silicon Valley] is like a hotel. There are always some teenagers staying with her. These teenagers are either her relatives or children of her friends. They come here for summer camps. If I cannot accompany my kids next summer, I will send them to my sister, too."

EIGHT

Building a Global City in My Backyard

In 1982 I was involved in an experimental dance performance at the Taipei Modern Dance Theater choreographed by Lin Huai-Min. The performance was an artistic statement on the fast pace of life, and on the international exposure and rapid urbanization that the Taiwanese had experienced since the 1970s. The performance was the first of its kind in Taiwan, integrating body movements, interactive sound, and avant-garde visual texts. The two-hour performance was staged as a series of dance vignettes.

The vignette I found most memorable was entitled "English First." This solo performance began when an actress dressed in a yellow-green suit and wearing a pair of white high heels pulled a sky-blue rolling suitcase to center stage. She then sat atop her luggage and began a monologue in Chinese in which she confessed her fear of speaking English and her admiration of those who did so well:

> My English has been bad since high school. English is our face. If we do not speak fluent English, we can't face the public. I was ashamed when I flunked my high school English tests. At my high school reunion, I heard my classmates joke about how they had failed in math, chemistry, or physics. I just smiled and didn't dare to say that I had flunked English. . . . Not speaking English fluently always embarrassed me. My high school English teacher constantly admonished me. "How can you go to college with such broken English?" she would say. "How can you possibly read all the English textbooks and study overseas?" . . . In order to improve my English I tried different En-

glish conversation programs. Well, they weren't as helpful as I expected, because those students with better English skills talked a lot. I couldn't interrupt their conversation at all. They joked around with our teachers and laughed loudly. I laughed right along with them even though I had no idea what was going on. But no one knew that I didn't understand the jokes, because I always dressed up in beautiful clothes. My clothes were high-quality, brand-name, fashionable designs imported from Hong Kong, Japan, and the United States.

The cynical wit in "English First" really resonated with audiences. It spoke for many motherlanders who had struggled with the humiliation of speaking "broken" English. Of course, one of the messages of the dialogue was that the Chinese who *could* speak English had no idea that the speaker *couldn't* because they had been so focused on her charming laughter and her beautiful imported clothes. Indeed, speaking fluent English was equivalent to dressing up in beautiful clothes.

In Taiwan today, even more so than in 1982, when "English First" was first performed, learning to read and speak English is mandatory for anyone seeking success and status. In March 2003 Mr. Si-quen You, the chief of the Executive Yuan (equivalent to the U.S. Department of State), visited a bilingual elementary school and admitted to the children there, "My English is bad." A few weeks later he announced that English would become the second official language of Taiwan by 2009. The new policy required that starting in 2009 all government paperwork and documents be written in English.

You's "English First" announcement led to heated debates about language policy in Taiwan. Public opinion on this controversial issue was split. One camp believed that making English an official language was a critical step the Taiwanese government must take in order to become a serious global player. The other camp vehemently opposed the policy, questioning whether it could really succeed given that the majority of Taiwanese citizens had not grown up in a bilingual environment. Calling the policy "nuts," they asked how the public could all be taught English? How could every piece of paperwork be translated daily? And if most government officials spoke and read Chinese, why did documents need to be translated into English (Tsai 2003)? After all, if Mr. Si-quen You were not fluent in English, as he had admitted to the elementary school children, what would he do when every document that crossed his desk was written in English?

Although the two camps held diametrically opposed opinions of the "English First" policy, both agreed that English was the bridge that would connect Taiwan to international society, and that there was an urgent need to establish English as the second official language of Taiwan. The mentality of the "English First" initiative not only dominated public policy, however, but it also influenced urban planning and community development in the Hsinchu region. For example, in 1997 developers in the Hsinchu region had come up with a new type of gated community, the bilingual community. The developers who came up with this idea believed that they would be able to attract buyers who associated speaking English with life in Silicon Valley. Living in a community where English was spoken would satisfy the desire of a growing market of potential homebuyers to achieve the "beautiful clothes" that would represent a high status.

The idea that living in a community of English speakers would confer upon residents "beautiful clothes" status was especially believable to Hsinchu residents, who were already familiar with their neighbors in Hsinchu Science Park who had high incomes, green card status, American educations, and, of course, mastery of the English language. Nevertheless, the conversations I had with the park's high-tech engineers and their wives were usually in Chinese, because that is the language they were more comfortable speaking. My interviewees sprinkled English-language words like "summer camp," "golf," and "shopping" into our conversations, using a sort of hybrid "Chinglish" rather than masterful English. What local residents in Hsinchu certainly did not know is that the same group of trans-Pacific commuters who spoke "Chinglish" in Taiwan preferred to stay within their Taiwanese social network when in Silicon Valley, where they would spend time with their Taiwanese friends and speak Chinese.

In previous chapters I discussed various achievements that symbolize the attainment of "beautiful clothes." Achieving American citizenship and receiving a PhD from a foreign (especially an American) university are *social* signs of having achieved high status, while *physical* signs include residing in an American-style suburban landscape, complete with the suburban shopping centers and single-family detached houses that are associated with that landscape. Following Dennis Cosgrove, who understood that "landscape is a social and cultural product" (1984, 269), I would argue that the ability to speak fluent English has also become a symbol of "beautiful clothes" in Hsinchu.

An analysis of two communities, Da-Ke-Ji (The High-tech Bilingual

Community) and Da-Si-Gu (Majestic Silicon Villa), supports this argument. Although the first, the Da-Ke-Ji Community, was never built, the fact that it was even proposed demonstrated that motherlanders were convinced that living in an English-speaking community in Taiwan would garner for them the same high status that they would achieve if they lived in Silicon Valley. The second project, Da-Si-Gu, was actually built, and its success was largely due to the fact that many of its residents spoke English and had homes in Silicon Valley. In both cases, the presence of trans-Pacific commuters in the Hsinchu area lent credence to the idea that the ability to speak English was a defining characteristic of Taiwanese identity, and that this characteristic could be achieved by living in a bilingual community.

Da-Ke-Ji: The High-tech Bilingual Community

In her book *Sex and Real Estate*, Marjorie Garber claims that real estate has turned into "a form of yuppie pornography" (2000, 3). But why do people love real estate and houses? Garber answers, "The house is the repository of our unmet needs, our unfulfilled dreams, or our nostalgic longings. It cannot really satisfy any of them, but perhaps that is why we have so much satisfaction in making the attempt" (ibid., 207). Similarly, the Da-Ke-Ji real estate project represents the "unmet needs" and "unfulfilled dreams" that motherlanders pursue.

Kenneth T. Jackson's statement that "Suburbia is both a planning type and a state of mind based on imagery and symbolism" helps me describe the interaction between local and global cultures that I have been discussing (1985, 4–5). As I described above, local motherlanders have a picture in their minds of what the lives of astronauts and returnees must be like in Silicon Valley. Real estate entrepreneurs have used that mental image to develop ways to market the Silicon Valley legend to an eager Hsinchu market. The elements that are widely regarded as contributing to the high quality of life in Silicon Valley are single-family detached houses, gated communities, and an English-speaking environment.

In the Hsinchu region, local governments and real estate developers caught the attention of potential buyers in the trans-Pacific housing market immediately. They quickly learned that images of suburban American communities represented the prestigious social status that both local residents and high-tech families were seeking. Developers advertised pedestrian-oriented gated developments containing "skyward houses," whose narrow multi-level interiors were familiar and attractive to Taiwanese buyers. In addition to the "skyward houses' " appealing interiors were their exteriors that were modified to convey an American suburban look. With their American exteriors and Taiwnese interiors, developers satisfied both the appearance of status and the recognizable physical form that high-tech families wanted.[1] Local developers also used words like "high-tech," "Silicon Valley," and "naturalism" to help them sell their projects to potential buyers. The majority of these new communities were gated, and they shared a feature that Packard criticized in American suburbs, "the mass production of homes" (Packard 1961, 28); the communities were extremely homogenous. There were no retail workers or laborers living in these communities. All the homeowners were either high-tech engineers or professionals working in related industries.

These types of communities had been mushrooming for more than a decade and had led to the suburbanization of the Hsinchu region. Since 1990, the transnational community phenomenon has led to proposals to build more than two-dozen American-style subdivisions in the area surrounding Hsinchu Science Park. Half of the proposals have already passed government review; others are in the process of being reviewed. According to the Taiwanese central and local governments' annual reports, in 2000 more than six hundred hectares of land were planned for development (Leu 1997, 75; Yang 1998, 38–40).[2]

Although many environmental researchers have criticized gated communities for exploiting the unrealistic hope for a modern utopia, which is related to the American dream of a safe and happy community (Davis 1992; Blakely and Snyder 1999, 15; Low 2003), every new project in Hsinchu emphasized their gated security system and that their residents would be composed of high-tech families returning from Silicon Valley.[3] Furthermore, advertising that the communities would be a bilingual environment became a critical element in the promotion of these communities and their Silicon Valley lure.

One high-profile example of a proposed community was Da-Ke-Ji (High-tech Bilingual Community).[4] Although it has not been built, its planned physical features and advertisements are worth analyzing.[5] According to the plan, it would have contained one thousand units of single-family detached houses, duplexes, town houses, and high-rise apartments. However, one of the reasons the community was never built was because the population density of the areas with the single-family homes and town houses was too high and violated local building codes.[6] In terms of landscape features and recreational facilities, it provided a golf course, a community center, a bilingual kindergarten, a business club, and a surrounding hillside green space.

The most striking claim of the Da-Ke-Ji promoters was that the fortress community fulfilled the "global bilingual" dream (Fig. 8.1). When I ran across the following real estate advertisement written in English, I was surprised by how Da-Ke-Ji's connection to Silicon Valley had been promoted (Da Bei Tou Media Corp. 1997).

The following descriptions are quoted exactly as they appear in the original ad:

- Find the *bilingual international* life
- Stunning the country, it's an one and only *international* construction;
- *Chinese and English* are never closer than now;
- The opening of *Bilingual* community living—the prototype of country's *first bilingual community . . . high-class living in an international global village* becomes a reality.
- That period when *Chinese & English* compliment one another.
- Bilingual Community Safety Viewpoint: The security guards at bilingual villa community are all *bilingual foreigners*, thus an *exotic foreign feeling* greets you in and out. Residents are required to carry *bilingual passes*, and the whole area has professionally trained *foreign guards* 24 hours a day, computerized disc control viewing system, *bilingual entrance microphones*, 365 days non-stop community security network, etc. Safety is there every second of the day. Worry free and carefree, you are free to go everywhere you want.

Reading the above advertisement I was struck by how many times the terms "bilingual," "foreign," and "international" were used. When I interviewed the chief designer of the project, I realized that all the members of the planning and design team had been trained in Taiwan. The advertisements, however, were printed in both English and Chinese, and different national flags were part of the graphic design. Western-style landscapes with Americanized skyward houses and driveways dominated the picture of the

FIG. 8.1. Real estate models for the High-tech Bilingual Community in the sale office. The Chinese signs on the wall at the backdrop are "Bilingual." Photo by author, 1998.

street, even though they described the community design as "pedestrian-oriented." Bilingual signs and systems were emphasized over and over again. Da-Ke-Ji was a very popular project when it was first advertised in 1996, and by February 1998 more than half of its properties had been sold,[7] but by the end of that year the project had fallen apart. Interestingly, all the potential homebuyers that had put money down on their dream properties were high-tech motherlander families.

Would bilingual high-tech families live in the bilingual community? Based on my survey, most bilingual high-tech engineers (astronauts, green card moms, and returnees) live in the Bamboo Village, inside Hsinchu Science Park. The majority of would-be homebuyers at Da-Ke-Ji, however, were motherlanders. The real estate developer's formula for selling the Silicon Valley legend in Taiwan had struck a chord with the motherlanders, who dreamed of achieving the status that would be conferred by living in Silicon Valley or Hsinchu Science Park.

Only a few high-tech motherlanders criticized this method of using the Silicon Valley legend to market the new community. Ken was one of these few. When I brought up the emphasis on bilingualism that developers had used to market Da-Ke-Ji, he pointed out the disjunction between imagination and reality. He believed that the concept of a bilingual community was strange and unrealistic. When he visited the office and model home of the Bilingual, he told the real estate agents that it wouldn't work. He explained to me, "All the people who dream about bilingual environments are those who don't speak English. The real bilingual high-tech families won't live here permanently anyway. They won't spend a huge amount of money to buy a pseudo-bilingual home here."

If Ken were right, it would mean that all the residents living in the so-called bilingual community would actually speak only Chinese. "So what is the purpose of providing those bilingual signs and foreign guards? Or why do we need to train those local guards to speak English? I think it would be a big joke if the bilingual system were really operated someday." Just as those on one side of the "English First" policy wondered why documents must be translated into English if the majority understood only Chinese, Ken's argument suggested that it was ridiculous to call an environment "bilingual" when few could speak or write English fluently.

Although the idea of selling bilingualism was a "big joke" to Ken, the idealization of the bilingual lifestyle reflects how the ability to speak English has become a symbol of the transnational life and has impacted the way local residents pursue their ideal community lives. Ironically, as indicated above, Taiwanese immigrants in Silicon Valley prefer to speak in Chinese. Even more ironic is the fact that the use of Chinese signs has been the subject of much debate in Silicon Valley. The Silicon Valley old-timers are often disturbed by the fact that many Chinese shops in Silicon Valley use signs in Chinese, which leaves them feeling as if their hometown has been unabashedly taken over by newcomers.

Da-Si-Gu: "A Real Bilingual Community"

Despite the fact that Da-Ke-Ji was never built, its developers had evidently tapped into a successful formula that linked their project with Silicon Valley in the public's imagination. Other projects promoting a similar set of Silicon Valley values were built, however, proving that the public's imagination could lead to a "real locus of growth and innovation" in Hsinchu (Fishman 1987, 190). Among recent developments, Da-Si-Gu, or the Majestic Silicon

Villa, was the most famous in the Hsinchu region. The development received from the Environment Bureau the Top Ten Model Community award in 1995, an award that was based on the excellent maintenance strategies and implementation that the community's homeowner association had put into place. Among the development's residents, however, their bilingual skills are the source of as much pride as the qualities for which they won the award. Contrasting his own community with the failed Da-Ke-Ji, Dennis, an on-site manager of Da-Si-Gu, told me, "The High-tech Bilingual Community is not really bilingual. They only proposed bilingual signs. Our Da-Si-Gu is a real bilingual community, though we have never promoted that. All the kids in Da-Si-Gu speak fluent English. I don't even understand what they are talking about. I feel I am in another country every weekend, when all the teenagers and kids play in the central open space."

A Model Gated Community

Da-Si-Gu is a hillside suburban community located in Chunglin Township, in Hsinchu County. The gated community contains American-accented Taiwanese skyward houses (Fig. 8.2), elaborate recreational facilities, and numerous other attractive elements that made it the benchmark for good community planning. Helen, Laura, and Joni were returnee housewives living in Da-Si-Gu. All of them had lived in the United States, and they all agreed that Da-Si-Gu was very similar to their American suburban communities. Their only complaint about Da-Si-Gu was the landscaping. They insisted that Da-Si-Gu would be a perfect community if only more trees could be added.

FIG. 8.2 Da-Si-Gu residents think of their community as very much like those in the United States, but with fewer trees. Photo by author, 2001.

Like many other new suburban communities in the Hsinchu region, Da-Si-Gu is very exclusive, enclosed by walls and attended by a guard at the gate. Hsinchu residents who are not part of Da-Si-Gu's social network are not allowed through the gate. Once through the gate, numerous houses of various building types can be seen, including 30 single-family detached houses, 108 duplex houses, 98 town houses, and a nine-story high-rise apartment.[8] In terms of public facilities, Da-Si-Gu provides a community center, a swimming pool, two tennis courts, baseball fields, and a large central open space for residents. There is also a store supplying residents with their daily groceries.

Dick, a resident and the homeowner association chairman, addressed various social issues when I talked with him. He thought that because the American-style housing design allowed everyone to drive their cars into their garages without passing any public spaces, the residents seldom spoke to one other. In fact, many didn't know who their neighbors were. Even worse, "If you knock on their door, they won't answer you," Dick said. "The community security guards have to call them for you first. Otherwise, they will call the police to kick you out."

The lack of communication between neighbors that Dick described was also mirrored in the relationships between the community resident subgroups. Residents arranged most of their social gatherings by phone, but anyone who wasn't a member of a particular small group might only learn what happened in the community by reading the newspaper. One of my interviewees, Helen, told me, "Our community has lots of activities, but I never heard about any of them until I read about them in the local newspaper one day. Now I know we have a housewives' club, a kids' group, and lots of other groups, but I don't have any idea what they are doing, because I don't have time to participate in their activities."

American Community Experiences
vs. Da-Si-Gu Community Participation

When I conducted my research, most Da-Si-Gu residents were Taiwanese American returnees and upper-middle-class locals. From the returnees' perspective, their experiences in the American suburbs had taught them how to participate in all kinds of community activities. For example, they contended that they were all much more concerned about public issues than other local Taiwanese; that their upper-middle-class neighbors were much easier to communicate with than local Hsinchu residents; and that they recycled their garbage. They were also proud of their homeowner association that had made the development one of Taiwan's model communities.

Dick, however, had an opposing view. He felt that the returnees did not contribute at all to the community-building process. In his view, community pride had been instilled by the local families who considered Da-Si-Gu their only real home. Dick portrayed the returnees as caring more about "keeping all [their] personal information private" than about public issues like "the establishment of a neighborhood help network or a neighborhood watch system."

Dick was frustrated because he had always wanted to build up a database that included basic information about each household, such as the number of people living in each unit and a list of emergency contacts. The returnees, however, considered his database an invasion of their privacy. Dick thus concluded that the returnees were "highly educated people [that] seldom participate in community activities."

According to Dick's point of view, there were four types of residents in Da-Si-Gu: the passengers, the short-term residents, the speculators, and the real residents. The first group, the passengers, was those who lived in Da-Si-Gu for only three to five months. They lived in the high-rise apartments and worked primarily as consultants for the high-tech companies in Hsinchu Science Park. Because their Silicon Valley companies had established joint ventures with Hsinchu Science Park companies, they came to Hsinchu on extended business trips but never got involved with the various local communities. Their apartments in Da-Si-Gu were rented by their companies in Hsinchu Science Park.

The second group, the go-between residents, lived in Da-Si-Gu for at least two years because of their term-work contracts with their Silicon Valley companies. They mostly rented skyward houses or apartment units. Most engineer families that moved back from Silicon Valley also fall into this category. The third group, the speculators, bought houses in the community to earn a profit. They did not live in Da-Si-Gu at all. In Dick's view, the only group that considered their Da-Si-Gu homes their real homes was the fourth group, the real residents. Dick did not have statistical data regarding the population of each group, but he estimated that each group, with the exception of the speculators, made up about one third of the total population.

Dick went on to tell me that only the real residents, those who considered Da-Si-Gu their permanent home, were willing to participate in community events. Most engineer families that moved back from the United States led very isolated social lives, and they did not want to talk to other residents. Gradually, they formed a very exclusive network. Their "ABC" (American-born Chinese) children played together, since they could communicate in English. In addition, they were mostly churchgoers. Through their shared language and religion, they formed an exclusive sub-subculture that alienated other local residents.

When talking about relationships with the local Hakkanese communities in the Chunglin area, Dick admitted, "Our community doesn't have a good relationship with local people in Chunglin." He viewed local Hakkanese as hard-working, industrious people. He told me that the Hakka locals disliked Da-Si-Gu residents because they led a life of luxury. As chairman of the development's homeowner association, Dick felt it was his responsibility to bridge the gap. He tried to coordinate a cultural festival in May 1998, hoping he could organize a performance that brought together Hakkanese and Da-Si-Gu children. "Then we can bridge the cultural differences by enjoying some fun times together," Dick said.

The Pu-yu New City Plan

In 2002 the National Chiao-Tung University (NCTU) initiated "the largest new-city project in Taiwan in the past 20 years," the Pu-yu New City Plan, which will be located in the hills at the foot of Da-Si-Gu (Fig. 8.3) (Chang et al. 2002). According to the Pu-yu Project Working Group (2002, 14), the Pu-yu site covers Chubei, Chudong, and Chunglin townships. Located a 20-minute drive from Hsinchu Science Park, the new Pu-yu city of 80,000 residents will provide infrastructure for the information technology industries and a high-quality residential community for high-tech personnel from around the world. The new city is planned to occupy 1,250 hectares (3,088

FIG. 8.3. A view from the Pu-yu New City Plan site toward Da-Si-Gu. The Pu-yu site is the location of a rural landscape and authentic Hakka culture. Photo by author, 2003.

acres) of farmland situated on both banks of the Tou-chien River, adjacent to the new high-speed rail station in Hsinchu. Professor Liu, the chief planner of Pu-yu, described the goals of the Pu-yu plan, which included the creation of:

1. A center for innovation leading to transformation in the rapidly changing IT industries,

2. A new type of university campus whose campus buildings blend with the building style of the surrounding community, thus symbolizing friendly interactions with both local communities and industries,

3. A high-quality residential community that addresses the desires of both relocated American high-tech personnel and the needs of long-term local residents.

In order to carry out this ambitious plan, NCTU established a partnership with the Hsinchu County government. When I was involved in the project as a consultant in 2001, the county chief and NCTU president explained that their main concern was how to provide the high-quality residential community and lifestyle that would attract trans-Pacific high-tech families. They considered Da-Si-Gu a very useful model that they could study to learn how to build the community they aspired to.

The Hakka Cultural Landscape as Unpolished Jade

The tensions between "real" local residents and returnees that Dick had sketched out in his portrayal of social relations in Da-Si-Gu were exactly the sort that the Pu-yu planners had consciously sought to avoid. From the start of the planning process, the primary actors—Hsinchu local government and NCTU—wanted to promote a "high quality of life," which they equated with a trans-Pacific lifestyle social structure and American suburban physical structure.

They named the development "Pu-yu," which means "unpolished jade" in Chinese, in a gesture that acknowledged the site's undeveloped agricultural landscape and the presence of the ethnic Hakka culture within that landscape. They believed that the site could be polished by installing an American suburban landscape, which in turn would attract a trans-Pacific commuter population.

Within the Pu-yu project site there were 9,000 households, with a total of 27,000 people (EDS International 2002). As in the Jin-shan-mian district adjacent to Hsinchu Science Park, most local residents on the Pu-yu site were Hakka farmers who had been there for several generations. The Hakkas are a subculture of the Han Chinese who came from mainland China beginning four hundred years ago. They mostly settled on poorer-quality land along mountainsides and flood plains, because the better farmland in flat areas had already been settled by the ancestors of Taiwanese natives who migrated to Taiwan earlier than the Hakkas. In the Pu-yu site along the riverbank, the ancestors of the local Hakka had used their traditional skill in constructing dikes and waterworks to channel and control the flow of the river, thereby creating rich alluvial rice fields that are still used to produce some of the highest-quality rice in Taiwan. Liu described the distinctive local Hakka cultural landscape:

> Along with the cultivation of the fields is the gradual refinement of villages following the waterways. Among the distinctive features of the Hakka settlements of this area are: lineage cluster housing grouped around a common central open space, earth gods and community gods which are housed in small temple structures strategically located to serve as guardian spirits, water-powered rice

mills as distinctive landmarks, parallel rows of wind-breaker bamboo and willow along the many narrow and wide canals to protect the fields, and most distinctively, an intricate system of water channels and water distribution devices to control the rate and amount of flow which form a rich web of connected fields all together forming an interdependent whole. (Chang et al. 2002)

However, as the chief planner of Pu-yu, Professor Liu pointed out that global events had impacted the Hakka way of life in recent years. First, there was a threat caused by the globalization of agricultural products, including rice. The entry of Taiwan into the World Trade Organization made the situation worse for Taiwan's rice farmers, and with the decline in rice production, rice farmers had been slowly fading away along with the Hakka rice landscape. Second, the proximity of the area in which the Hakka lived to the highly successful Hsinchu Science Park caused it to face development pressure, as high-tech industries and high-end housing for industry personnel began to expand. The proposed Pu-yu New City was a case in point. Third, a new high-speed railroad line was under construction, with a station planned adjacent to this area. The high-speed rail station would bring large-scale development to the area, which in turn would speed up the decline of the agricultural use of the land.

For or Against the Global City?

In contrast to Hsinchu County and NCTU, which viewed the Pu-yu plan as a vehicle for the production of a suburban "American dreamscape" (Martinson 2000), Professor Liu deemphasized the product and focused on the process. He believed that the Pu-yu proposal could only be successful if local residents participated in the planning process in partnership with government officials and NCTU. His team held dozens of grassroots meetings and workshops to discuss the Pu-yu plan with locals. The different townships that participated in the planning process expressed both support for and objections to the plan.

In Chubei Township, which was closest to the built-up urban area and adjacent to the high-speed rail station, about 80 percent of the people supported the new development. In Chudong Township, the number was lower, at around 70 percent. In Chunglin Township, however, the township furthest from the station, fewer than half the residents supported the project.

Liu pointed out that the various cultures of the local communities as well as the differing physical settings of each township caused the differences in

attitude toward development. Residents of Chubei and Chudong were a little younger, and there were more newcomers to these areas. They were less
attached to the agricultural landscape because fewer of them had actually
worked in the rice fields. These younger newcomers knew less about the significance of the earth gods, the water canals, and the rice mills, for example.
At the same time, because they were younger and newer to the area, they
had a greater expectation of future growth and prosperity. Young people
considered that the development would create new jobs, jobs in the high-
tech industries, in which the rapid accumulation of wealth was likely. On
the other hand, older land-owning farmers were resigned to the eventual decline of rice farming, and they accepted development as their fate. They
weighed the arrival of future development against the money that could be
made if they sold their land immediately. The lure of profit to be gained
from land development was so strong that in most community meetings
people's uppermost concern was how much they could gain by participating
in the project, rather than whether a better environment or a better school
would result from the development.

The people of Chunglin Township reacted quite differently. Generally
older than those in Chubei and Chudong, people in Chunglin were more
attached to the place they had grown up in. Their community was more ho-
mogeneous, with fewer newcomers, and therefore its residents were more
motivated to hold on to what they had, less willing to change, and less prepared to imagine a different future. Their conservatism also manifested itself
in an almost zealous desire to protect the beauty of the local landscape, including the canals, the earth god shrines, the rice mills, and the clustered
courtyard houses.

From a physical point of view, Chunglin Township had a much better
preserved landscape than the other townships. There were fewer new developments dotting the landscape, and the streams, vegetation, and riverbank
seemed richer. Thus, in response to the new development project, the residents of Chunglin were the most vocal in their opposition. The project's potential to destroy Chunglin's assets outweighed the potential benefits.
Chunglin citizens were less interested in monetary gain and more concerned
about whether they could maintain their quality of life.

It is particularly interesting that during community meetings in Chunglin residents simultaneously voiced their desire to maintain their existing

lifestyle and suggested the possibility of having outsiders come to live in their community. They embodied a strong sense of a balanced relationship between the host and the guest, and this construct extended to their view of the physical environment. In other words, there was an existing host environment composed of natural ecological elements and cultural artifacts, and there was a guest environment of new spatial needs. The people of this community seemed to be saying, "Come and live with us in our way, and feel the beauty of our environment."[9]

Indeed, Pu-yu's participatory planning process and the attitudes that residents in Chunglin Township expressed open up a new way for outsiders and insiders to share the process that leads to negotiating a community identity together. Everyone in this negotiation process was equally important, and the existing cultural landscape was also considered part of the dialogue. Cultural landscapes, which include residents within those landscapes, "are storehouses for these social memories, because natural features such as hills or harbors, as well as streets, buildings and patterns of settlement, frame the lives of many people and often outlast many lifetimes" (Hayden, 1995, 9).

Silicon Valley Landscapes in Shanghai, China

After I completed my preliminary investigation of the lives and landscapes of Taiwanese high-tech trans-Pacific commuters, I presented the results to my Berkeley colleagues in 2000. Clara, a Portuguese friend, was very surprised to learn of the trans-Pacific home phenomenon, and she revealed that a very similar phenomenon occurred among Portuguese high-tech trans-Atlantic commuters who fly back and forth between San Jose and Lisbon. They also have two American-style suburban homes and hang out with the same group of friends in both San Jose and Lisbon. She claimed, "You only need to change the titles on your slides from Chinese to Portuguese. Then, if you presented the slides to Portuguese communities, nobody would know whether the images were taken in Hsinchu Science Park, Silicon Valley, or Lisbon." Her remarks made me aware that the high-tech commuter culture does not exist only among the Taiwanese, but is in fact a global phenomenon.

Later, in the summer of 2001, I experienced another variant of trans-

FIG. 8.4. A single-family detached house may cost from US$700,000 to US$2,000,000 here, while the ordinary Shanghai resident's annual income is between US$100 and US$250. Photo by author, 2001.

Pacific commuter culture when I traveled to China and visited the newly developed Zhongguancun Science Park in Beijing and the Zhang-Jiang Science Park in Shanghai. The newly developed suburban communities surrounding these science parks demonstrated that trans-Pacific suburbanization had started flowing from Silicon Valley to Shanghai and Beijing.

My interviewees and friends in Shanghai all recommended that I visit the Tang-chen (Luxury Mansion) project in Poudong New District, because it was considered the most prestigious real estate development. Many transnational migrants and high-tech engineers had established their Shanghai homes there. The project was located across the street from the main entrance of the Zhang-Jiang Science Park. It was a model golf resort that consisted of multi-million-dollar single-family detached houses surrounded by two eighteen-hole golf courses. One golf course, designed by an American, applied a wild and naturalistic style. A Japanese designer had laid out the other course in an Asian style. The project consisted of seven hundred homes that were constructed during two phases (Fig. 8.4).

The homebuyers of the first phase, which took place in 1995 and 1996, were predominantly residents from Taiwan, Hong Kong, and Macao. The second phase of construction took place in 1999 and 2000, after the Shanghai economic boom. Therefore, the majority of these homebuyers were domestic Chinese businessmen who had established their companies in Shanghai. Additionally, there were international businessmen who had established their careers in Shanghai.

"This is a 'united nation,' " said Ziva, who is the manager of the Tang-chen project. According to her, the residents of Tang-chen included the CEOs of Coca-Cola and GM and top-level managers and senior high-tech engineers of global corporations located in Shanghai, especially Zhang-Jiang Science Park. These families were global citizens who migrated from different countries such as the United States, India, Brazil, Hong Kong, Macao, Taiwan, and Singapore, as well as from different provinces in China.

There were also community activities, like housewife clubs, within the Tang-chen development. Iris, a housewife living there, explained to me that the real estate company helped organize different classes for different age groups. There were diverse courses for housewives who wanted to learn Chinese, painting, calligraphy, embroidery, tai chi, ballet, ornamental flower arranging, or Chinese opera. There were also activities for senior residents. Playing mah-jongg was the most popular, and both Iris's mother and her mother-in-law were members of a mah-jongg club. She added, "It is really convenient. The community shuttle comes to pick us up. We don't need to go anywhere outside Tang-chen. Everything is here" (Hester and Chang 2002; Chang and Zhang 2001).

I asked Iris about the relationship between Tang-chen and the local rural communities in the Poudong New District or the Shanghai area. Iris proudly explained, "We create many job opportunities for local people. All the Tang-chen residents hire *ah-yi* [female housekeepers]. *Ah-yi* can live with us because there is an *ah-yi* bedroom in our house design. We hire local people and help the local economy. I feel that we contribute to local society greatly!" (Chang and Zhang 2001).

Iris's experiences were very similar to those of the wives we encountered in previous chapters. From Taiwan to Portugal, from China to Israel, there are many high-tech global communities sharing the same story. According to the membership data of the International Association of Science Parks (IASP), 63 countries have already established 251 high-tech parks around the world (International Association of Science Parks 2003). In contrast to IASP's prodevelopment stance, numerous researchers, reporters, planners, and policy makers have criticized the rapid increase of suburban developments in technopoles on a global scale (to name a few: Castells 1989; Scott 1993, 1996; Wu 1997, 1998a, 1998b; Hsu 1998a, 1998b; Rosenthal 1998, 2003). These transnational suburban landscapes provide their residents with the *jin-yi* (beautiful clothes) that the global commuters seek. But, as we have seen, those who live inside the walls of the new developments are not the only ones who have felt the impact of these landscapes. The view that development of high-tech global communities engenders only positive economic growth, technological advances, and higher levels of social status is a narrow view that turns a blind eye to the people and places that are negatively impacted by such growth. In this chapter I have tried to convey the need for a clear and inclusive view of the development of global cities within local contexts, a view that recognizes that when a global city has been built in someone's (or some group's) backyard without their participation in the planning and building process, it can lead to resentment and the separation of social identities and cultural values.

Homes

.

NINE

Mirror Homes

Doreen Massey has criticized postmodern geographers for conceptualizing place identities as specifically "place-bound" entities that interlink with particular locales and are defined by particular times and societies (1994a, 111). She argues that, in the era of globalization, "the identity of place is formed out of social interrelations, and a proportion of those interrelations . . . will stretch beyond that 'place' itself. . . . [T]he identity of a place is also necessarily unfixed" (ibid., 115). Massey claims that there is "no one essential past" for a place, and that it is also problematic to characterize any place by counterposition to another place that is outside (ibid., 116–17). In this chapter I will be introducing a concept that I call the "mirror home," and I want to be clear that my conception of Silicon Valley suburbia is *not* in counterposition to newly developed single-family detached houses in Hsinchu. The concept of the "mirror home," as you will see, does *not* suggest that trans-Pacific commuters' identities are bound to a particular place, or places, in the United States or Taiwan. "Mirror home" captures the set of "unfixed" (in Massey's terms), intermingling, and constantly changing relationships that trans-Pacific commuters experience in their process of shaping their homes and landscapes.

I use the term "mirror home phenomenon" to refer to various aspects of the identity struggles that are experienced by dozens of Silicon Valley–to–Taiwan commuters who live in two homes on both sides of the Pacific. I found that for some trans-Pacific commuters, their mirror homes are actual existing homes, while for others they are constructed through psychological processes in which memory, fantasy, desire, and dreams intertwine with reality. No one I spoke with thought of one of their homes as an exact mirror image of the other, so the "mirror" in my "mirror home" conceptualization of the relationship between trans-Pacific commuters homes and their selves is better understood as a mirror that has been broken into many pieces, or the mirror of a kaleidoscope, or even a carnival fun house mirror. It is a mirror that changes, alters, and modifies, not a mirror that takes one's home or home identity and reflects it to precisely reproduce another.

The mirror home phenomenon is one in which trans-Pacific commuters make use of home and landscape forms embedded within their memories, cultural norms, and social relationships. A familiar home and landscape form experienced in one of the cultures they commute between might be transplanted to the other culture, or the familiar form of one culture might be changed, rearranged, reformed, or completely transformed in interaction with the one other or many other cultures that these commuters experience in their "go-between" lives (Chang 2000, 73–111).

In the previous chapter I discussed the trans-Pacific commuters' pursuit of "beautiful clothes," the status symbolized by American suburban houses and landscapes, and how that pursuit influenced the home identities of Taiwanese high-tech engineers in both Hsinchu and Silicon Valley. Through my conversations with these high-tech engineers, I found that the similarity of transcultural lifestyles, transnational community networks, and the mirror images of suburban houses were three key factors that influenced trans-Pacific commuters' shifting home identities. We explored the transcultural lifestyles in Part 2, and addressed the transnational social network in Part 3. Here we focus on the mirror home phenomenon from the perspective of building physical and psychic home environments. We will visit the Hsinchu region first, and then move on to Silicon Valley.

Dreaming the American Lifestyle: Image vs. Experience

Some authors who, like me, are interested in the relationship between places and identities have studied the relationship between identity and the bodily experience of place (Bloomer and Moore 1977; Altman and Low 1992; Lyndon and Moore 1994) or the relationship between identity and the images of place (Lippard 1997; Hayden 2003). The images that one is attracted to say a lot about one's view of oneself, or one's identity. In my conversations with trans-Pacific commuters they often talked about their memories and embodied feelings, and they often talked about their identities in terms of images—images of house forms, landscape types, or even shopping centers. As discussed in previous chapters, American suburban landscapes, which have come to symbolize highbrow cultural status, have influenced landscapes in both the Hsinchu region and Silicon Valley.

The gated communities containing American-style single-family detached houses that now dominate high-tech areas in Taiwan are other images that these commuters identify with. For global commuters, the image of the gated community, separate and detached from its local neighbors, is a defining symbol of the status they have acquired. For both local residents and trans-Pacific commuters, the image of a detached American house embodies the glory that is conferred by American citizenship, higher education, and a high-level position in a transnational corporation. The detached suburban American house has become an image representing status on both sides of the Pacific.

Who Are the Actors? What Are the Actions?

Following Donald Appleyard, I think it is useful to think of the process of creating an ideal home place as a collective "environmental action" (Appleyard 1979, 143–45). Ideal places are built, or imagined, as part of collective processes that involve many actors in many sectors of the home and community building industries. In the case of the Hsinchu Science Park, the actors, such as the planners and developers in the public and private sectors, realized that the creation of a pleasant image of the home environment was critical in order to attract a high-quality workforce. Returnees, green card moms, and astronauts were pioneers who have tried to make one place a mirror of another. Other actors, including motherlanders, local residents, design professionals, and policy makers, were also major driving forces in the construction of the mirror home phenomenon.

In the 1990s real estate developers discovered an eager market of buyers in Hsinchu who were very attracted to images of American suburban homes

TABLE 9.1

Home Types and American Experiences

Hsinchu	Project name	Interviewees	Hsinchu housing type	American experience
Hsinchu Science Park	Bamboo Village	2	house	1 New Jersey, 1 California
	Lakeside Village	1	townhouse	1 California
	Lakeside Apartment	5	apartment	4 California, 1 Illinois
Hsinchu City	Longshan Village	2	house	2 Taiwan
	Kuangfu Community	1	apartment	1 Taiwan
	Kuangming Village	1	house	1 Taiwan
	Chenghuang Temple	3	house	1 New York, 2 Taiwan
	Plum Bamboo Villa	3	high-rise apartment	1 Virginia, 1 Texas, 1 Taiwan
Suburbs Chunglin	The Majestic Silicon Villa	4	house	1 Texas, 2 New Jersey, 1 Taiwan
Boushan	Treasure Mountain Villa	2	house	1 New York, 1 Taiwan

NOTE: The data of this table include the motherlanders I interviewed in Hsinchu. Since motherlanders do not have American experiences, I use "Taiwan" to categorize them.

and landscapes. The trans-Pacific commuters I spoke with were part of that market, but these high-tech go-betweeners constituted only a minority of the residents in the area. The group of returnees was only 10 percent of the population, or about nine to ten thousand people, and the group of astronauts was even smaller, about 2 percent. However, their presence in the Hsinchu area and the public's perception of their high status inspired developers interested in supplying local homebuyers with the American suburban image they wanted.

The high-tech families I visited in the Hsinchu area of Taiwan lived in Hsinchu City, Boushan Township, and Chunglin Township and were both returnees and motherlanders. Table 9.1 shows my trans-Pacific commuter interviewees' home types and their American residential experiences. We can easily identify that the motherlanders and returnees live in similar communities outside Hsinchu Science Park.

Osman, a principal of a local architecture and construction firm, made clear to me just how large an impact the small number of returnees had made on the local Hsinchu market. His company was well known for developing new hillside communities for high-tech residents. He pointed out that, for most homebuyers, "Images are more important than experiences." Local homebuyers just want to have something that looks like an American home. Three types of homebuyers have played major roles. The first group is the astronauts, who have had the most experience living in American but are in the minority. Many of them did not buy homes locally. Instead, they usually rented temporary places,[1] because their families and their primary homes were in Silicon Valley. However, they became the models that set the standard for local homebuyers and builders.

The second group, the returnees, was also a minority. They had studied or worked in the United States but had moved back to Hsinchu. They generally appreciated the quality of life available in America, and considered moving back to the United States for jobs and their children's education.

The third group, the motherlanders, constituted the majority of the population. Although some had traveled to the United States, others had not even visited. Osman told me, "However, as home buyers, 80 percent of them shared similar tastes, especially those motherlanders who had never lived in America. They would bring books, magazines, or photos, then point out the images they preferred."

Speaking with Osman helped me to better understand how the production of symbolic forms, the American suburban landscapes dominating the Hsinchu hillsides, was a collective environmental action cooperatively produced by various social actors. The creators of these forms, from high-tech policy makers to local real estate developers, agents, and architects, all tried to duplicate the sense of suburban Silicon Valley on the Hsinchu hillsides. The residents, whether they had lived in the United States or could only imagine the American dream, saw as their ideal an American single-family detached house standing on a fenced-in lawn and protected by a guarded gate. The creators of the home forms, then, industriously attempted to create mirror images of American homes in response to consumers who idealized such imagery.

Since the early 1990s, developers have proposed and marketed two different types of residential projects. In one type, developed by the high-tech

FIG. 9.1. A completed single-family detached house designed by Osman's office for the Winbond project. Photo by author, 2005.

companies themselves, American suburban images were transplanted into local landscapes (Fig. 9.1).[2] In the other, driven by real estate developers, a modified Taiwanese skyward house was installed into an American suburban landscape (see Fig. 8.2). Although the former introduced the symbolic forms of home environments in exclusive enclaves, the latter type of projects dominated the Hsinchu local housing market. Together they superimposed the image of suburban Silicon Valley onto the hillsides surrounding Hsinchu Science Park. In the following sections I will analyze these two types of home-building processes in Hsinchu. Then, I will examine how the images, the desire for personal comfort, and the need for daily convenience constitute a response to trans-Pacific home identities.

Transcultural Transplantation:
Taiwanese-Style Single-Family Detached Houses

Where do all these home images originate? How have they been produced locally? And how did their production satisfy the psychological
processes of clients whose memories and desires caused them to seek out
mirror home imagery? Osman, the Taiwan-trained architect engaged in both
types of hillside residential projects, explained the mirror home transplantation process in detail.[3]

In Osman's experience, the process of producing homes usually took
from five to ten years.[4] To start, a high-tech company had to organize potential homebuyers, primarily from among current employees of the company, though some employees may change jobs and leave the company during the long process. As future residents of a development, the potential
buyers had to select representatives to form a committee to advise on their
dream community. The CEO of the company would chair that committee,
which was responsible for finding potential sites and hiring professional
planners and architects.

Imagining America. The second stage of home production included three
steps: (1) an American house slide show, (2) a lottery to determine property
locations, and (3) a participatory home design workshop. Osman proudly
explained the first step:

> If you were a designer of residential projects for the high-techers in the
> Hsinchu region, you should know all the trendy housing types in the United
> States, especially those on the West Coast. Of course, California is a very im-
> portant one. My wife and I travel to the States to update our slides once a year.
> We drive all the way from Canada to San Diego. We visit not only places like
> Orange County, in Southern California, but also those cities surrounding Sili-
> con Valley, like Daly City. Then we introduce the new housing forms to our
> clients through slide shows.

Slide shows were the main vehicle for presenting ideal forms to potential
residents. The shows were presented many times, both in Taipei and in
Hsinchu. During each presentation architects explained the details of each
house form,[5] and also showed new computer-generated designs, which even
further expanded the possibilities in the imaginations of all the participants.
Architects eliminated certain forms from the slide show. Osman explained,
"Japanese styles can be removed from the list first. These guys are all from

America. They like American taste. . . . In my opinion, Southern California styles fit Taiwan best. The choice of color is very important. Although they like American home styles, they still prefer Chinese colors. This seems very hard to change. Mostly, they like a red roof with white walls, or very light gray is acceptable. Black has to be avoided.

The property location lottery. After the slide shows the potential residents participated in a lottery to determine who would receive which home lot. It seems that the principles of feng shui were less important to them than participating in a fair and equitable process. Osman described how the lottery worked:

> They have science backgrounds, so feng shui is not their major concern. However, equality is essential to them, maybe because they had come back from America. We don't need to worry about their status in the company. All of them follow the "first-come, first-served" rule. And none of them, including the CEOs, will ask for an exception. However, we also have to consider social relationships, because certain people would like to live close to each other. We have to design each house in our subdivision with a sense of closeness and neighborliness. Our lottery is group-based. Each person can be a group, while nine families can be another group. After they get their group lottery numbers, they still don't know the location of their lots. They don't know how many households are in each group, so it's impossible for people to cheat in this process.

The participatory design process. The participatory design process included three parts: ideal home questionnaires, standard house form presentations, and hands-on group and individual design. Following the slide shows, the professional group—the architects and designers—designed questionnaires, a form of market survey, to understand what types of houses would fit buyers' needs. The questionnaires provided detailed information regarding the homebuyers' needs in terms of square footage, number of rooms, and type of rooms. Designers then used this information to create five or six standard prototypes. The prototypes served as a point of departure for the designers. Each individual family chose one of the prototypes, but they had the right to negotiate variations to the interior spaces. All facades, however, were fixed.

Wives tended to be much more engaged in the design process than their husbands. His CEO clients always asked him to play golf after dinner, Osman told me, but he couldn't play with them most of the time. He had to talk to their wives to work out design details. Since most participants picked out a house form based only on images, they used their imaginations when conceiving of design variations. Osman said, "They don't know what they really want. Some participants will come to me, for example, to request a California-style kitchen. I will draw three stereotypical California kitchens and say, 'There are three types here. Which one do you really want?' Then the guy gets confused."

In a way, this participatory process was more an art of representation than a process of negotiation and communication. It integrated the social status embodied with each form and the way designers presented the form. Designers had to know how to combine the images in their clients' imaginations with the experiences that members of the high-tech groups valued, and then they had to present their designs to the participants in a professional style that was respected by their high-tech clients. Osman's virtuosity in the "art of representation," his skill at tapping into his clients' memories and desires for a mirror home, were clearly evident when he told me, "We have to use real spaces, but do not talk about materials. I would use a five-star hotel lobby as an example. If I tell them their living room is going to look like the lobby of the Hyatt Regency in San Francisco, they can imagine it. Dealing with them, you have to be precise. When you say 'the Hyatt Regency,' it just clicks and they get it!"

Transcultural Modification: Americanized Skyward Houses

The Winbond project, designed and developed by Osman, has started a new trend in the construction of dream homes for high-tech residents. Many other high-tech companies, such as TSMC and Acer, have begun to follow the same steps to create communities for their employees. Due to the complicated government review process required and the rapidly changing policies regarding hillside development, only a few of these projects have been completed. In contrast, communities of modified Taiwanese skyward houses (*tou-tian-tzu*) have been mushrooming rapidly. These residential developments driven by real estate companies provide a large quantity of new homes.

Instead of transplanting American-style buildings, some builders have created "Americanized skyward houses." The Americanized skyward house is an example of the new hybrid forms developed to satisfy both the American and Taiwanese look that consumers want. It is a modified home form that combines the footprint of a Taiwanese skyward house and the freestanding form of an American single-family detached house (see Fig. 8.2). The American suburban house and the Taiwanese skyward house share an essential characteristic: both are single, detached forms. But the Taiwanese form was not a pure form, not a pure mirror or a perfect reflection of the original American suburban house. It was a mirror home form, an altered and re-arranged form that met the needs of both its producers and consumers.

Bill, a local architect, explained why the majority of Hsinchu residents, whether they had lived in the United States or not, could adapt easily to the Americanized skyward houses. He pointed out two ways that Taiwanese residents viewed the situation:

> Two phenomena are quite interesting. First, the form of recently built single-family detached houses in Hsinchu is a transformation of the form of modern Taiwanese rural houses, the so-called skyward house. Or, you can generally relate them to Taiwanese urban shop houses. Second, the American idea of living in a single-family detached house is the same as the old Taiwanese or Chinese rural custom of owning a piece of land before industrialization and urbanization.

Creating an Americanized skyward house. The typical residential house form in rural Taiwan is the skyward house, a multistory walk-up building constructed of reinforced concrete. Its unique characteristics are its narrow but deep shape and the uncut rebar tails on its flat rooftop. The square footage of these houses varies depending upon the size of the property, but in some cases the lots on which the houses stand are extremely narrow (see Fig. 4.3).

The floor plans of these houses are simple, because they are too narrow for elaborate arrangements. Each floor typically has only one or two rooms. The ground floor is often divided into two sections, the front section consisting of a living room or public space and the back consisting of a kitchen and dining area. The second floor and those above are reserved for bed-rooms and private areas. In old skyward houses there is only one bath, on the ground floor, so residents have to climb up and down in order to use the bathroom or get water. An interior staircase, perhaps three feet wide, is typically located at the side of the house. This private staircase is usually hidden between walls and has no handrails; it somewhat resembles a tunnel. In some cases the ground floor has been converted into a garage, in which case all the other rooms have been moved up one floor. In order that more floors might be added in the future, the owners of skyward houses seldom cut off the house's rebar tails. From the street level one can often see small sections of rebar protruding from the rooftop.

Most city dwellers, especially landowners, in Hsinchu have traditionally lived in urban shop houses. Shop houses and skyward houses are similar in appearance, but shop houses are always attached to one another. They are usually found in old urban centers lining both sides of a street. The front section of the first floor is traditionally a family-owned shop. Shop houses look like row houses, although each of them has a different owner and may have been constructed at a different time and in a different style (see Fig. 4.2).

Owning land. Because Taiwan has traditionally been an agricultural society, land ownership is very highly valued. Residents of upper-story apartment units generally do not feel that they own the lot where they live, even though legally they partially own it. Only ground-level residents consider themselves to own the entire lot. This is why the price of ground-level apartment units has always been much higher than that of apartments on upper floors in Taiwan, whether or not the ground-floor residents have permission to convert the apartment to commercial use.

With the exception of the narrow shape, the form of a skyward house is similar to that of an American detached house. A shop house, on the other hand, more closely resembles a town house or a row house. Typically, adapted stem families have inhabited multistory skyward houses, with each nuclear family of the adapted stem family living on one story. However, the residential patterns of the nuclear high-tech family are more similar to those of American families. In other words, one nuclear family tends to live alone in a house or town house. Bill explained:

> Local residents feel they are upgrading their Taiwanese skyward house with an American facade. To those who migrate back from Silicon Valley, they don't want to downgrade their standard of living by moving to an apartment. It seems okay for them to get a home like this. Compared to an apartment unit, an Americanized Taiwanese skyward house is more expensive. Today, people don't consider living in an apartment conducive to a high quality of life. These high-tech guys want to have something more valuable, with higher quality. They want to feel the value of their home environments.

The Challenges of American Lifestyles

In his book *Body*, Don Hanlon Johnson (1983, 13–14) argues that although we are "gripped by ideologies," our bodies have "different needs." He claims that our bodies have "wisdom, justice, intelligence and love," but all of these have "to be won through patience." Similarly, the trans-Pacific commuters have also discovered that their bodies have different needs than their dreams. These high-tech families dream of American suburban houses before they move into their homes, but their bodies have to adjust to their ideas after they settle down. The question remaining for environmental researchers is what is really going on in the lives of those who live in their dream homes, homes that are structured by suburban images?

Three typical adjustments necessary when moving into an Americanized skyward house are worth some attention. First, the high-tech residents who have lived in the United States but have never experienced a Taiwanese skyward house must learn to manage climbing up and down staircases every day. Second, they have to cope with the size of their gardens and learn how to maintain them. Third, Taiwanese high-tech residents who used to live in the city now have to drive to and from their suburban neighborhood.

The "nightmare" of stairs. The defining characteristic of a skyward house is its vertical arrangement, with each floor dedicated to a specific function. Many Taiwanese are used to living in this type of house, but others are not used to climbing stairs many times a day. Helen, for example, moved back to Taiwan from the United States and lived in an Americanized skyward house. She complained:

> My husband used to live in a skyward house, so he feels quite comfortable here. However, it's such a nightmare for me to climb up and down stairs so many times every day. It's depressing. Sometimes I just forget to bring with me whatever stuff I need for domestic chores, and then I have to climb three stories and come down again. In a way, I feel I am doing nothing but climbing the staircase everyday.

This young woman also worried about having a baby in the future. "How am I going to carry my baby up and down every day? I cannot just leave it on the upper floor when I am downstairs. I cannot hear or see what is happening to my baby."

Jessie, whose family returned to Taiwan from Silicon Valley, lived in an apartment inside Hsinchu Science Park. She recalled that they had bought an Americanized skyward house when they returned and had lived there for six months. They sold the skyward house and moved into an apartment unit, however, because they could not adjust to living in the towerlike space. Jessie described her experience:

> As soon as we moved into that house, I felt that my family life was packed into a tower. It's just like catching a train together with my two boys. You can hardly imagine. Whenever and wherever I wanted to move, all my kids wanted to follow me. Nobody wanted to be alone on one floor. It seemed that we were all bound together every minute. Though we had a sixty-ping house [2,142 square feet], we were always crowded into a fifteen-ping space [535 square feet]. The rest of the house was empty.

How big should a garden be? In *The Meaning of Gardens*, Mark Francis reveals that people in different cultures express their personal values and feelings through their gardens (Francis 1990, 206), a theory that can also be applied to hillside Hsinchu. Most urban Taiwanese grew up in apartments, where a tiny balcony was the only place for cultivating plants. Many Taiwanese, then, dream of having a large garden. Few, however, have any experience in tending a garden. Ken told me that his dream house would have a high ceiling with a skylight and a nice garden in the front yard. Once he owned the space for that garden, however, he started to realize that gardening was a labor of love. He told me:

> I like to live here. My kids can ride their bikes on the weekends, while I can do some gardening. I have tried to weed my garden for at least two or three years, but there are still so many weeds. I'm a very picky person. Before I really plant anything in my garden, I'll have to get rid of all that irrelevant stuff [weeds, rocks, pebbles, stones]. I also think it's important to dig deep. I dug my yard for two seasons, but I haven't finished it. In the summer it is too hot, while in the winter it is too cold. If I work too hard, I hurt myself. Now most of the weeds have been plucked out, but the best season for planting seems to have passed already. Forget it! I used to dream about a huge yard or garden when I lived in an apartment. The bigger the better. Now I know that it's very tiring to maintain a large yard. You just never have enough time to take care of it. In my case I can only hire some professionals to design my garden and build it. However, that's different. I would like to take my time to nurture it, but the problem is that it really takes time.

Ken's garden was really quite empty. If I hadn't spoken with him, I would not have imagined that he had already invested two to three years of work in it.

Ken was not the only one troubled by his garden. Most Taiwanese were not used to tending a garden or mowing the lawn. This was evident both in Hsinchu and in the Silicon Valley suburbs, where some Taiwanese immigrants had even turned their lawns into AstroTurf lots.

The disaster of driving. Hillside communities were Hsinchu's highbrow landscape, and those that lived there were considered to hold a higher social status. However, for residents who had formerly lived in cities, where everything was within walking distance, the location of these suburban communities created a driving disaster. They now had to drive everywhere, and driving along the rolling, meandering hillside roads made many of them carsick. Those who didn't drive or ride motorcycles found daily shopping inconvenient, and transporting their children to after-school programs and weekend activities was even more problematic.

Most Taiwanese children from kindergarten through high school attend after-school classes, but most of the centers where these classes are held are located in Hsinchu City. No public transportation connects most hillside communities to the city center, so parents living in the suburbs frequently have to drive to pick up their children. On weekdays parents drop their children off at school at 8 A.M. and pick them up from after-school centers around 9 P.M. If the children also attend weekend classes, the parents might spend half of their Sunday driving back and forth. Some families rent apartments in Hsinchu City where they can spend time when they don't want to drive back to their homes. Others ended up moving back to city apartments, frustrated in their attempt to create a home that mirrors the suburban Silicon Valley home. Considered from the perspective of the mirror home phenomenon described above, this sort of move could be understood as a symbol of a family's resilience and flexibility as they transform their family identity to adapt to newly emerging physical and psychological constraints.

Hannah, Ken, and Carol all went through this process. Hannah, a female high-tech engineer, painted a picture of the stressful situation. Two of her colleagues had rental apartments. The family of the first colleague used the apartment as a place to gather and rest between daily activities. The young couple dropped their children off at school every morning. After school their children went to the apartment to eat a dinner their mother had prepared before going to their evening classes. After the evening classes they returned to the apartment and waited for their father. When he arrived, they all drove to their hillside suburban home. The family of her second colleague ended up living in their city apartment on weekdays, returning to the hillside home every weekend. "Their gated hillside community is more like a week-end resort!" Hannah exclaimed.

Asian American Suburban Dreams Under Construction

My conversations with high-tech families in Hsinchu helped me to understand their daily experience of residing in the hillside region. On the other side of the Pacific, my conversations with the astronauts helped me to gain insight into their jet-set lives. After flying back and forth across the Pacific many times myself as I conducted my interviews, I began to imagine what it would be like to lead a trans-Pacific life. If I were interviewed by a researcher such as myself, I might describe my experiences like this:

> During the flight, attendants treated me with nice Chinese instant noodles, fried rice, and Taiwanese rice soup. After twelve hours in flight I had crossed the Pacific Ocean. When I finally approached the San Jose Airport in the San Francisco Bay Area, I had a great bird's-eye view of the South Bay and Silicon Valley. Through the clouds I could see the boxy buildings of high-tech companies lined up along the highways, and newly developed gated communities everywhere. The highways, like concrete rivers, ran from the ocean to the dry and brown Californian mountains. Before the plane landed I got a closer view of the urban landscapes. Thousands and thousands of cookie-cutter single-family detached houses sprawled for miles and miles away from the city of San Jose to the edge of the salt marshes that connect to San Francisco Bay and the foothills of the mountains [Fig. 9.2]. After getting out of the airplane, I encountered mostly Asian and Latino passengers at the airport. Mandarin and Spanish seemed to be the background soundtrack played against the English announcements at the San Jose Airport.

My imagined experience of being a trans-Pacific commuter helped me to consider how the Taiwanese American high-tech immigrants participate in the process of integrating their Silicon Valley experiences into their Hsinchu homes. As sketched out earlier, many returnees and motherlanders have ac-

FIG. 9.2. A bird's-eye view of thousands of cookie-cutter houses in Silicon Valley. Photo by author, 2001.

quired Silicon Valley dream homes that developers have transported to the Hsinchu region. These new Americanized houses tend to dominate the region's hillsides. But while some high-tech Taiwanese families integrated a modified form of the Silicon Valley detached house into the Hsinchu hillsides, others were searching for a Silicon Valley suburban house that would fit their preconceived image of the American dream home: new, spacious, in a good school district and close to shopping. Table 9.2 shows the home types of thirty-seven interviewees that I spoke to in the major cities in which many high-tech Taiwanese immigrants reside.

The process of searching for, finding, and buying a home that the trans-Pacific commuters shared with me gave me further insight into the way that they constructed their home identities. Images of single-family detached houses played an important role in this process. Jessie, Kelly, and many other interviewees explained that they had seen American suburban houses in movies and on television before traveling overseas. They envied the sub-

TABLE 9.2

Home Types and the Chinese American Population in Silicon Valley

City or County	Number of Chinese	Chinese as % of total population	Number of interviewees	Housing type
Atherton	373	5.2	1	house
Cupertino	12,031	23.8	8	7 houses, 1 apartment
Fremont	29,240	14.4	2	2 houses
Los Altos Hills	1,006	12.7	4	4 houses
Menlo Park	885	2.9	1	1 apartment
Milpitas	8,098	12.9	1	1 house
Palo Alto	5,450	9.3	3	2 houses, 1 apartment
Sunnyvale	12,579	9.6	3	3 apartments
San Jose	51,109	5.7	6	6 houses
San Francisco County	152,620	19.6	1	1 house
Total Chinese Americans in Silicon Valley[a]	429,403	9.3[b]	30	
Hsinchu, Taiwan[c]			7	3 houses, 4 apartments

[a] According to the 2000 U.S. Census, the Silicon Valley Chinese population included 115,781 in Santa Clara County (6.9%), 48,996 in San Mateo County (6.9%), 112,006 in Alameda County (7.8%), and 152,620 in San Francisco County (19.6%).

[b] I divided the total Chinese population of the four counties by the total population of the four counties to get this number. According to the 2000 U.S. Census, the total population of the four counties is 4,610,220, which includes 1,682,585 from Santa Clara County, 707,161 from San Mateo County, 1,443,741 from Alameda County, and 776,773 from San Francisco County.

[c] I interviewed thirty-seven high-tech engineers and their families. However, seven of them were in Taiwan when I conducted my interview.

urban houses they had seen in movies because most Taiwanese lived in high-density urban apartments. However, they would not have believed that the homes they saw in the movies actually existed if they had not seen them for themselves. Their first encounter with actual suburban houses was quite dramatic. Jessie said, "I suddenly realized that these kind of beautiful houses are everywhere in America. I felt that this is the place where I would like to live."

The experience of living in suburban America clearly dominated the preferences of the trans-Pacific commuters I spoke to. The astronauts considered their Silicon Valley home more important than the one in Taiwan. But, as highly as they valued their homes in the United States, they would still re-mark excitedly, "Silicon Valley is very similar to Taiwan. Sometimes, I get confused about where I am." The length of their American residency was a key factor for the astronaut interviewees, who tended to mention their Tai-wanese residential experiences less frequently the longer they had resided in the United States. On the other hand, some of their customs and behaviors were significantly influenced by their convenient lifestyles in urban Taiwan, where they could walk to nearby shops and offices to complete their daily chores. It surprised me that all the trans-Pacific commuters I spoke with live in Silicon Valley suburban houses but live in the parts of suburbia that are closest to shopping malls, and especially close to Asian markets. So although they live in the suburbs, they have, as much as possible, replicated a Tai-wanese life-style of close proximity to shopping, or what I call "an urban convenience life-style."

The Search for a Home

In contrast to transplantation and modification, a search for a home was a symbolic act for Taiwanese high-tech immigrants who were in the process of rebuilding their lives, because the home itself symbolized their new start. In Gish Jen's *Typical American* (1991, 156–58), she describes the process by which Chinese American immigrants buy a new house to make a new start in life, to lead to a "paradise." Jen's use of "paradise" to convey the sense of searching for perfection is also applicable to the Taiwanese Americans I spoke with who often talked about finding their "perfect dream home."

In Silicon Valley, the Taiwanese American trans-Pacific commuters I spoke with regarded suburban single-family detached houses as their dream home. Based on my interviews, the four criteria they considered most im-portant when choosing a house were: (1) whether the house was safe, afford-able, and in a predominantly white neighborhood; (2) whether the house was in a good school district; (3) whether it was recently built; and (4) whether it was convenient to shopping and one's workplace.[6]

It has not been easy for trans-Pacific commuters to acquire suburban houses in Silicon Valley. Due to the housing supply shortage in the 1990s (Wu 1997), house hunting in Silicon Valley was a painful experience for every potential homebuyer, including the trans-Pacific commuters. The out-rageous cost of homes and cutthroat bidding tactics became notorious nationwide. Those I spoke to who had been lucky enough to purchase a home shared their house-hunting stories. Their stories made me realize that they conceived of bidding on a house as analogous to setting up a home page. If they lost the bid, they had to move on and construct a new home page.

When Bob was house hunting, he drove his entire family, including his parents, his wife, and two-year-old son, from house to house every weekend for about six months. Sam, Bob's father, said, "I feel very sad that my son has to take us to see so many houses but hasn't worked out a contract." Every time they saw a house they all liked they would picture themselves living there. They were stressed out about the mortgage payments, but they did the best they could to make an attractive offer. When they heard that the seller had rejected one offer that they had been particularly hopeful about, they got depressed; their dream had been dashed. Then, next weekend, they started the cycle over again.

Many younger transplants have had experiences much like Bob's. They constantly checked real estate databases, looked at every ad in the Sunday paper, and drove to every open house. Most of them emphasized that finding a home in a good school district was their top priority and that the style of the house did not matter that much. If they liked a house, they were willing to pay top dollar for it. They preferred new houses, but did not mind the fixer-upper that held more potential for disaster than delight. They would do whatever it took to place their children in a good school district.

Younger couples were willing to use all their savings and go deep into debt for a house. Many ended up becoming so "house poor" that they couldn't afford furniture, silverware, and the other basics needed to outfit a new home. When Ted and Liz invited me to visit them at their new home in Palo Alto, Liz warned me, "I am sorry that our home is pretty empty. I hope that you won't mind." I told her, "Of course not." I thought that she was being polite. However, when I got to the house I was amazed by how empty it was. One chair was standing in their living room, and piles of books lay on their bedroom floor. Their computer was on the floor of their family room. Ted explained, "Everything you see here is from Cornell, my graduate school years. We do not have money to buy couches, tables, and other things, because we put all our money into this house." Liz added, "We will make it better within a couple of years, and we will invite you again!"

Bob's family got themselves into a similar situation. They got the

$120,000 down payment they needed to outbid other homebuyers by sell-ing their townhouse in New Jersey. Their empty savings account and hefty monthly mortgage payments made them aware of every penny they spent. When I had dinner at Bob's home, I noticed him tearing each paper napkin in half as he set the dinner table. "The size of an American napkin is too big," he said as he smiled and handed me my portion. "We only need a half-size one."

Although buying their house resulted in enormous debt for them, Bob and his wife, Kris, both admitted that they really loved their home. Kris ex-citedly told me, "It's our dream home. The school district is pretty good, the house is only two years old, and the location is great. Ranch 99 is right down the street. So is the park where we walk our dog. It's so convenient. Where could we find a house better than ours?"

Mapping Taiwan onto Silicon Valley

Talking to trans-Pacific commuters in Silicon Valley, I realized that four so-cial-psychic aspects were critical in their construction of trans-Pacific home identity: relocating to suburbia rather than Chinatown; prosperity for the younger generation; the extension of transnational family life; and a subur-ban home with inner-city convenience.

Relocating to suburbia rather than Chinatown. Perceiving themselves as a marginalized group in American society, Taiwanese Americans consider pur-chasing a home in the United States a key to escaping a life of insecurity. Taiwanese high-tech families prefer all-American suburbs to inner-city Chi-natowns, and none of my interviewees particularly cared about having Tai-wanese neighbors. Some of them even mentioned that they would prefer not to live in an Asian neighborhood, especially one dominated by Chinese.

For Taiwanese trans-Pacific commuters, predominantly white suburban neighborhoods embody a sense of home for two reasons. First, a suburban home provides socio-spatial security. The high-tech Taiwanese recognize suburbs are much more highly valued in mainstream American culture than inner cities, which leads them to believe that living in a suburban house will greatly enhance their chances of improving their social status. Second, good school districts are primarily associated with white suburban communities. Like the Cupertino couple we met in chapter 5, many Taiwanese high-tech families consider their suburban homes in good school districts a sign of the success of their migration.

A prosperous future for the younger generation. Imagining a prosperous future is an important part of the trans-Pacific commuter's search for a home. The process of searching for a home holds the promise that one's children will someday enter mainstream American society. All of the married astronauts that I interviewed told me that a location in a good school district was at the top of their list of qualities they wanted in a home. What motivated many of them to fly back and forth between the United States and Taiwan, or in some cases to relocate permanently to Silicon Valley, was their perception of the higher quality of American education. Some, however, worried that even if they moved to a good school district, other Asians moving into their neighborhoods would lower their neighborhood's status, which they perceive as a high status because it is a predominantly white neighborhood.

Most of my interviewees, however, were not worried about an influx of Asians into their neighborhoods. Most, like Melanie, whom I spoke with at her Cupertino home, were happy to be located in an American suburb with a good school district. Melanie and her family had lived in Silicon Valley, moved back to Taiwan, and then moved back to Silicon Valley again after discovering that the schools in Taiwan were "still as bad" as they had been when Melanie was a child. For Melanie, as for most of the parents I spoke with, the sacrifices necessary to live in Silicon Valley were a small price to pay for the promise of a prosperous future for their children.

Melanie's relocations back and forth across the Pacific were a response to the value she placed on her children's education. For her, owning a single-family home was not as important in the construction of her identity as enrolling her children in a good school. Seen from the perspective of the mirror home phenomenon, her constant relocations exemplify how personally embodied cultural values can become "unfixed" and override place identity (the relationship between home and self).

The extension of transnational family life. How moving into a new home might affect their extended family relationships is an important consideration for high-tech Taiwanese Americans as they search for a new home. For many, their travel between Taiwan and the United States has resulted in family ties being reconfigured. For example, some Taiwanese Americans in

Silicon Valley maintain one bedroom in their homes as the "grandparents' room," since the grandparents might frequently travel between Taiwan and Silicon Valley to meet the family's childcare needs. In this variation of "fluid family arrangements," described earlier, the grandparents are willing to make sacrifices to preserve an extended family pattern, even if they might feel isolated by taking up residence in suburbia.

Suburban homes with inner-city convenience.   Most trans-Pacific commuters emphasized that the location of their home was very important, and that they specifically preferred a quiet neighborhood that was close to a busy commercial district. When they described their ideal lifestyle to me, their descriptions closely resembled the urban lifestyle they had enjoyed in Taiwan. The only difference was that now that they were in the United States, their house had to take the form of a single-family detached house. Melanie told me that the Cupertino home that she and her family had bought *was* her ideal home. As she described the qualities of her home, I realized how closely aligned they were with the qualities that other high-tech families in Silicon Valley were seeking:

> Here is my ideal home. We were very lucky to get this suburban house. . . . I like the location of the house the best. It is adjacent to the Noble Hill Shopping Mall, but the house itself is in a quiet neighborhood. It is very convenient. Everything is within walking distance. I can buy fresh groceries and Chinese newspapers every day. Those Chinese restaurants are really my kitchens, while the nursery close to the highway exit is my garden. I enjoy taking walks and stop by each place every day. I like to hang out at the nursery and watch those beautiful flowers. I just want to watch them. I don't need to take care of them. Then I go to Noble Hill Shopping Mall and pick up Chinese newspapers and browse Chinese novels. At the same time, I can bring some fresh vegetables and milk back home. Isn't it terrific?

The "terrific" urban convenience of her home's location was the quality that the San Jose Starlite Court advertised when marketing its townhouses (Fig. 9.3). Their ad emphasized the fact that a Ranch 99 supermarket was right next door to their newly developed townhouses. Living in the San Jose Starlite Court, one could walk to Chinese markets, bakeries, bookstores, the post office, a jewelry store, a video and music store, an ice cream parlor, a karaoke bar, and a beauty salon. Restaurants within walking distance in-

FIG. 9.3. "San Jose Starlite Court located adjacent to Ranch 99 II [Pacific East Mall]: you are close to shopping, restaurants, post office, bakery, bookstore, and beauty salon." Source: Chinese New Home Buyer's Guide, November/December 1997, p. 17.

cluded several Chinese restaurants and others serving Thai, Vietnamese, and Hong Kong–style cuisine.

My interviews, observations, and photographic analyses revealed how their frequent commute between their suburban homes in Silicon Valley and their suburban-style replicas in Taiwan plays a significant role in the construction of Taiwan-born immigrants' nontraditional, multiple, and shifting identities, identities that reflect their multiple home ownership and cross-cultural lifestyles. Those whose homes in Taiwan did not replicate the residences they occupied in the United States engaged imaginative processes to flow between past and present experiences and sustain both the Asian and American parts of their identities (Graham and Marvin 1996). The traditional logic that one's place identity is shaped entirely by monocultural context, or unchanged and unaffected by transcultural contexts, did not hold in the cases I studied (Relph 1976; Tuan 1974, 1977; Appleyard 1984). What I found was that living within actual or imagined mirror homes enabled trans-Pacific commuters to embody, rather than transcend, their dual contexts and to construct multiple and culturally mixed rather than singular and culturally pure identities (Bourdieu 1993; Massey 1994a, 1994b). The mirror home conceptualization of the relationship between identity and place is meant to challenge the traditional notion that equates a coherent self with a determinate place. The trans-Pacific commuters that you have met in this chapter have revealed how shifting selves are possible, and even prefer-able in instances where new circumstances demand change and flexibility. The voices of Melanie, Osman, Helen, Ken, Bill, and many others pointed me in a new and surprising direction that enabled me to understand that a broken mirror reflects a hundred new possibilities that could not have been seen when it was whole.

TEN

Homes Across the Water

Home Everywhere; Home Nowhere

My investigation of how trans-Pacific commuters' jet-set frame of mind affected their perceptions of themselves and their homes began in 1998, when I began documenting the everyday lives of high-tech Taiwanese families who traveled back and forth between Silicon Valley and Taiwan. Since then I have moved across the country from California to Maryland. I have carried my manuscripts wherever I have traveled, including Berkeley, Portland, Chicago, London, Tel Aviv, Taipei, Hsinchu, Beijing, and Shanghai. Packing a suitcase, speeding to the airport, passing a security checkpoint, and running to a departure gate are common activities for almost all the passengers I encounter in different airports. Each of us arrives from different directions and heads down our different paths. Nevertheless, one moment in our lives when we share the same joy and excitement is when the flight attendant announces that our plane is arriving at the destination. Finally, we land.

Although the moment of landing is extremely brief compared to the length of the flight, the emotional transition that takes place upon landing is extraordinarily complicated. We might thank God that we safely landed; we might miss the loved ones we left behind or become excited about those we are going to embrace in a few moments; we might be cheerful or nervous about the adventures and challenges ahead; or we might be replaying our memories of the trip that we just completed. One of the most significant moments we experience just after we land is the one we feel in our hearts when we return home. An inner voice that tells us "I am home" anchors us, giving us a feeling of stability and security. As we transition from "being away" to "being home" we begin to take in all those familiar sights and sounds that provide a structure to our daily lives. We relax without being consciously aware of it. Our mundane chores (putting out the trash, walking the dog), which we had momentarily forgotten about, become ritual acts of return that make our bodies conscious of being back home.

Whatever else our return home may be, it is a ritual that resuscitates the feelings that we associate with the particular place we call home—feelings that we might never experience anywhere else. Although every place has its unique characteristics, our homes have inimitable qualities that we can experience only there. During the time that I lived in Berkeley, I enacted one little ritual every time I returned to my parents' apartment in Taipei. Soon after putting my luggage away and catching up with my father and mother over a meal I would drive my father's old manual-shift Sentra through the extremely chaotic traffic of the streets of Taipei.

This ritual that I played out on every return visit to Taiwan was a way for me to reclaim my identity as a Taipei driver. The pleasure that I feel while driving through the urban jungle of Taipei is a sensation that I don't experience any other place, not even when I drive in New York City. When I switch gears, my feet dance on the clutch, the brake, and the accelerator. The up-and-down, left-and-right rhythms of my feet in tandem with the circular movements of my left hand as I steer and the back-and-forth motion of my right hand as I shift gears are the familiar choreography that gradually reminds my body that I am home.

No matter what personal rituals one might engage in, the reunion with family and friends is a defining moment of the return home. Indeed, the people are what make our homes unique. Our loved ones and local friends want to know about the adventures that we have had, the things we have seen, and the changes we have gone through since we left home. At the same time, returnees want to know what changes have been made to their homes. And just as important as learning about any physical changes that might have taken place, we also want to catch up on the life events that may have affected our loved ones since last we saw one another.

If we return home after a very long time away, our loved ones might treat us like special guests for the first couple of days. My parents usually volunteered to drive an hour and a half to the airport to pick me up. Back at home, they would prepare plenty of my favorite foods, such as stir-fried noodles, fish-cake tempura, silky tofu soup, chicken dumplings, meatballs stuffed with black mushrooms, and sliced fresh pineapple. This special treatment reflects the fact that our loved ones have been waiting for us to return. When we are away from our homes, we long to return to them. Similarly, waiting for our loved ones to return home to us is an exciting and anxious experience. To sum up, returning home is a process that involves specific landscape changes, intimate emotional transformations, unique bodily adjustments, and individual personal interactions.

However, the trans-Pacific home phenomenon is very different from the experience of returning home that I just described. For example, when I first entered Jessie's living room in her Hsinchu Science Park apartment, I felt as if I were in a suburban house in the United States. Her displays of paintings, family photos, and antique furniture suggested to me that she was very proud of her American middle-class taste. A couple of months later I met Sara in the suburbs of San Jose at a social gathering for Taiwanese high-tech housewives who had homes in both Hsinchu and Silicon Valley. Sara and her husband had just moved to Silicon Valley two years prior to our meeting. She claimed:

> There isn't any difference between Hsinchu and here [Silicon Valley], though my husband and I just moved here two years ago. I run into some of my friends here at Ranch 99 or in Chinese restaurants, and I meet them in the park [Hsinchu Science Park] when I fly back to Hsinchu. Though I have lived in the park for more than a decade, America is a new country to me. I get really confused sometimes. I feel I have never left Taiwan.

All the high-tech Taiwanese families and individuals described earlier in this book have revealed their confusion about their experiences of their two homes that they have on each side of the Pacific. They seamlessly and simultaneously coexist in two societies and on two continents as they commute between their new and old homelands. Inevitably, their residential experiences from these two places blend together. They enjoy their Hsinchu Science Park homes because when they are there, they feel as if they are in their suburban American homes. Similarly, they enjoy their Silicon Valley homes because they blend the convenience of the Taiwanese urban lifestyle with their suburban dream house. They apply their specific Taiwanese habits when running daily errands at the Ranch 99 market in Silicon Valley. Moreover, they encounter the same friends at both locations, while their individual family lives remain separate on the two sides of the Pacific.

The confusion of their daily rituals and the ambiguity of the people and landscapes that surround them dramatically challenge the intimate relationships between Taiwanese high-tech immigrants and their two homes. "Where is my home?" is the critical question that many of the trans-Pacific commuters I spoke with ask themselves. In their minds, they never leave either their Hsinchu home or their Silicon Valley home, because the moment they leave one is the moment they return to the other. They virtually live at both homes because these two home environments are very similar to one another.

The trans-Pacific commuter phenomenon rewrites the *jin-yi-huan-xiang* (beautiful clothes returning home) narrative that I introduced at the beginning of this volume. The traditional version of the *jin-yi-huan-xiang* story emphasizes the reunion ritual that engages the entire family as a whole. The trans-Pacific *jin-yi-huan-xiang* narrative instead emphasizes the in-between relationship of the two homes on either side of the Pacific. The *jin-yi* (beautiful clothes) in this case have been transformed into suburban American houses and modern Chinese shopping centers. The forms of single-family detached houses and modern megastores symbolize the specific quality of life that the trans-Pacific commuters experience in both locations. The *huanxiang* (returning home) has been transformed into the convenient urban lifestyles and the transnational social networks that have been supported by the technology revolution. Moreover, instead of reuniting with their entire families, the trans-Pacific commuters conduct their fluid transnational family lives in both places.

In Part I of this book we visited three women: my grandmother, representing the static home identity, Joni Mitchell, representing the mosaic home identity, and Melissa, representing the shifting home identity. We explored their desire to return home and drew from their situations three prototypes related to returning: returning as a stranger, the identity crisis return, and virtual returning. We also met Winnie and Julie, who explained how bigration patterns influenced their home identities. Now we will meet with another three trans-Pacific women: Jane, Jessie, and Kelly. We will visit their homes, listen to their stories of virtually returning to their childhood homes, and learn about their dream homes across the water.

The experiences and memories that these three women portrayed in their conversations with me encompassed all three prototypes of home identity—static, mosaic, and shifting. Listening to their stories I realized that they had pieced together various memories of their homes and landscapes from different periods of their trans-Pacific lives. Their pieced-together memories (which I call mosaic imagination) became a source they drew upon when they described their present (as well as when they imagined their future) homes and landscapes. The mosaic imagination integrated the contradictory values and fragmented experiences. Home is something that exists simultaneously in multiple places. At the same time, multiple home memories exist in one home. Their memories ebb and flow like the Pacific Ocean as they run their daily errands, while their imaginations fly like kites in the sky, tethered to their sentiments, desires, and emotions.

Jane: Viewing Chinese Stars Through a Bungalow's Skylight

Jane, in her early fifties, was an art teacher at Hsinchu Science Park's bilingual school. She rented an Americanized skyward house outside Hsinchu Science Park, in a gated community on a hillside with a stunning view toward a reservoir. Furthermore, she had opened an organic food store in Hsinchu City in February 1998.[1] She designed the interior of her home and the store herself, and all of her friends admired her artistic talents. When I interviewed her at her home, it seemed to be something of a community center. She kept answering the phone, mostly in English, every five to ten minutes during our ninety-minute interview.

Jane told me that the home she remembered best from her childhood was surrounded by a rice field. Although she would never be able to return there, she told me, "I always remember watching the stars after our dinner with my father in our yard in my childhood, so my ideal home has to have a skylight." This childhood home was a courtyard house against the mountains, with a fishpond in front of the house. The layout was typical for a courtyard house in rural Taiwan. She said, "I really miss those worry-free times living with my parents. Instead of saying I miss that house, I feel I really miss the people in that house. Because of those people, I experienced those activities. Because the houses contained those activities, I miss those houses."

Jane's experiences in the United States influence the way she decorates her home. When she lived on Long Island, all her friends were Americans. They mostly decorated their homes by themselves, and she learned from them about do-it-yourself projects. "Here, you see, everything in my home is my artwork. People call me an *interior artist*.[2] They have all been fascinated by my seasonal home decorations," Jane said. She suddenly brought up her relationship with her mother when she related her memories of the interior of her home. She declared, "My mother was the last person in the world who could arrange our household. She didn't know how to run the domestic errands at all. In my memory, my home was forever chaotic, so I envied all my friends' homes whenever I visited them. I always felt their homes were very beautiful."

She told me that she liked her current home only because of what she called the "multi-million-dollar view" of the reservoir. She complained, however, about the "stupid and ugly" design. She felt that the design of the house didn't fit the beautiful reservoir site, and she was frustrated to be living in a house that "didn't make sense at all." She made a list of all those things that didn't "make sense":

> The entrance should be wider. . . . The window to the lake should be a larger bay window. . . . All these chandeliers are unbearably vulgar. . . . There are too many strange outlets and panels on walls. . . . All my paintings hang on the walls chaotically. It's because I want to cover this strange stuff [outlets and panels]. None of the walls are completely without holes.

After criticizing her home, Jane told me that she liked New England a lot and had been enchanted by its fall colors. She hoped she could buy a barn in New England some day and enjoy the surrounding maple trees, or she would like to have a bungalow by the sea. "The bungalow must have a skylight so I can watch the stars on a peaceful night, like in my childhood memories."

When I talked to Jane, I realized that she seemed to maintain two contradictory values simultaneously. On the one hand, she seemed to consider the social experience associated with a house more important than its form. On the other, however, she seemed to have an urgent need for a pleasant physical home environment. She asserted in the beginning of her interview that her family life is at the core of her memories of home. However, she also discussed her mother's failure as a housekeeper throughout our conversation. And, in the end, Jane spent her own life creating beautiful interior spaces to please herself and others. Jane also merged the most memorable landscape experience of her childhood—watching stars in the old courtyard house—with her current American house form preference, dreaming of a house by the sea with a skylight. In other words, she wanted to preserve certain essential memorable experiences, but felt that she could change the form containing the experiences.

Jane's story challenges the modern notion that specific forms evoke specific experience. According to the notion of experience following form, the form of Jane's childhood courtyard house should be essential for Jane's dream home, because that courtyard house is the place where her worry-free memories originate. However, she does not want to "reproduce" her childhood courtyard house (Marcus, 1995, 35). She chose to install her Taiwanese childhood memories in her trans-Pacific dream home, the New England seaside bungalow.

Jessie: A Silicon Valley Home in Taiwan

Jessie, who is around forty, lived in an apartment in Bamboo Village. She used to live in an Americanized Taiwanese skyward house outside Hsinchu Science Park, but she did not like it because her two children were always following her around from floor to floor. They finally decided to move to the Bamboo Village apartment, because "all the rooms are on the same floor."

Both of Jessie's children studied at the Hsinchu Science Park bilingual school, where she worked as a part-time teacher. When she spoke about her children's education she became emotional, saying, "I may stay in Taiwan, but it's my life. My children will definitely go back to America . . . and get their education there, because the higher educational quality there will provide them with a brighter future."

"When I was young," Jessie said, "I believed that I would be able to find the things [a certain quality of space] I preferred someday and somewhere. However, I lived in a rural area, so I had never seen my dream house till I studied overseas." "I think a home shouldn't be so dirty," she added. Jessie's childhood impression was that every kitchen and bathroom in Taiwan was sticky and damp. "I really didn't like this feeling. I believed that a home could be clean, neat, and comfortable." When Jessie went to America to study, she rented a room in a suburban house and lived with her American landlord's family. "I suddenly felt that I had found what I had always dreamed of—the high quality of life, with a neat kitchen and a clean bathroom where you can enjoy your bath, but you do not have to flee right away after you go to the toilet."

After finishing her studies, Jessie decided to stay in the United States. During her ten-year residence, she lived mostly in the San Jose area. Moving back to Hsinchu Science Park was not an easy decision for her family. "We almost moved to Los Altos, but we finally decided to come back here [Hsinchu Science Park]." Although Jessie said that she and her family finally came back "here," they had still virtually stayed at her Silicon Valley home for the past seven years.

> Though I have lived here for seven years, I don't quite feel I'm in Taiwan. I seldom leave home, and the interior decorations are the same as in my previous home in the States, except the space itself is much tinier. My father-in-law always told me, "Though it is very chaotic outside, as long as I enter your home, I feel I am in America." I seldom walked outside before I moved into the park. The public spaces in Taiwan are hopeless. They are just too chaotic. Garbage, plus illegal parking and food stands, is everywhere.

Without a doubt, Jessie longed for her Silicon Valley life.

> I miss Silicon Valley very much. . . . I have many friends there. We always hung out together. My housewife friends and I always indulged ourselves by dining at diverse restaurants, and we enjoyed our American life together. It was a lot of fun. I could get whatever I wanted, whether it was Chinese or Western style. *Actually, I enjoyed Western food, but I didn't want to miss Chinese life.* So when I lived in Silicon Valley, I didn't miss anything.

Jessie was dissatisfied with her life in Hsinchu and she missed "certain things" about Silicon Valley. To remedy her longing for American life, she would frequent Hsinchu restaurants whose interiors reminded her of Silicon Valley. It didn't matter that the food didn't taste American; what was critical was that the Hsinchu restaurant provided her with an American interior décor. She explained:

> Here [Hsinchu] is different. There are certain things I'm missing, so I mostly eat Western-style food. I don't care for the taste of food too much, but I'm "eating" the interior design, furniture styles, and Western atmosphere. It is very fun to be there [Silicon Valley]. Many nice friends are there. Some of them are here [Hsinchu Science Park], but others are there. I visit there every year. It wouldn't be as much fun if they were not there.

After "eating" the interior design and fashions of Silicon Valley, her dream home had become an American-style single-family detached house. She said, "Actually, I have collected pictures. I like browsing those home and garden books and design magazines and clipping the images I prefer." Browsing through her collection I recalled the "scrapbook houses" that were popular with American children between 1880 and 1910, when young girls would cut out pictures of furnishings and arrange them in room settings before pasting the pictures into an album (Roth, 1998, 301).

How would Jessie arrange her scrapbook house? She doesn't want a big house or a big garden, but she definitely wants a "colorful garden." "A garden is very important. . . . There should be varieties of flowers and it should be well arranged. I would like to have a colorful front yard, but only a lawn in my backyard." Jessie also clearly described her dream house and lifestyle. Her house should be sunny and spacious. The living room should have a high ceiling and room for a piano. There must also be a deck where she could have her coffee every morning. Maybe she could also do some community volunteer work or read novels on the deck. "It's my ideal life: listening to music, sitting in the garden, watching beautiful flowers in the morning, and playing piano in the afternoons. Plus, playing with my dog. Relaxed, but not luxurious and decadent."

As she described her dream home and dream life, she looked around the interior of her apartment and told me with pride, "Most things I have here are of American style. I prefer the American style. It's simple and elegant. . . . I am Americanized. I like a simple style, not too colorful. Most stuff in Taiwan is too colorful for my taste. American things are different. They are simple and harmonious."

She also shared her shopping experiences with me. She felt that it was easy to find the things she wanted in the United States because more people study interior design there. She said,

> If you try hard, you still can find good stuff you like here, but it will take you a lot of time and energy. I usually start my search from the Hsinchu area, but it's too local. Hsinchu is just a small town. Maybe there will be more choices in Taipei, but Taipei is too far away, and not convenient for me. I go shopping in Silicon Valley every year, since my son has to attend summer camp there every year, and I have lots of friends there. Most of the stuff you see here comes from there. It is much more convenient for me to look around there. Besides, the price is affordable. You see, I brought all this stuff back last summer. For example, this mirror is an art piece. This tea box is not only beautiful, but also very convenient. You can put tea bags and sugar inside to make the table very neat. This chiffonier is actually a cabinet for shoes. I put in a special order for it, since I wanted something that fits my style.

Jessie believed that living in Silicon Valley was an experience that was crucial in opening her eyes to a new world. She said that learning from the United States is the path that people in Taiwan should pursue. She concluded:

> I consider the quality of life the most important value in my life. After living there [Silicon Valley] for more than ten years, I think Taiwanese can learn from Americans. The only problem here [Hsinchu] is that people don't have this sense. Before experiencing life in the United States, I didn't have this sense either. Most Taiwanese never think about it. It's nothing but a simple concept, i.e., maintaining a clean bathroom and a neat kitchen. Of course, it takes time to maintain them.

Sitting and talking with Jessie in her Hsinchu home, I felt that she was virtually staying in her American home. Just as Jane's childhood experiences influenced the type of home she dreamed about, Jessie's unpleasant memory of domestic places from her childhood influenced her ideas about the home she wanted to build. Of all the homes I visited, hers most closely resembled the photos in American design magazines. Unlike Winnie and Julie, who lived in a duplex in the Hsinchu Science Park, or Jane, who inhabited a skyward house on the hillside, Jessie lived in a Taiwanese-style apartment in a park. However, everything inside the apartment, including the furniture, silverware, glassware, lights, candles, paintings, and flower arrangements—

even the decorations in the bathrooms—was Americanized. The most stunning attribute of her apartment was her American-style dining room, a rectangular pine table with six walnut chairs. On the table, six sets of dinnerware were arranged on blue cotton napkins. Two scented candles lit the table. I felt as if I were in a Western restaurant when I first sat there, and it seemed that I should order some stylish food and drink rather than interview her.

She pointed out that she had brought most of the furnishings from Silicon Valley. Compared to shopping in Hsinchu and Taipei, she found shopping in Silicon Valley much more convenient and enjoyable. Shopping there is especially convenient because she has to take her children to summer camp there every year. Many middle-age high-tech families living in Hsinchu have similar arrangements, shuttling between Silicon Valley and Hsinchu so that their children can take advantage of the American education system.

Kelly: Two Homes or No Home?

Kelly is the youngest of the housewives I have introduced. In her late thirties, she had two children who attended the bilingual school in Hsinchu Science Park and participated in summer camps in Silicon Valley every year. I met with her in both Taiwan and Silicon Valley. Her home in Hsinchu Science Park was a "sandwich apartment," a two-story residence with an interior staircase. It was larger than most Taiwanese apartments. Her home in Silicon Valley was a single-family detached house in a newly developed suburb of San Jose.

"Of course, I prefer living there [Silicon Valley]. Living here [Hsinchu] destroyed my health." Kelly told me that she blacked out three times last month because living in one of Taiwan's highly polluted urban areas caused her eyes to swell, which in turn caused her entire body to weaken. She explained, however, "My husband likes to stay here [Hsinchu], so I have to fly back and forth between these two homes." It was not easy to be an astronaut, she admitted. She really could not stand the apartment where she and her family lived inside the park. "I like big houses. They are much easier to arrange." She recalled different places that she had resided before she studied overseas. She said:

I used to live in a single-family detached home in my childhood. It was not a traditional Taiwanese courtyard house. It was a Western-style detached house with front and back yards. It wasn't bad; I felt quite comfortable. To me, this is what is meant by *huo* [living]. After I entered college, my family moved to an apartment in Taipei. I hated it. I haven't liked to go home since then.

For Kelly, like Jessie who you met earlier in this chapter, American movies, images, and pictures influenced the type of home she preferred even before she arrived in the United States. The high quality of life that she had actually experienced in the Silicon Valley, lived up to the Hollywood version of life that she had expected. The high-quality, Hollywood-type of life that she had grown used to added to the frustration she felt by the low quality of life in Hsinchu. Kelly complained, "The quality of life is too depressing in Taiwan. My American experiences were much better, even when I was a graduate student." Before she moved into her Silicon Valley home, she and her husband were graduate students at Stanford University, where they lived in a dormitory for married graduate students. "It was quite spacious for me, since we didn't have children at that time."

Her husband acknowledged that having a large house was important to Kelly, so they decided to buy a single-family detached house in the Winbond project, described in the previous chapter. However, they learned they would probably have to wait for at least two more years to acquire a house there. Kelly felt that it was fine to wait, because having a sense of ownership was very important to her. "I prefer living in a house that belongs to me. I like to do the interior design and garden." She was irritated by the fact that housewives had to endure unpleasant domestic environments and sacrifice their pleasant homes in Silicon Valley because their husbands wanted to advance their careers.

It's so important for a housewife to have a comfortable domestic environment. We are the group staying at home the whole day. . . . My husband, he invests 90 percent of his energy in his career. He can endure a low-quality home environment much more than I can. It's unfair! On the other hand, we are the ones who are always here. Why do our husbands have their right to pursue their careers while we have to suffer from a low quality of life?

Talking about her Silicon Valley home, Kelly got excited again. It was near IBM in San Jose, in a neighborhood where many Chinese lived. Unlike many Taiwanese housewives who flew back to Taiwan every year, she seldom came back before moving back to Taiwan. After her husband decided to accept an attractive job offer from Winbond, they rented out their San Jose home. "Now I am going to stop renting out the house and stay there longer and more often. My children are growing up. I would like to send them back [to Silicon Valley] to study." Her choice is just like that of other women who have teenage children; they bring their children to Taiwan to study Chinese while the children are young. Then, when their children are in high school and college, then send them back to Silicon Valley to receive a high-quality English education.

She acknowledged that her dissatisfaction with her current life was a result of comparing it with what she had before. She said, "Those who have never lived in the United States are very satisfied by the Hsinchu Science Park environment. To me, it's still not good enough. I like to garden, shop, or look around in supermarkets. It's much more convenient in Silicon Valley. It is much easier to make money here, but the living environment is so depressing."

She was the last housewife I met during my visit home to Taiwan. After the interview, I packed my bags and returned to Berkeley. While in the San Francisco area, I was able to meet many of the high-tech housewives in Silicon Valley. Two months later Kelly called me and told me that she was in Silicon Valley, at the home she really loved, a suburban house with a high ceiling located in San Jose. Another two Taiwanese high-tech families lived on the same block. She showed me around her house and garden, claiming, "When I was there [Hsinchu], I felt I was nothing but a Filipino maid. From dawn to night, I had to do the domestic chores, sweep dust, and cook. More important, I had to arrange all our stuff in our tiny apartment. It was so depressing."

I asked her why she was so unhappy at her Hsinchu home. She explained, for example, that she and her husband had mailed thirty to forty boxes of books back to Taiwan. "It's only one third of our total books here [San Jose]." However, Kelly had not had enough room to store them in her Hsinchu home. Instead of looking for local storage spaces in Hsinchu, she ended up mailing them back to San Jose. She continued, "Remember when you interviewed me there? I was packing all those books. When I tried to store them on our balcony I couldn't open the windows on the balcony, and the apartment became very hot and humid. Tell me, don't you feel here is much larger than there?" Without waiting for my answer she continued, "It's much more comfortable for a housewife to live here. The surrounding landscape is neat. It's very convenient for me to drive to shopping malls and easy to park. I'm sick of the crowded streets and marketplaces in Taiwan. I can go nowhere. I mostly stay at home. It's too crowded, too dirty, too chaotic."

Kelly showed me around her spacious two-story house. She said that she was the mastermind behind all of the interior design, and she had personally picked out accessories such as the curtains, carpets, and lighting. "I really enjoy designing my home," she said before she led me to her garden. She explained, "You see, this is my garden. I designed the whole place myself. I planted all the flowers and shrubs, too. This floral pattern represents the Olympic circles. I'm very proud of it." Kelly usually does some housekeeping in the morning and then goes shopping.

> It's such a relaxing life. I hate to cook in that small kitchen there [Hsinchu], but I quite enjoy cooking here. My children will enter the eighth grade next year. I'll bring them back here for a better high school education. I plan to fly back to Taiwan and stay there for one week per month. I don't need to have a job. No company would like to hire a person like me. I can still be a housewife. However, I'm very worried about my marriage. My husband has thought about starting up his own company. However, if he quits his job at Winbond we would have to move out of our apartment in the park. Many people don't change their job just because they want to live in the park.

At the end of my visit I asked Kelly how she would distinguish her Silicon Valley home from her Hsinchu home. She said that American houses provided the spaciousness that she had always craved as a result of her childhood experiences in Taiwan. Although she emphasized how much she liked living in Silicon Valley, she kept reminding me "Please, don't tell anybody else. Otherwise, people will criticize me and say that the only reason for me to be in Hsinchu is to make more money."

> Every time I complain about my home environment there, my friends will simply reply, "your home is much better than many other people's homes in Taiwan." However, my home is indeed very small. Why can't they see it? Some people also told me, "If you like America so much, why don't you go back? Are you just here making more money?" I feel it's quite unfair. I'm not used to the

horrible environmental quality there. Why can't I complain? Why do we housewives have to sacrifice our lives to fulfill our husbands' career goals?

During my conversations with her at both her homes I got a profound sense of her loss of home during her bi-gration experience. The quality of her home environment seemed to play the most important role in her life. However, it seemed impossible for her to simultaneously achieve the social home (family life) and physical home (the house structure, design, and locale) that she desired. When I interviewed her in Hsinchu Science Park she was packing to move to another unit. Piles of stuff and boxes filled her home. She kept complaining that she could not stay at home any more, so we ended up having our interview at the sculpture garden in the lakeside park adjacent to her home. She was much calmer and happier in that environment. When I visited her at her Silicon Valley home there was nothing inside the house except for a square dining room table and chairs. She was wondering if she should stop renting out the house and move back to Silicon Valley from Taiwan.

During our conversations she brought up the topic of her trans-Pacific marriage every thirty minutes, as she kept reminding me how people like to gossip about this topic. The fact is that if she brought her children back to San Jose to study, she would have two physical homes and a transnational family life. Her husband would stay in Taiwan and work in Hsinchu Science Park to make a good income while she and her children would live in San Jose, enjoying the educational and recreational opportunities. However, she was concerned about losing control of her transnational family life if she were to commute between two homes.

Identity Shifting Toward Ambiguity

We have just finished our short visit with Kelly, who we found experienced anxiety about having to search for her cross-ocean homes. Her anxiety represents that of many young high-tech housewives. The ongoing journey will not be stopped by national boundaries as long as their family lives are tied to the rapid economic growth and technological transformations that are set against the backdrop of the global Silicon Valley landscape.

All three of the women you have just met have homes on both sides of the Pacific. The question that immediately poses itself, then, is which home would they choose if they had to decide. I intentionally avoided asking this question directly, and instead I asked them to describe their ideal home. By asking this question I was able to see that there was no simple answer to the question "Which do you consider your true home?" but instead their thoughts about themselves in relation to their homes were complex.

In analyzing Jane, Jessie, and Kelly's stories, we can reexamine the modern notion of idealized and coherent relationships among identities (self), experiences (lifestyle), and forms (home/landscape). The idealized and coherent relationships are dissolved by the three women's "global sense of place" (Massey 1994a, 146–73). The new relationships between themselves, their lives, and their homes and landscapes do not need to follow a traditional conception of self related to place. A new "global sense of place" breaks from the traditional conception of life lived within a specific place. The new "global sense of self" similarly breaks from the traditional notion of a self whose essence must be associated with one specific place. The new set of relationships between self and place that these women reveal is not bound by the unambiguous one-to-one (self-to-place) logic of the past. New self-to-place relationships are shifting, ambiguous, contradictory, and unsystematic. Jane, Jessie and Kelly's "global sense of self" allowed each of them to easily adapt to the constant changes that a global lifestyle demands.

Although all three of them dressed up in "beautiful clothes," in this case American single-family detached houses, for their homecoming in Hsinchu, they disclosed different ways of integrating personal histories, memories, overseas experiences, and personal preferences into their future dreams. In Jane's case, she had precious childhood memories of watching stars with her father in their courtyard house in Taipei almost half a century ago. Unlike my grandmother, Jane does not want to return to that specific courtyard house at that particular place. Neither does she want to reproduce the same style of courtyard house in her current community. Instead, it is her dream to create a mosaic home landscape that incorporates all the forms that she appreciates: a bungalow, a skylight, and the New England coastal landscape. In our conversation, the first thing she emphasized was that family means more than a physical house to her. If she had followed the traditional Chinese set of rules that clearly define how the size and shape of a house relates to the extended family inhabiting it, she would have talked about a Chinese courtyard house located in coastal New England. Had she talked about wanting a traditional Chinese courtyard house, the form of the house would not only have embodied her childhood memory, it would have related to the culture of her Chinese family.

However, she did not want a Chinese courtyard house, but instead wanted a bungalow. She was not aware that in the 1910s, when those bungalows were first produced, they were designed for "business girls" or "girl bachelors" as domestic spaces that could be maintained with a minimum of effort, which in turn enabled women to engage in professional and social work (Wright, 1981, 173). Gwendolyn Wright explains that a "large proportion of unmarried independent women" lived in these sorts of houses (ibid., 174). Jane, however, probably never even considered that the social history of the bungalow was contradictory to the value she placed on family life. Her love of the bungalow was unrelated to its history, but was instead related to current culture, in which a bungalow is considered an appropriate home for an artist or a member of the counterculture. Within this postmodern nonessentialist construction of material culture (Ward 1998), the meaning of home, like the meaning of a popular fashion or musical trend, does not reflect the meaning of the form itself, but rather the meaning that people assign to that form.

The way Jessie described her childhood home as very dirty was very similar to the way trans-Pacific commuters talk about San Francisco's Chinatown or communities outside Hsinchu Science Park. She did not want to return to the Chinese space in which she grew up, but she was also certain that she wanted to maintain both her American and her Chinese life-styles simultaneously. Her longing to retain both the American and Chinese parts of life she loved most was captured when she told me, "Actually, I enjoyed Western food, but I didn't want to miss Chinese life." In contrast, Kelly grew up in large detached houses in Taiwan. Because of that experience, she could not stay in a two-story apartment home in Hsinchu that she considered "tiny," even though most Taiwanese families lived in less than half of the space. Ironically, although Kelly grew up in Taiwan and loved her spacious childhood home landscapes, she cannot stay in Taiwan any longer. The spacious home landscapes that she longs for can only be found across the Pacific.

Like Jane, Jessie and Kelly have ambiguous and shifting relationships with their selves, their lifestyles, and their homes and landscapes. The meanings that they make of their homes are parallel to the meanings they make of their own selves. The ambiguity and uncertainty of their identities as they relate to their lives and landscapes could first be seen as a deficit, yet to them properties of ambiguity and uncertainty are the very contingency in their lives and homes they view as an asset. Although each of these women had two homes, they felt no pressure to decide which was their real home, nor did they feel as if they had no home at all. Their experience of moving across national borders, their memories of both of their current homes as well as other homes they have experienced in the past, and their experience of moving freely from one home to another as it suits their needs—like selecting clothes or a song that fits a particular mood or event—is an asset rather than a deficit when one considers that they are creating their senses of self on their own terms. Their new practice liberates them from thinking that the home is the basis of their identity, and opens up new possibilities for the construction of identity. At the same time, intriguing complications emerge when the self is constructed: when the beautiful clothing one chooses to express one's self-image meets up with the image that others have. I will discuss these complexities in the next chapter.

ELEVEN

Leaving and Returning
in Trans-Pacific Commuter Culture

My mother, who taught fifth and sixth grade in Taipei, loved shopping for new clothes. She always felt that the clothes that she wore were important—to her students, their parents, and the other teachers and administrators—and that her attention to her clothing encouraged others to respect her profession. When I was very young, she used to make many dresses for me, and of course I wore them, not yet old enough to realize that constructing one's self in one's own terms was possible. During my teenage years, after I had developed my own taste in clothes, I began wearing jeans, oversized T-shirts, shorts, and sandals—outfits that were comfortable, sloppy, and low maintenance. These choices, however, didn't meet my mother's standards. In fact, the comfortable clothes that I wore during my teens and early twenties were diametrically opposed to the neat, clean, color-coordinated suits that she preferred.

When, in my late twenties, I left my Taipei home for graduate school in the United States, my mother developed a new approach to getting me to wear the clothes that she wanted. She would buy for me clothes in the style that I preferred, while also buying items that she liked, as if they were for herself. Then, after she had worn the clothes that she liked a few times, she would say, "If you like these, why don't you take these back to America with you?" Although I did, I rarely wore most of them, because they were too formal for me. However, taking the clothes with me was my way of bringing a piece of my mother with me, a way of bringing my Taiwanese identity with me whenever I traveled from Taipei to Ithaca. Once the beautiful clothes that my mother had given me found their way into my American closet, I was able to touch the Taiwanese family I had left behind. Even though I rarely wore the clothes, when I opened my closet and saw them, touched them, and smelled them, the distance that separated me from my parents disappeared, and at that moment I felt at home.

Things that can be seen and touched—things like homes and landscapes—gain their meaning through a process that engages memory, feeling, and the process of leaving and returning, things that, although they can't be touched, are nonetheless deeply felt. Here I would like to revisit the ritual of "beautiful clothes returning home" as it relates to the themes and people that I have introduced in this book. The phrase "beautiful clothes returning home" embodies both the material aspect of clothing and the experiential aspect of returning home. Even though the experience of returning home may not seem as tangible as the clothes one carries in a suitcase, it is nonetheless deeply felt and requires reflection and analysis to be fully understood.

The narrative of "beautiful clothes returning home" helps to convey the culturally defined set of expectations about leaving one's home and returning in the Taiwanese experience. The crisp, clean, crimson uniform that clothes the returnee is a symbol of all the things that he has gained since he departed: status, money, fame, family, and education. His return to his hometown is an important moment, both for the returnee and for those that he left behind.

Tensions in the Global Commuter Culture: Our Neighbor's Beautiful Clothes

When returnees arrive at their old home, their clothes symbolize the status and material riches that they have acquired elsewhere—a large and luxurious estate, a prestigious education, an enviable career—all the things the onlookers wish they possessed for themselves. The clothing is seen as the undisputable proof of what the returnees have acquired but could not bring along to show to those in their hometown. But in the new era of global commuting, the practical limitation of being unable to carry one's new house or one's new community on one's back has been virtually overcome. Today houses and communities are imported and exported as easily as silk or cotton. Bricks and mortar, trees and gardens, roads and shopping centers are the materials that attest to success. In the new global commuter age, a mansion, a garden, an office building, or even an entire community is easily imported into the existing fabric of the place left at the beginning of one's journey.

In other words, the ritualized encounter in which the splendidly clothed returnee is enthusiastically greeted by aged and humbly attired residents of the community is no longer a single occasion; instead, the encounter persists, and has a long-term impact on the community. The seemingly permanent imbalance and the inequality between two spheres of a community when the returnee arrives create a tension. The permanence of the homes and landscapes that take the place of the returnee's beautiful clothes also inspires a new set of needs for the wearers—needs that did not previously exist. There is an urgent need for the returnees to invent new ways of thinking about themselves as they flow between two distant lands. The returning-home ritual creates, in some cases, the longing to be in one's new home while occupying the old home. Why? Because in today's version of the "beautiful clothes coming home" ritual, the returnees have not only new clothes, but also unique homes, novel commodities, and brand-name diplomas to go along with the status they have acquired.

The tension between local residents and the trans-Pacific commuters who live adjacent to one another is one way that the "beautiful clothes returning home" ritual has changed in the era of global travel and communications. Other tensions reveal other ways in which the traditional ritual is being played out quite differently in the twenty-first century than it was when the returnee arrived in his hometown on a white horse to the cheers of children and elders. The dissonance that global commuters feel when commuting between homeland and new land (a tension I call "the body beneath the beautiful clothes") and the stress caused by status seeking (what I call "following the fashion trend") are both examples of these tensions. Exploring how trans-Pacific commuters have been able to cope with, overcome, or resolve these tensions enables a better understanding of the different notions they hold about what identity is, how one's identity gets played out through one's home and landscape, and, finally, how a new shifting identity has emerged.

The "heaven and hell" clash, as one Hsinchu local termed it, is one example of the tension between the old and the new versions of the relationship between landscapes and identities. In many of the conversations I had with trans-Pacific commuters, they described themselves as happy to be separate from the local culture that they had grown up in. I found myself wondering, "Why do so many become disengaged from their own homecomings?" This question brings me back to the poem by the poet He that I introduced in the first chapter. Returning to his home village after his travels to many distant places, He is surprised to find himself greeted by youngsters who ask, "Where did you come from, my guest?"

As I reflected on the poet's surprise and confusion in response to the children's question, I came to understand the variety of ways that trans-Pacific commuters attempt to transcend the aged notion of fixed identity as they establish their careers and families and pursue other achievements. If you were in He's shoes and found yourself at a place where you considered belonging your birthright but the locals saw you as a stranger and treated you as a guest, you would almost undoubtedly face some sort of struggle. But by dropping the essentialist notion that one's self is grounded in one place, members of the global commuter culture have resolved this traditional struggle. More important, within trans-Pacific commuter culture, the status of a guest, or a go-between, is higher than that of a local. Therefore, returning home as an outsider who is disconnected from the local community carries with it a sense of pride.

Although many members of high-tech commuter families make a concerted effort to adjust to living in communities on both sides of the Pacific, the local members of those communities often view them as alien. Ken, the local engineer residing in Hsinchu, complained that "those Americans" only talked about their memories and experiences of California, but they never shared their Taiwanese childhood experiences with other motherlanders; the former congresswoman Marie and the community activist Pat called Bamboo Village an "American colonial town" because residents celebrated only American holidays and ignored local cultural festivals; John, a venerable block leader who had fought for a cleaner environment in Hsinchu, accused high-tech returnees who commuted between Taipei and Hsinchu in the 1980s of turning into go-betweeners who flew back and forth across the Pacific in the 1990s; and Dick, chair of a community board, was upset by the fact that most trans-Pacific commuters living in Da-Si-Gu formed an exclusive network and seldom engaged in local activities.

On the other hand, Peter, a Taiwanese-born Silicon Valley transplant who worked as a computer engineer, claimed that the Ranch 99 market near his home represented his Taiwanese identity. He didn't feel that he was an outsider, nor a member of a minority culture. In other words, for Peter, Ranch 99 contained the cultural codes only people from Taiwan, China, or other Asian countries were familiar with, so even though he lived in an American suburb, he was able to shift from American to Asian thoughts and experiences whenever he shopped.

Peter's construction of a shifting, as opposed to static, identity led me to wonder if it would be possible to alter the relationship between the Taiwanese locals and the trans-Pacific commuters. The participatory planning process for the Pu-yu project that Professor Liu was instrumental in implementing is one example of an event that resulted in a positive alteration of the relationship between locals and commuters. While Chunglin residents voiced their desire to maintain their existing lifestyle, they also suggested the possibility of having "outside people" live within their community in the future. The participatory process allowed them to maintain their sense of ownership and control over their community, a sense that was clearly reflected when they announced, "Come and live with us in *our* way and feel the beauty of *our* environment."

The Chunglin example illustrates the difference between *consumption of* and *participation in* the ownership of one's local community. The inclusive process that Chunglin residents engaged in was a stark contrast to the exclusionary process of building and marketing Bamboo Village. One result of the planning process that excluded the voices of local residents was the construction of an eight-foot wall dividing Hsinchu Science Park from its local community. Inside the Bamboo Village section of the park, clean streets, neat rows of Silicon Valley–style homes, gardens, and various community amenities suggested an American suburb and the high quality of life associated with that sort of neighborhood. Outside Hsinchu Science Park, however, the less fortunate local residents endured hellish traffic congestion, air pollution, impure water, and other inconveniences. The success of Bamboo Village spawned the development of other gated communities throughout the Hsinchu region. These gated communities that have been carved into hillsides since the late 1980s have resulted in the transformation of the Hsinchu region into a broken mirror image of the Silicon Valley suburban landscape.

During the same time, developers were providing trans-Pacific commuters with California-style images to be consumed. In addition, individual members of the newly emergent culture of global commuters were inventing new ways of constructing the relationship between the image they held for themselves and the images of the homes and landscapes that they readily consumed. The "mirror" lifestyle components included: (1) recycling and gardening services that reflected environmental awareness; (2) shopping areas that enabled residents to keep up with fashion trends; (3) shuttling children back and forth to school and activities; and (4) participating in sports and forms of recreation that helped solidify residents' high-tech identities. These experiences that mirrored both sides of their home environments enabled trans-Pacific global commuters to manifest both their Asian and American identities. Their construction of a day-to-day set of mirror activities enabled them to see themselves as embodying hybrid, rather than the singular and fixed, identities. They didn't see the hybridization of their selves as a deficit, as a sign that they had lost essential features that made them uniquely who they were. Instead, their everyday enactments of continuity between the two cultures they commuted between—the everyday set of communication practices (email, internet access, telephone) that engendered a sense of connection between their two homes, a sense that they were involved with their life at one location, while physically being in the other location—enabled them to cope with the cultural discontinuities that they faced on a daily basis.

Furthermore, everyone participated in the act of consuming the materials (homes, landscapes) that they perceived as giving them a higher status. This was the case with those who had lived in Silicon Valley, but also those who had not. Motherlanders who had never been to Silicon Valley were more eager to buy American single-family houses than astronauts. Their desire to own a detached house embodied the conventional belief that "the American moon is larger than our local one."

Meanwhile, returnees reconstructed their American homes within their Hsinchu homes. In Jessie's case, she transplanted the interior of her Silicon Valley home to Taiwan. Any time she traveled from California to her apartment in the park she would arrive at a home that mirrored the one she had come from. Jane, as you will recall, who has childhood memories of watching the stars with her father from their courtyard house surrounded by rice fields, wanted to relive those peaceful, starry nights in a New England bungalow. Her approach to reconstructing her American home didn't require transporting the New England bungalow style to Taiwan, but instead involved demonstrating the interior decorating skills she had learned from the Americans she had befriended. She reconstructed her American home by using tie-dyed fabric, arrangements of dried flowers, and bottles and beach rocks she had found to decorate her Taiwan townhouse. For her, applying the skills she had learned while in New England was a way of transporting her American home identity across the Pacific.

The Beautiful Clothes Fashion Trend: Clothes as the Object of Status Seeking

In the traditional "beautiful clothes returning home" story, success is a shared phenomenon. Not only do the clothes broadcast the success of the one wearing them, but they also reflect the hometown residents' yearning to participate in the celebration of a homegrown hero who has done well in a foreign land. The returnees' success speaks for the entire village, and when they return they immediately engage with their home community. This ritual of returning home points to the returnee's belief in a static home identity—a belief that one's identity is always coupled with one's birthplace. Within the process of the homecoming celebration, the beautiful clothes that returnees wear reflect both the community's collective identity and longing and the returnee's individual identity. Everyone within the community can claim ownership of the beautiful clothes.

In the age of trans-Pacific commuting, however, homecoming takes on a very different character. The trans-Pacific commuters' shifting home identity enables them to seamlessly transform from one version of their identity to another as they travel from one set of geographies and cultures to another. They are able to claim ownership of their Taiwanese personal and home identities by living in subdivisions close to Asian shopping centers in Silicon Valley, and they also display their American home identities as if they were dressed in beautiful clothes when they return to their Taiwan homes. Their "beautiful clothes" are sewn from three types of fabric: social (advanced degrees and American citizenship), cultural (the ability to speak English and experience living in American suburbs), and physical (owning suburban homes and visiting shopping malls and corporate campuses).

More important, even though they return to their Taiwanese home, they continue to identify themselves as trans-Pacific commuters, and they associate their status with the American suburban home. Taiwanese global commuters tend to associate with other Taiwanese global commuters. They do not engage motherlanders in the ritual of returning home. Their message to the motherlanders is that the objects that represent their "beautiful clothes"—houses, gardens, shopping centers, educational facilities, and recreational facilities—belong to the trans-Pacific commuters alone. The "beautiful clothes," then, take the form of a fashion trend rather than a community identity. Jessie clearly demonstrated this when she declared that she could not find high-quality furniture in local Hsinchu and that Taipei was too far away for shopping. Instead, she would shop in Silicon Valley every summer when her son attended summer camp there.

My Own House-Hunting Experience

Trans-Pacific commuters are not the only group that has been trapped by the trend toward "beautiful clothes." My husband and I have recently gone through a struggle to find a house in the Washington, D.C., area. We searched in several different neighborhoods and bid on several different houses. All the houses we made offers on had charming curbside appearances and were located in a trendy neighborhood. Every time we made an offer, I was consumed by the thought of the status that I would gain by owning such a cute house in a neighborhood that would excite my friends' envy. While waiting to hear the response to our offer, however, I would begin to hear my internal voice interrogating me. "Do you really like this house and neighborhood? Or are you too concerned about how chic the community is? Why do you want to spend so much money in order to be hip?"

In the end, we lost all the bids on those homes in "super-status" neighborhoods, and we ended up falling in love with a little rambler located in Wheaton, a rather anonymous township endowed with a peaceful park and a lively array of multinational marketplaces. After we bought the house, we strolled along the tree-lined streets adjacent to a little creek that ran in front of our house. That walk led us to the Wheaton Plaza Metro station, a typical American mall, and dozens of small ethnic shops and restaurants. We loved the chaos of the commercial area, while we simultaneously appreciated the soothing wilderness close to our home. We were surprised by the comfort and the peace that we experienced in this house and its surroundings. At that moment, we felt proud to own our modest home in an undiscovered neighborhood, and we were thankful that we had bought a home and a neighborhood rather than our friends' jealousy.

My Trendy Apartment in Taiwan

I do not mean to suggest that those who live in very trendy neighborhoods are simply consuming the fashionable status of their homes. Nurturing an identity involves a process of creating a personal history rooted within a place. My apartment home in Taipei, by chance, is located in the prestigious and affluent Dr. Sun Yat-sen Memorial Park district. Whenever people learn that my apartment is adjacent to the park, they say to me, "Wow! It's the best neighborhood in Taipei. It must be very expensive!" In response to their jealousy, I have always said, "I grew up there. When my family moved there, the area was nothing but an abandoned rice field and muddy marshland. My home was the only building that stood there for many years." While outsiders envied the status of my family's address, I felt sentimental about all the places I remembered from my childhood that had been washed away by the tides of real estate development: the narrow alleyways where I used to hang out with kids from the neighboring apartments, the basement parking lot that my brother and I used as a bicycle racecourse, the corner store where I liked to buy snacks and lottery tickets.

The memories we have of our bodily experiences change over time as we grow and come to new understandings of our selves. Memory conceptualized as constantly transforming (as opposed to static) makes it possible to conceptualize a changing self that transforms who, what, and where we identify with. We are part of the landscape we encounter, and our daily landscapes are part of our selves. Speaking from my childhood experiences, before the Sun Yat-sen Memorial Park was developed, there was a railroad track a block away from my old apartment. This railroad track was my lab where I collected samples for my biology class in middle school, because many wildflowers, insects, and other little creatures made their home there.

Now the area is a parking lot where fashionable cars are parked. Similarly, in order to make room for a new city council building, a slum located adjacent to my apartment complex was removed during my college years. I regret that I never documented anything about this makeshift community, and I don't know where my silent neighbors were relocated.

"Consuming" or "Experiencing" Our Home Identities?

While my vision of the Taipei neighborhood in which I grew up is based upon memories and experiences, my friends' vision of it tends to be based on the hip reputation that it has only recently acquired. The contrast between my account of the neighborhood and that of my friends led me to wonder whether the trans-Pacific commuters that I spoke with were "consuming" or "experiencing" a home identity. Let's revisit some of them. Julie, for example, who lived in Bamboo Village for more than sixteen years, declared that the form and the legal ownership of her home did not mean as much to her as her participation in the process of making her home. She treasured her memories of her childhood home so much that she refused to return to witness the dramatic changes that took place after her family moved away. Julie's process of making changes to her home was a sign that her experiential interaction with her home was the basis of how she constructed the relationship between her self and her home.

But while Julie's interactive process was a fairly clear sign that she was experiencing, as opposed to consuming, her home identity, most other situations were not as clear-cut. Winnie is a good example of the blurred line between an experienced and a consumed home identity. Winnie appreciated her Bamboo Village home, and she tried to mobilize her neighbors to decorate their gardens to improve the quality of their public environment. Her transcultural effort consisted of an attempt to persuade her neighbors to display Taiwanese national flags on Nation Day (as her father did during her childhood) and to hang Christmas lights for Christmas Eve (as she experienced in Palo Alto). Only the latter effort, however, succeeded. Winnie happily embodied both the consumption and the experience of home identity. Her flag project arose from her childhood experiences, while the Christmas lights were a sign of her having consumed and imported an American landscape archetype that she acquired while living in Silicon Valley. Experiencing our home identities and consuming our identities play out in our daily lives as intricately intermingled processes. Most of the time we aren't aware of their complexity. For example, when Winnie promoted trick-or-treating and Easter egg hunts in Bamboo Village, she felt that she was transplanting something she had learned from her American experiences. However, from the point of view of local residents like Pat and Marie, people like Winnie failed to pay attention to the local Hakka heritage and Taiwanese cultural festivals.

Winnie is representative of almost all the Taiwanese trans-Pacific commuters I spoke with, who believed that American suburban culture is superior to their traditional Taiwanese culture. They seem to think that they have completely embraced all aspects of American society; however, they are often unaware of the traditions and behaviors they have retained from their Taiwanese homes. On the one hand, these trans-Pacific commuters choose the physical forms that are marketed to consumers who want objects representing highbrow culture and social prestige. On the other hand, the consumers of these highbrow artifacts still maintain the social networks, bodily experiences, and memories that are a result of the daily practices and behaviors acquired in their home communities. These two discrete forces drive the trans-Pacific home phenomenon as "a constantly shifting and changing milieu of ideas, events, appearances, and meaning," as Soja puts it in his third-space framework (1996: 2–3).

When experiencing one's home identity intermingles with consuming the identities, they transform into a new driving force that results in reshaping the physical landscapes that we reside within. For example, although trans-Pacific commuters enjoy the ability to shop for Asian groceries and the convenience that they used to experience in their urban Taiwanese communities, they certainly do not adore San Francisco's Chinatown. They regard it as a "marginal community," backward and unhygienic. They prefer the high-end suburban communities blessed with the modern Chinese shopping center, Ranch 99, which provides all the Asian merchandise they want in an American megastore atmosphere that they are comfortable with. Ranch 99 has thus emerged as a Taiwanese community and commercial center where friends and family gather, young professionals go on dates, and grandparents reunite with friends.

The blurring of the boundary between the experience and consumption of home identity does not suggest that we are powerless to shape our identities when we encounter the mainstream values broadcast by the mass media. Shaping one's identity is a continuous negotiation between self and others. It is a complex process that integrates what we believe with how we go about choosing the homes and landscapes that give meaning to our sense of our selves. It is an individual decision to believe in identity as a static sphere, as my grandmother did, or that our identities are constantly changing and shifting within a complex process of shaping and reshaping one's version of one's self, as is the trans-Pacific commuters' experience.

The Body Beneath the Clothes

With respect to identity choice, I do not wish to suggest that we choose an identity that has a predetermined shelf life, like a box of cereal or the latest fashions (Mirochnik 2002, 7). The story of "beautiful clothes returning home" is not a story about a fashion trend. Instead, it is a metaphor for the process by which Asian American immigrants construct their identities within the context of a life lived within two homes and two cultures. The clothes in this process do not merely cover up the body underneath. Nor are the clothes worn only as a sign that the latest status trend in housing or landscape has been consumed.

The "beautiful clothes" are a metaphor for the process of the construction of identity, but it is not as simple as "the clothes make the man." Choosing the "beautiful clothes" (a home, a landscape, a lifestyle) in which to clothe oneself is a complex process of negotiating the relationships between the "beautiful clothes" we choose to cover our bodies with and how our bodies feel wearing the outfits that we have chosen. In some cases, we might wear traditional clothes, but our bodies might behave in contemporary ways. The modern dancers of Cloud Gate Dance Theatre described in chapter 5 dressed in traditional Chinese costumes while their bodies performed the modern dance movements of Martha Graham. Their bodies beneath their traditional clothes exposed their audiences to new sets of movements and nontraditional choreography. Through body movements that broke away from the rigidity, symmetry, and predictability of ballet, they introduced audiences to a new way of dance, but also to a new way of seeing one's self as a flexible, improvised individual.

What I want to emphasize here is that changing the way one's body moves and behaves is a process that evolves slowly, over time. The Cloud Gate dancers took a long time to become familiar with Graham's new set of bodily movements, and even longer to internalize the movements to the point where they seemed natural and comfortable. The new environment that modern dance introduced to dancers can be seen as a metaphor for the new environment of the American suburb that was introduced to a Taiwanese market that was hungry to "try on" the American lifestyle. The homes looked wonderful in the newspaper ads and brochures, but once the eager Taiwanese population moved in, they began feeling the dissonance between the convenient urban/pedestrian life they had come from and their new suburban/car-dependent life. They began to realize that the image of the dream home they had consumed was rubbing up against the concrete discomforts of a suburban life and landscape.

From Disneyland to Mother's Lap

Kore-eda Hirokazu's film *Afterlife* (1998) seems to me to convey the dissonance experienced during the process of finding the fit between one's sense of self and one's experience of place (a complex process that the phrase "the body beneath the clothes" attempts to convey). The film is set in a transit station between heaven and earth. There, guides have five days to help the newly deceased filter through their memories for one defining moment to take with them to heaven. One of the new arrivals is a teenage girl. When her guide asks her for the defining moment of her life, she promptly replies "Disneyland!" She eagerly goes on to explain her excitement at riding the roller coasters and other rides. Her guide quietly writes down every detail. Afterwards, her guide chats with her casually, saying, "You are the thirtieth girl talking about Magic Mountain. Many teenage girls brought up their Disneyland experiences when they first talked to me." The guide's comment caused the girl to realize that her experiences at Disneyland were a generic pleasure that all girls her age might enjoy. More important, they enjoyed their experiences there because they identified Disneyland as *the* cool place to go. On her last day in the transit station, this girl substitutes for her Disneyland experience the first time she felt her mother's lap—a time when her mother was cleaning her ears for her. This time as she told her story, her voice was calm and she smiled like a baby. She simply recalled her mother's soft touch, warm body, and sweet smell.

The poetic point that Hirokazu makes is that her memory of mother's lap is more reflective of the teenage girl's sense of herself than her memory of Disneyland. I see the teenage girl's process of choosing mother's lap over Disneyland as a process of finding a fit between her sense of self and her experience of place. Disneyland may be the popular and fashionable place of moment, but mother's lap is a unique place; a place that reflects her unique self, and metaphorically reflects her unique "body beneath the beautiful clothes."

A Taiwanese Body in an American Home

In the daily experiences of trans-Pacific commuters, there are many moments when Taiwanese bodies perform a dance while dressed in American "beautiful clothes." One of the most obvious of these dances occurs when those who live in Silicon Valley—those who adore the single-family detached suburban house—simultaneously relish the convenience of living an urban lifestyle (e.g., living near Ranch 99). They have American "beautiful clothes"—here referring not only to their homes and gardens but also Ranch 99's modern design—but inhabit Taiwanese bodies, which are comforted by the familiar goods and services available at the market. All of Ranch 99's amenities—from restaurants to Chinese bookstore to teahouses selling pearl tea drink—make them feel at home in Silicon Valley, because their Taiwanese bodies feel relief.

Ironically, while the Silicon Valley Taiwanese enjoy their "Taiwanese life," the motherlanders in Hsinchu suffer the consequences of having acquired the details that go along with living in an American dream home. They find they have to spend time weeding their huge lawns, or that they have to climb long flights of stairs to get from floor to floor. What they had imagined as an American dream in many cases turns out to be an American nightmare of unwanted chores and unfamiliar spatial arrangements. In chapter 9, Osman, the Taiwan-trained architect designing homes in Hsinchu, claimed that motherlanders are crazy about the mirror images of American suburban homes, and they show him magazines and pictures to make sure that their dream will come true. However, those who move into the Americanized skyward houses in the hillside community don't feel the comfort they had imagined they would, as if their clothes were not a good fit for their bodies. Helen, for example, worried about having to carry a baby up and down the stairs all the time. Ken was uncomfortable with the size of his garden, as he constantly battled the weeds and was unable to improve it beyond a dirt lot. Hannah's co-worker moved into a gated hillside community, but they discovered the entire family got carsick when they had to drive in and out of the neighborhood.

The overpowering influence of American "beautiful clothes"—not only detached houses, but also the ability to speak English and participation in American holidays and festivals, for example—significantly affected local communities in Hsinchu. The clearest examples of how American "beautiful clothing" affects locals are the stories of motherlanders who were trained in Taiwan but work with astronauts and returnees. They adored the bilingual real estate project that advertised the fact that English would be widely spoken in the community, even though most of them spoke only Chinese. The housing project failed because of certain legal restrictions regarding population density, but, barring this problem, it seems it would have failed anyway, as it would require Chinese-speaking motherlanders to speak English; the motherlanders would have been wearing imaginary beautiful clothes that did not fit their bodies.

Motherlanders were not the only group that wished to speak perfect English. Everyone within the trans-Pacific commuter culture embraced this dream. Although they were unable to fulfill this dream in their lifetime (because English was not their mother tongue), they wanted to make sure that their children would be able to achieve this goal. Many high-tech families developed transnational family lives to accommodate the educational needs of their children. The need to switch home locations when the children reached a certain age resulted in their possession of homes in multiple locations. These homes mushroomed in California and Taiwan, reflecting the fluid family arrangements that were being developed within these transnational families.

Much to their parents' delight, second-generation Taiwanese American children speak perfect English. During my research I was surprised to discover that many of the Taiwanese families I spoke to in both California and Maryland recorded their children's perfect English voices to use for the greeting on their telephone answering machines. This greeting in perfect English reflected how the children had acquired an American voice. At the same time, however, it reflected the ethnic stereotyping that their first-generation parents had experienced, and how they soothed their suffering by presenting to the world their children's American voices instead of their own, which still reflected Mandarin or Taiwanese folk languages.

Transcultural Outfits on Trans-Pacific Runways

My analysis of the trans-Pacific home phenomenon reveals that the ease and frequency with which commuters travel between Silicon Valley and Hsinchu has resulted not only in the cultivation of new family and social relationships, but also in the invention of new and innovative ways of constructing the relationship between self and home and its material equivalents—the trans-Pacific landscape. The reconceptualized relationship between self and home that derives from this study of the Asian American trans-Pacific commuter holds implications for the actors who will shape the future of science parks in the United States and Taiwan, and for environmental design and planning professionals and public policy makers in general.

Thinking in response to long-term implications leads to a set of key principles that can potentially shape a culturally sensitive and ecologically sustainable transcultural landscape for newly emerging trans-Pacific populations. Daily convenience plays a crucial role for most Taiwanese trans-Pacific commuters. Although they have moved to suburban Silicon Valley, they still prefer to have every service they might want to use within walking distance. This preference stems from their having experienced an urban Taiwanese lifestyle and their desire for an American pedestrian-oriented lifestyle. However, as a marginalized social group, most Taiwanese immigrants seek out suburban homes that conform to mainstream American imagery and forms. They embody their newly acquired suburban American lifestyles and preferences as they commute back and forth from California to Taiwan. One of the outcomes of their embodied desires is the transplanting of American suburban low-density auto-dependent housing into a Taiwanese landscape composed of high-density, pedestrian-oriented housing. This has led to an erosion of social, cultural, and ecological values in many communities.

Can we reverse this process? Instead of exporting suburban residential patterns to Taiwan, designers and planners need to advocate for small-town and pedestrian-oriented American urban patterns. These land-use patterns result in mixed-use environments—the kind of environments Taiwanese Americans are accustomed to and prefer. Four sets of applications are essential for creating transcultural home landscapes for trans-Pacific commuters.

The Integrative Development Approach

Combining Asian urban mixed land use patterns and the high quality of American small-town life could be a new and vital direction for transcultural community developments around the Pacific Rim. Six components are essential for achieving this integrative development approach: (1) mixed land use patterns, (2) mass transportation plans, (3) transit-oriented housing developments, (4) housing within walking distance of markets, retail shops, and entertainment, (5) encouraging in-fill developments in towns and cities, and (6) applying green architecture technology in housing design.

Researchers have already criticized the suburban sprawl in Silicon Valley, and some have suggested learning from the mixed land use patterns common in Asian countries (Wu 1997, 165). The increase in Asian-Pacific high-tech migration opened up a great opportunity for the integration of mixed land use patterns with small-town lifestyles and the creation of transcultural and sustainable community development models. A few examples of such development were initiated by Asian developers, such as the San Jose Star-lite Court. Some high-end housing and retail projects have already been developed in Silicon Valley (for example, Santana Row in San Jose), but more mixed-income affordable housing is needed.

Meanwhile, green architecture, solar energy, and sustainable landscaping technologies should be applied to new housing and community developments. Governments should provide incentives and policies that promote these green developments. Designers in Japan, the Netherlands, Germany, the United States, and other countries have already successfully integrated green technologies with elegant buildings in many well-known projects.

Promoting, Designing, and Planning Transcultural Retail Areas

The analysis of the Ranch 99 phenomenon reveals that retail areas function as family gathering places and community centers for Taiwanese in Silicon Valley. The Ranch 99 story is an example of how modern shopping malls have replaced traditional urban markets in both Silicon Valley and the

Hsinchu region. These market areas, however, are dominated by specific cultural groups. It is crucial for the emerging transcultural society to develop transcultural retail areas shared by various groups.

A threefold strategy that integrates planning, design, and policy making is essential. First, on a planning level, the retail areas should be located close to public facilities, especially parks, libraries, and historical main streets. The shopping center in the city of Walnut Creek, California, provides a good example. Walnut Creek encourages private investors to develop shopping areas within walking distance of the main street district by providing multistory public parking structures for shoppers.

Second, on the design level, creating an active interface between streets and shopping areas is critical. Jane Jacobs (1992) observed that the diverse activities occurring on sidewalks stimulates the best-quality city life. Her principles can and should also be applied to the design of transcultural retail areas. The location and design of parking lots are also essential. Instead of providing parking lots around a shopping area, designers should lay out parking courts or multistory garages surrounded by shops. Connecting shopping activities with sidewalks and creating green features to link the interfaces are much-needed steps toward diversifying urban activity.

Third, at a policy level, local governments should establish regulations that support multicultural shops. Ranch 99 shopping centers intentionally targeted the pan-Asian population, especially the overseas Taiwanese and Chinese. The analysis of global commuters' tendency to exclude locals from their social networks points to the potential for ethnic shopping centers to heighten social tensions among different cultural groups living near these centers. If local governments were to develop multicultural commercial districts via local regulations and financial incentives, such as transfers of air development rights and tax exemptions, this monoculturality might be avoided.

Negotiating Cultural Diversity in Public Spaces

In several chapters I described how transnational networks within gated communities segregated local residents from trans-Pacific commuters, inspiring the NIMBY (not in my back yard) syndrome in both Silicon Valley and the Hsinchu region. Today, there is an urgent need for face-to-face interactions in public spaces. Negotiating cultural diversity often begins with providing diverse populations with places that support daily interactions, places where they can meet and socialize with one another. Two issues are critical. First, multicultural community events lead to community participation and collaboration. Second, parks and open spaces are often seen as the heart of multicultural community life.

In his Monterey Park study, Horton (1995) elaborated on the concept of negotiating cultural diversity. He asserted that cultural diversity did not exist naturally. In every immigrant society, old-timers, newcomers, and various cultural groups might not accept each other at first. Multicultural community events help display cultural diversity and allow different groups to understand each other through a playful process. Environmental professionals and policy makers should be more aware of the importance of community activities, cultural festivals, and holiday events.

In contrast, the wall outside Hsinchu Science Park reflects a rigid boundary approach to social interaction (or noninteraction). The wall that separates local residents and high-tech families ultimately increased the social tension between the two groups. Instead of walls, designers could develop soft boundaries, using elements like green belts and public parks. Public parks and open spaces could become the center of multicultural community life. Replacing a wall with landscaping and open spaces would invite various people to communicate and negotiate cultural diversity.

Creating Interactive Communities and Home Places

Trans-Pacific commuters have redefined the roles of family members as well as what house and landscape mean in a location that hosts many cultures. Family members pop in and out of each other's lives with great frequency. At the same time, their constant travel across cultures has resulted in family members adopting multiple cultures in the formation of their identities. Their family and lifestyle relationships point to new design approaches: first, the creation of versatile home places (house and garden patterns) for transnational family life, and second, the design of property boundaries that enhance the potential for social interactions, and for connecting private, semipublic, and public spaces by pedestrian circulation systems.

Designers should create versatile home places for transnational family life that intertwine multiple cultures within one home. I anticipate that transnational family life will continue to be a trend for high-tech Taiwanese Americans in the twenty-first century. Developers have sold this emergent population on trendy house forms, but these forms tend to be prepackaged and expressive of a single culture, usually the California suburban one. This marketing approach is not reflective of the multicultural lens through which members of the trans-Pacific culture view themselves. Instead of emphasizing monocultural home imagery, designers should help residents reveal the multicultural experiences of their daily experiences, for example, inventing versatile interior spaces that integrate different residential cultures.

Furthermore, designers should create "shared gardens," "common greens," and "parking gardens" (Groth 1990) that integrate with property boundaries and provide the potential for social interaction. Shared gardens and common green areas that connect across individual properties allow for interaction among, rather than separation between, neighbors. As Dick pointed in chapter 8, high-tech families who parked their cars in private garages had no contact with their neighbors. But parking spaces for cars need not lead to isolation from one's neighbors. Designers and planners could also reevaluate the function and location of parking garages.

If we connected private yards and garages and established shared gardens and common green spaces connected by pedestrian pathways, social interactions would be encouraged rather than eliminated. These design and planning principles are offered as alternative visions of transcultural design to facilitate shifting home identities, mixed lifestyles, and multiple cultural values in the era of globalization.

Conclusion: Suitcase Packed

Throughout the book, my investigation of the relationship between home identities, lifestyles, and building forms explicitly demonstrates how economic transformations impact cultural transformations and consequent landscape transformations. Trans-Pacific commuters' new schemata for constructing the relationship between one's personal sense of self and one's home have enabled them to develop new sets of social and family relationships that are based on nontraditional conceptions of self, place, and migration. Instead of relying on the traditional notion of the existence of a singular static self, they think of themselves as hybrid identities composed of pieces of their Taiwanese homeland identities and their American Silicon Valley identities. They have dissolved the purity and essentiality of ethnicity within their daily residential lives, where they constantly cross the borders between cultures. They have relinquished the need to adopt either a pure Taiwanese urban lifestyle or a completely American suburban lifestyle. Their regular commutes between their Silicon Valley and Taiwan homes, land-scapes, and communities have engendered the emergence of a transcultural lifestyle that allows the Asian *and* American cultures and identities that they embody to shift, separate, interconnect, entangle, and meld into each other, depending on the changing flow of their complex lives.

The many stories that were told to me of leaving and returning have af-fected me in many ways. As I listened to these stories, I recalled a practice that Eudora Welty (1984) describes as her way of listening "for" the emer-gence of characters in her fictional stories. By listening "for" the person—for ways in which they themselves construct the deep and significant meanings in their lives—I began to realize that there was much more to their trans-Pa-cific lives than I had originally conceived. Their stories challenged me to re-think my own ideas about what a self is in a world where one experiences multiple homes simultaneously. Their stories showed me that there was much more to having multiple homes than deciding which home was the true home and which were the secondary ones. In many cases my precon-ceptions did not apply at all to how the trans-Pacific commuters thought of themselves, and in almost all cases their behaviors pointed to a new concep-tion of self that was multiple and shifting rather than singular and static.

I conclude with the hope that you will dance with the people whose sto-ries I have told; dance to the sound of their voices, their homes, and their gardens in order to see the spaces and places within your own life in a new way. As a teller of other people's stories, I became more and more aware of how their tales have shaped the one that I tell about myself.

I want to conclude with one such story about myself that emerged dur-ing my investigation. The intricate mother-and-daughter ritual my mother and I performed, in which I brought back to the United States the clothes that she said she had bought for herself, was a sort of inversion of the "beau-tiful clothes returning home" ritual. On all of the trips that I made from the United States to Taiwan, I never felt that I had to show off my status as a student at Cornell and UC Berkeley, and when I arrived at the Taipei airport my mother and father would see me in my everyday outfits—the faded and frayed blue jeans and sandals—rather than in the beautiful clothes that my mother had given me during my last visit. In my case the beautiful clothes made their appearance at my *departure*, when my mother and I enacted our private exchange ritual and I neatly packed the clothes alongside the jeans and books and field notes that filled my suitcase. As I flew back to the United States with my mother's beautiful clothes that I knew I was not likely to wear, they were still symbolic of the need of both my mother and me to enter into a dance that allowed us to blur the boundaries between arriving and leaving, a dance that allowed each of us to play out our different selves while still feeling that we had created our relationship together.

Today's technologies have enabled thousands of people to participate in a dance performed across a stage that is as wide as the ocean that separates Taiwan from the United States. And, as in the dance that my mother and I engaged in, the clear-cut distinctions between departure and arrival have become less rigid than in the past. Homeland for my grandmother was a specific place. She never overcame the longing she felt for China because, for her, the departure was permanent. The act of returning to one's homeland through the virtual means of the information age, and the speed and ease with which one can fly across the Pacific, have made possible what was unimaginable to my grandmother. Her idea that one's essential identity is rooted in a permanent homeland no longer applies in the high-speed information age. A new generation of global commuters is developing new ways of understanding the relationship between identity and landscape, forms that shift day by day and person by person. With no essential definition that everyone has to follow, and no rigid distinctions between places of departure and places of arrival, this new generation has set into motion the possibility of boundless and diverse ways of shaping the relationship between where we live and who we are.

Reference Matter

Notes

Preface

1. The literal meaning of "Tienlou" is "Tien's tower." Tienlou is a very small rural village of Pu-cheng County (Shandong Province), in northeast China. It is a 90-minute drive from Confucius's hometown, Qu-Fu.

2. I conducted environmental observations in several Silicon Valley neighborhoods (Fremont, Milpitas, Cupertino, San Leandro, Atherton, Walnut Creek, and Oakland) and seven communities outside Silicon Valley. The seven communities include Bamboo Village and Lakeside Village in Hsinchu Science Park, the Majestic Silicon Villa and Treasure Mountain Villa in Hsinchu County, Tang-chen (Luxury Mansion) in Shanghai, Zhongguancun Science Park in Beijing, and Shan-Shui Villa in Beijing.

3. Among the 148 interviewees, I interviewed 77 in 1998 (42 in Hsinchu and 35 in Silicon Valley), 31 in 2000 (in Hsinchu), 22 in 2001 (12 in Shanghai and 10 in Beijing), and 20 in 2003 (4 in Hsinchu, 10 in Beijing, and 6 in Silicon Valley).

Chapter 1. Returning Home in the Information Age

1. Ranch 99 (Tawa 99) is the name of a supermarket chain specializing in Chinese food and home supplies. It is often the anchor for dozens of other Chinese restaurants, bookstores, and groceries in the same complex.

Chapter 2. Toward the Trans-Pacific Home

1. In contrast to those scholars who focus on urban ethnic enclaves, urban sociologist Mark Gottdiener (1994) discusses the ethnic suburban phenomenon in

his recent book *The New Urban Sociology*. He specifically points out that Asian newcomers have modified the traditional American suburban landscape (172–74).

2. In *House as a Mirror of Self*, Clare Cooper Marcus (1995) follows a modernist tradition that I am calling the construction of the essential self. There are numerous feminist and postmodern critiques of the essential self view. Two of the most influential are Jaggar and Bordo 1989 and Rorty 1989 (23–43).

Chapter 3. Made By Taiwan: The Trans-Pacific Commuters

1. The online survey was conducted between May 15 and July 13, 2001. A total of 2,273 responses were received from 10,837 questionnaires sent out by Customer Sat.com. The respondents included 2,000 (88 percent) foreign-born engineers and 273 (12 percent) U.S.-born engineers. Of the 2,000 that were foreign-born, 43 percent were born in India, 30 percent in mainland China, 12 percent in Taiwan, and 15 percent in other countries (including 11 percent who were born in other countries in Asia).

2. The phrase "made *by* Taiwan" is currently trendy in the high-tech field. From the 1960s to 1980s, many labor-intensive manufactured products were made in Taiwan. Therefore, the term "made in Taiwan" suggested that Taiwan played a marginal role in the global economic market during that period. Since the 1990s, however, the development of the high-tech industry in Hsinchu has been transforming the country from a site of labor-intensive production to a new center for information technology. Many trans-Pacific Taiwanese therefore use the new term "made *by* Taiwan" to suggest their pride in their high-tech talents.

3. In terms of age, they fall into three generational categories: the senior group (fifty years and older), the junior group (forty to fifty years old), and the youth group (younger than forty).

4. According to the Hsinchu Science Park data, there were 244 companies in the park in 1998. Ninety-seven of them were funded by entrepreneurs who returned from overseas, and 147 were funded by Taiwanese local investment. If there are 5 to 10 astronauts in each company, the total population is about one to two thousand.

5. In September 2004 the Hsinchu Science Park employees included 1,291 PhDs (1.2 percent), 19,317 with Master's degrees (17.94 percent), 23,771 with bachelor's degrees (22.08 percent), 25,499 with junior college degrees (23.69 percent), 30,134 with high school diplomas (27.99 percent), and 7,645 others (7.10 percent). In addition, 5,220 of the employees were legal foreign laborers from Southeast Asia, such as Malaysia or the Philippines.

6. In September 2004 there were 378 companies established in Hsinchu Science Park. I estimate that every company has five high-level managers who do not

hold a PhD. Therefore, there are 1,890 managers altogether. If we add 1,890 and 1,291, the total is 3,181, which is about 2.8 percent of the total Hsinchu Science Park employee population.

7. There are also green card grandparents who commute by air to take care of their grandchildren. However, their impact is not as great as that of the green card wives because they are mostly isolated in suburban settings. I will address this issue in chapter 5.

8. It is not always easy to identify which engineers were trained in Taiwan because they all speak in Mandarin or the Taiwanese dialect with a few English phrases thrown in.

9. This situation has changed in the past couple of years. The recent trend is toward recently graduated college students choosing to stay in Taiwan or work in China. Those in the Taiwanese government worry about this new trend, because more mainland Chinese students have been choosing to study in the United States. The Taiwan government is concerned that the Taiwanese will not be able to compete with the mainland Chinese in the future.

10. This was reported by Tein-hwei Chang in *Sin Tao Daily*, March 5, 1997.

11. This was a 13 percent change compared to the survey in 2000. There were more Taiwanese who preferred to migrate to Shanghai instead of the United States after September 11, 2001. See Commonwealth 2001.

12. This data is quoted from Chen's report "Over 500,000 Taiwanese Sneak in the United States," in *China Times Evening* (Taipei), November 8, 1994.

13. The total number of Chinese high-tech engineers is 19,218 (Saxenian 1999, 13).

14. Saxenian's 2002 report revealed that 25 percent of Taiwanese high-tech engineers settled in Silicon Valley before 1980, compared to 13 percent of Indians and 7 percent of mainland Chinese who settled during the same period. The majority of Taiwanese engineers (42 percent) moved to Silicon Valley in the 1980s. Only 29 percent of Indians and 21 percent of mainland Chinese moved to Silicon Valley in the 1980s. In contrast, while only 33 percent of Taiwanese arrived in Silicon Valley in the 1990s, the majority of Indians (58 percent) and mainland Chinese (72 percent) arrived during this period.

Chapter 4. The Emerging Transnational Family Life

1. This number is converted from the Ministry of the Interior's December 2003 *Population Affairs Monthly*. According to the 2000 U.S. census, an urbanized area (UA) is: An area consisting of a central place(s) and adjacent territory with a general population density of at least 1,000 people per square mile of land area that together have a minimum residential population of at least 50,000 people

(Ministry of the Interior 2004). I converted 1,000 people per square mile to 386 people per square kilometer (1 square mile = 2.59 square kilometers).

2. The seven cities include (from north to south): Keilong City, Taipei City, Hsinchu City, Taichung City, Jiayi City, Tianan City, and Koushoung City.

3. The Japanese colonized Taiwan from 1895 to 1945, with Japanese elite living in urban areas during this period. Following World War II, the Japanese in Taiwan were forced to move back to Japan, leaving many empty Japanese houses in urban areas. However, only upper-class mainlanders or those who had close connections with Chiang Kai-shek's government could get the permits needed to live in those vacant Japanese homes.

4. According to my field notes, twenty-four out of twenty-eight interviewees commuted between Silicon Valley and the Hsinchu region.

Chapter 5. Transcultural Lifestyles Across the Pacific Rim

1. The founder of the Cloud Gate Dance Theatre, Lin Huai-Min, studied modern dance in the United States at the Martha Graham School of Contemporary Dance. He returned to Taiwan in 1972 and established the first modern dance group in a Chinese-speaking country. Lin, who enjoyed perennial acclaim in both Taiwan and the United States, blended Graham's techniques with Chinese opera, tai chi, and ballet in his choreography.

2. Morris Chang was born in China, moved to Hong Kong during World War II, and then went to the United States to pursue his education when he was eighteen years old. When he came to Taiwan he was fifty-four years old (Chung-Mou Chang 1998).

3. Traditional Chinese patriarchal society is very much built upon extended families. Husbands, especially the eldest sons, lead the families. The *traditional* extended family includes not only the grandparents on the husband's side, but also siblings, uncles, and cousins on the husband's side. The *modern* extended family, on the other hand, consists only of parents, children, and grandparents from the husband's side.

Chapter 6. Ranch 99: A Virtual Chinatown

1. Only one of my thirty-three Silicon Valley interviewees told me that he felt attached to San Francisco's Chinatown. He had been a parachute child, and his mother had shopped in Chinatown when they moved to the San Francisco area; she still shops there today. San Francisco's Chinatown is part of his daily life as well as his childhood memories.

2. The Chinese horticulture industry primarily involved chrysanthemum cultivation.

3. Unlike the migration history of the old-timers in Chinatown, which has been well documented, the history of Taiwanese high-tech immigrants to Silicon Valley has been studied by few researchers.

4. Most Chinese high-tech engineers who have been hired in Silicon Valley recently were trained in the United States. Based on the graduation data of Stanford University, in the heart of Silicon Valley, 21.7 percent of the computer science students who graduated in 1998 were from China, Hong Kong, Taiwan, and Singapore. If all Asian Americans are counted, the percentage of computer science students was 49.3 percent. Meanwhile, 22.5 percent of electrical engineering students were from China, Taiwan, Hong Kong, and Singapore. The total percentage of Asians was 40.8 percent.

5. I have performed three informal experiments to determine how Taiwanese and Americans respond to the Ranch 99s. I explained to some Americans how Ranch 99 symbolizes home to Taiwanese immigrants. Their typical response was, "Oh! I never realized Ranch 99 is so different, though I pass it frequently." I also brought three groups of Taiwanese tourists to Ranch 99. The first had just arrived in San Francisco. The second group of people had been in the United States for a while, but they did not live in the Bay Area. The third group had been traveling in California for more than three weeks. All of the groups had the same response: "This is just like Taiwan!"

6. From September to November 1997 I observed how people used the Ranch 99 in Milpitas on both weekdays and weekends.

7. All young, single interviewees admitted that if one church friend were to discover that they were going out with somebody, then everyone would hear the news immediately.

8. Grocery shopping together is a special dating ritual of Taiwanese students in the United States, although it does not take place in Taiwan. Most female students in the United States need a ride in order to go grocery shopping, so driving them to the store is the easiest way for male students to demonstrate that they are interested in someone. As a result, young men without cars might have problems courting young women.

Chapter 7. Heaven and Hell

1. According to the 2002 data provided by Ministry of the Interior in Taiwan, Hsinchu City has a population of 378,125 and covers 104 square kilometers. Hsin-

chu County has a population of 452,097 and covers 1,427 square kilometers (MOI Statistical Information Service 2003).

2. According to the club guidelines, employees and residents of Hsinchu Science Park are eligible for membership. Those outside this circle must be introduced by three or more members of the club for membership, and the board members must review their applications. The founding member and some other interviewees have admitted that this rule creates a boundary between the local community residents and residents of Hsinchu Science Park, but they do not intend to change it. Instead, they declare, "Our members should participate in the local communities more."

3. Although some of high-tech wives had formerly been engineers or programmers, they seldom checked email or used the Internet after they become housewives. One told me that "computer technology changes so fast, it is totally different than what I learned before. I don't even bother to understand it now."

4. High-tech engineers working inside Hsinchu Science Park use these nicknames themselves.

5. The Taiwanese public believes that the high-tech elite, the best-educated group in Taiwan, can get rich overnight by inventing cutting-edge technology.

6. In terms of administrative districts, part of Jin-shan-mian belongs to Hsinchu City and part to Hsinchu County. Six neighborhoods make up Hsinchu City. Hsinchu Science Park is one of them.

7. Before the Hakkanese migrated to this area, aboriginal people occupied Jin-shan-mian. Many confrontations occurred during the Hakkanese migration period. For more on this see Lee et al. 1997 and Wu 1998.

8. Coincidentally, the Chinese term for the San Francisco Bay Area is Jiou-jin-shan, which means "old golden mountain."

9. According to Lee et al. (1997, 77), all the irrigation ponds, each of which supported one nearby neighborhood, are associated with their own legends, but only local seniors remember these stories.

10. After many negotiations between grassroots groups and the express train development company, in 2001 the railroad was rerouted, preserving the dragon feng shui for Jin-shan-mian.

11. As described in Byster and Smith's article "Toxic Lifecycle of Electronics Production," not until 1983 was it widely recognized that "the semiconductor and circuit-board industries had devastated both the pristine reputation of the industry as well as much of the groundwater in Santa Clara County." In the case of Hsinchu Science Park, it took a toxic fire in 1997 to awaken its neighbors' environmental consciousness.

12.   My field notes show that the Hsinchu Science Park employees who have PhDs, Master's degrees, and bachelor's degrees are likely from outside the Hsinchu region. Employees who have only junior college or high school degrees—usually manufacturing workers employed on assembly lines—are generally from the local Hsinchu region. According to the September 2004 employee data, 60 percent of the workers were locals (Hsinchu Science Park 2004b).

13.   In 1998 Charles estimated that about 50,000 of the 72,000 Hsinchu Science Park laborers were local Hsinchu residents. The total population of Hsinchu in 1996 was 345,000, with 120,000 between the ages of twenty and thirty-five (Ministry of the Interior 1998). There were 95,000 citizens in that age group in 2002 (Population Affairs Administration 2003).

14.   Jan was the first Taiwanese planner to specialize in industrial park planning, according to her because she was "the only Taiwanese who had professional experience in planning and designing high-tech industrial parks at that time." The park chair invited her to work with them when her husband accepted a job in Hsinchu Science Park.

15.   Careen, a housewife I interviewed in Hsinchu whose family moved back there in 1989–91, said, "From 1989 to 1991, many Silicon Valley engineers moved back to Taiwan." According to Wang's report (1998), Silicon Valley and Hsinchu continued to compete for Taiwanese high-tech engineers for about a decade.

16.   Most of the families, however, still want to send their children to America for a better education. The ability to speak English is considered the most essential prerequisite for their success.

Chapter 8. Building a Global City in My Backyard

1.   An Americanized skyward house combines an American suburban house facade with the interior layout of a Taiwanese skyward house. I will explain the details of constructions of Americanized skyward houses in chapter 9.

2.   My field interviews revealed that some of the developers of these projects experienced financial crises and ended up going bankrupt. Those projects may be sold and transferred to other investors hoping to make a profit. However, these second investors may also declare bankruptcy and sell the projects to a third agent. The process can continue on and on, and certain developments may end up not being built at all.

3.   Because of a series of recent kidnappings, many higher-income Taiwanese prefer to live in secure gated communities.

4.   The project, which was planned and designed by the chief architect of the Winbond Home projects, is analyzed in chapter 9.

5. As of the spring of 1998, when I conducted my fieldwork, there was no clue whether the project might be built in the future.

6. The chief architect did not want to discuss this project with me because the Hsinchu County government was suing him at the time.

7. However, one of the architects told me that down payments had only been placed on one-third of the properties.

8. Only 5 units—3 detached houses and 2 duplexes—out of the total of 320 had not been sold as of March 1998. The price of a single-family detached house was about US$760,000, a duplex unit about US$460,000. Local architects and some real diaspora high-tech engineers—astronauts who live in the low-density suburbs in Silicon Valley—pointed out that the development's density was too high because it lacked enough green space and it contained the high-rise. The high-rise apartment was not advertised during the first development phase, so homebuyers assumed they would be living in a community with only houses and large green spaces. However, after most of the houses were sold the developer added the high-rise in the open space adjacent to the gate. Naturally, this addition upset many residents.

9. This is from Liu's notes from community meetings with local residents conducted over an eighteen-month period from 2000 to 2002 (Chang et al. 2002).

Chapter 9. Mirror Homes

1. Of the seven astronauts I interviewed, one lived in a rented house in a hillside gated community outside Hsinchu Science Park. All the others lived inside Hsinchu Science Park.

2. Residential developments driven by high-tech companies are open exclusively to their employees, not to the general public.

3. Since 1990 he has been involved in two of the earliest projects, the Winbond Sweet Home project and the Homeland project. These two projects will provide 441 new homes, primarily for Winbond employees.

4. The proposals were submitted in early 1990s, but project was not completed until 2004.

5. For example, only steep roofs are suitable because of the accumulation of snow in the winter; wood structures will typically require higher maintenance in a humid climate like Taiwan's; and setback walls violate local building codes.

6. Some interviewees mentioned they would follow conventional feng shui principles, while others declared that those principles were not important to them at all.

Chapter 10. Homes Across the Water

1. ·Another interviewee told me that her store was very successful. More than two hundred high-tech housewives visited her store on the afternoon of the grand opening, even though it was a cold and rainy day.

2. Her work was also exhibited at a local museum last year.

References

Akhtar, Salman. 1999. *Immigration and Identity: Turmoil, Treatment, and Transformation.* Northvale, NJ: Jason Aronson.

Altman, Irwin, and Setha M. Low, eds. 1992. *Place Attachment.* 12 vols. Vol. 12, *Human Behavior and Environment: Advances in Theory and Research.* New York: Plenum Press.

Amersfoort, Hans van, and Jeroen Doomernik. 2002. Emergent Diaspora or Immigrant Communities? Turkish Immigrants in the Netherlands. In *Communities Across Borders: New Immigrants and Transnational Cultures,* edited by P. Kennedy and V. Roudometof. London: Routledge.

Anderson, Kay J. 1987. The Idea of Chinatown: The Power of Place and Institutional Practice in the Making of a Racial Category. *Annals of Association of American Geographers* 77, no. 4: 580–98.

———. 1991. *Vancouver's Chinatown: Racial Discourse in Canada, 1895–1980.* Edited by D. H. Akenson. McGill-Queen's Studies in Ethnic History. London: McGill-Queen's University Press.

Anderson Appleyard, Donald. 1978. Home. Berkeley: Institute of Urban and Regional Development.

———. 1979. The Environment as a Social Symbol: Within a Theory of Environmental Action and Perception. *Journal of the American Planning Association* 45, no. 2: 143–45.

———. 1984. Identity, Power and Place. Unpublished manuscript.

Bachelard, Gaston. 1958. *The Poetics of Space: The Classic Look at How We Experience Intimate Places.* Translated by M. Jolas. 1994 ed. Boston: Beacon Press.

Barringer, Herbert, Robert W. Gardner, and Michael J. Levin. 1995. *Asians and Pacific Islanders in the United States*. New York: Russell Sage Foundation.

Barthes, Roland. 1988. Death of the Author. In *Twentieth-Century Literary Theory, A Reader*, edited by K. M. Newton. New York: St. Martin's Press.

Belenky, Mary Field, et al. 1997. *Women's Ways of Knowing: The Development of Self, Voice, and Mind*. New York: Basic Books.

Bhabha, Homi. 1994. *The Location of Culture*. London: Routledge.

———. 1996. Culture's In-between. In *Questions of Cultural Identity*, edited by S. Hall and P. D. Gay. London: Sage.

Bih, Herng-Dar. 1992. The Meaning of Objects: A Contextual Analysis of Experiences of Chinese Students in Their Home and Host Country. Ph.D. diss., Department of Psychology, The City University of New York, New York.

Blakely, Edward J., and Mary Gail Snyder. 1999. *Fortress America: Gated Communities in the United States*. Washington, D.C.: Brookings Institution Press.

Bloom, Harold. 2000. *How to Read and Why?* New York: Scribner.

Bloomer, Kent C., and Charles W. Moore. 1977. *Body, Memory, and Architecture*. New Haven, CT: Yale University Press.

Bourdieu, Pierre. 1993. *The Field of Cultural Production: Essays on Art and Literature (Edited and Introduced by Randal Johnson)*. Edited by L. D. Kritzaman, *A Series in Social Thought and Cultural Criticism*. New York: Columbia University Press.

Brab, Avtar. 2003. Diaspora, Border and Transnational Identities. In *Feminist Postcolonial Theory: A Reader*, edited by R. Lewis and S. Mills. New York: Routledge.

Briggs, Anne Theodore, and Stephen Watt. 2001. *Technology and Research Parks*. MBA Class of American University. http://www.american.edu/carmel/ab5293a/techparks.htm.

Brown, Patricia Leigh. 2003. The New Chinatown? Try the Asian Mall. *New York Times*, March 24.

Butler, Judith. 1990. *Gender Trouble: Feminism and the Subversion of Identity*. New York: Routledge.

Byster, Leslie, and Ted Smith. Forthcoming. The Toxic Lifecycle of Electronics Production. In *Challenging the Chips: Labor Rights and Environmental Justice in the Global Electronics Industry*, edited by D. N. Pellow, D. A. Sonnenfeld, and T. Smith. Philadelphia: Temple University Press.

Castells, Manuel. 1989. *The Informational City: The Space of Flows; Information Technology, Economic Restructuring and the Urban-regional Process*. Oxford: Basil Blackwell.

———. 1997. *The Power of Identity*. 3 vols. Vol. 2, *The Information Age: Economy, Society and Culture*. Oxford: Blackwell Publisher.

Castells, Manuel, and Peter Hall. 1994. *Technopoles of the World: The Making of Twenty-First-Century Industrial Complexes.* New York: Routledge.

Catanese, Anthony V. 1999. *Haitians: Migration and Diaspora.* Boulder, CO: Westview Press.

Chang, Chi-Yuang. 1997. The Migration Wave Reaching the New Ten-year High. *China Times,* April 21.

Chang, Chung-Mou. 1998. *Chang, Chung-Mou.* 2 vols. Vol. 1. Taipei: Commonwealth Publishing.

Chang, Jaw-ling Joanne. 2003. *Managing U.S.-Taiwan Relations: 20 Years After the Taiwan Relations Act.* Institute of European and American Studies Academia Sinica. http://www.taipei.org/tra/sinica/sinica–02.htm.

Chang, Michael S. 1997. 150 Years of Chinese Lives in the Santa Clara Valley. In *Toward the Golden Mountain: The History of the Chinese in the Santa Clara Valley; An Exhibit at the Cupertino Historical Society & Museum,* edited by H. John. Cupertino, CA: Cupertino Historical Society & Museum.

Chang, Shenglin. 1998. Fieldwork Notes and Interviews from Hsinchu and Silicon Valley, 1997–98. Berkeley.

———. 2000. Real Life at Virtual Home: Silicon Landscape Construction in Response to Transcultural Home Identities. Ph.D. diss., Department of Landscape Architecture and Environmental Planning, University of California at Berkeley, Berkeley.

———. 2002. Transcultural Home Identity across the Pacific: A Case Study of High-tech Taiwanese Transnational Community in Hsinchu, Taiwan, and Silicon Valley, USA. In *Urban Ethnic Encounters: The Spatial Consequences,* edited by A. Erdentug and F. Colombijn. London: Routledge.

Chang, Shenglin, and Randolph T. Hester Jr. 1998. When Landscapes Are Transplanted across the Ocean: Multicultural Community Design in Technopoles. Paper read at 1998 ASLA Annual Meeting, October, 2–6, 1998, at Portland, Oregon.

Chang, Shenglin, Huamei Chiu, and Wenling Tu. Forthcoming. Breaking Silicon Silence: Giving Voice to Health and Environmental Impacts Within Taiwan's Hsinchu Science Park. In *Challenging the Chips: Labor Rights and Environmental Justice in the Global Electronics Industry,* edited by D. N. Pellow, D. A. Sonnenfeld, and T. Smith. Philadelphia: Temple University Press.

Chang, Shenglin, K. C. John Liu, Tian-Xin Zhang, and Margarita Hill. 2002. Building a Global City in My Backyard: Case Studies of Pu-Yu New City Plan (Taiwan), Gateway Arts District (USA), and Shanghai Xin-Tian-Di (China). Paper read at Fourth Annual Pacific Rim Participatory Community Design Conference, at Hong Kong.

Chang, Shenglin, Wen-Ling Tu, Wen-Chuan Yang, and Li-Fang Yang. 2001. A Study of the Environmental and Social Aspects of the Taiwanese and US Companies in the Hsinchu Science-based Industrial Park. Policy report for California Global Corporate Accountability Project. Berkeley, California: Nautilus Institute for Security and Sustainable Development, the Natural Heritage Institute and Human Rights Advocates.

Chang, Shenglin, and Tianxin Zhang. 2001. Fieldwork Notes and Interviews: Shanghai, Hsinchu, and Silicon Valley, 2001. College Park, MD.

Chang, Tien Hwei. 1996. How Come Chinese Commercial Signs Take Over Cupertino's Streets? *Sing Tao Daily*, December 14.

———. 1997. Cupertino's Multicultural Community Meeting, March 1st and 2nd. *Sing Tao Daily*, March 5.

Chang-chen International Planning and Construction Consultant Company. 1990. Wind-bong Sweet Home Community—Design Patterns for Single-detached Houses. Hsinchu, Taiwan: Chang-chen International Construction.

———. 1997. *Advertisement of Grand High-tech International Bilingual Villa Community*. Hsinchu, Taiwan: Chang-chen International Planning and Construction Consultant Company.

Chen, Kwan-Fu. 1988. High-tech Industry Development and the Spatial Division in Taiwan: A Case Study on the Hsinchu Science Park, Taiwan. Master's thesis, Graduate Institute of Building and Planning, National Taiwan University, Taipei.

Chen, Shiang-Lan. 1994. Over 500,000 Taiwanese Sneak in the United States. *Independent Daily*, November 8.

Chinese Historical Society of America. 1991. *Chinese America: History and Perspectives 1991*. Brisbane, CA: Fong Brothers Printing.

Chow, Esther Ngan-ling. 1987. The Development of Feminist Consciousness Among Asian American Women. *Gender & Society* 1, no. 3 (September): 284–99.

Cloud Gate Dance Theatre. 1978. Legacy. Chiayi: Cloudy Gate Dance Theater.

———. 2003. *What Has Been Said About Cloud Gate Dance Theatre of Taiwan*. Cloudy Gate Dance Theatre 2003. http://www.cloudgate.org.tw/english/cgdt.htm.

Cohen, Robin. 1997. *Global Diasporas: An Introduction*. Edited by R. Cohen, *Global Diaspora*. Seattle: University of Washington Press.

Colic-Peisker, Val. 2002. Migrant Communities and Class: Croatians in Western Australia. In *Communities Across Borders: New Immigrants and Transnational Cultures*, edited by P. Kennedy and V. Roudometof. London: Routledge.

Cosgrove, Denis E. 1984. *Social Formation and Symbolic Landscape*. Edited by R. A. Butlin. *Croom Helm Historical Geography Series*. London: Croom Helm.

Da Bei Tou Media Corp. 1997. Da-Ke-Ji High-Tech Bilingual Community. Taipei: Da Bei Tou Media Corp.

Davis, Mike. 1992. Fortress Los Angeles: The Militarization of Urban Space. In *Variation on a Theme Park: The New American City and the End of Public Space*, edited by M. Sorkin. New York: Hill and Wang.

Deng, Hay-Ju. 1998. *Legends of Silicon Valley*. 2 vols. Taipei: Yuan-shen Press.

Department of Statistics, MOI. 1997. Taiwan-Fukien Demography Quarterly. Taipei: Ministry of the Interior ROC.

Ebrey, Patricia Buckley. 2001. *A Visual Sourcebook of Chinese Civilization*. http://depts.washington.edu/chinaciv/home/3garintr.htm.

EDS International. 2002. Pu-yu Development Plan, Final Report. Taipei: EDS International.

Egnall, Marc. 1996. *Divergent Paths: How Culture and Institutions Have Shaped North American Growth*. New York: Oxford University Press.

English-Lueck, J. A. 2002. *Cultures@Silicon Valley*. Stanford, CA: Stanford University Press.

Findlay, John. 1992. *Magic Lands: Western Cityscapes and American Culture after 1940*. Berkeley: University of California Press.

Fishman, Robert. 1987. *Bourgeois Utopias: The Rise and Fall of Suburbia*. New York: Basic Books.

Fong, Timothy. 1994. *The First Suburban Chinatown: The Remaking of Monterey Park, California*. Philadelphia: Temple University Press.

Francis, Mark. 1990. The Everyday and the Personal: Six Garden Stories. In *The Meaning of Gardens: Idea, Place, and Action*, edited by M. Francis and R. T. Hester, Jr. Cambridge, MA: MIT Press.

Garber, Marjorie. 2000. *Sex and Real Estate: Why We Love Houses*. New York: Pantheon Books.

Glennon, Lorraine, et al., eds. 2000. *The 20th Century: An Illustrated History of Our Lives and Times*. Dighton, MA: JG Press.

Gottdiener, Mark. 1994. *The New Urban Sociology*. New York: McGraw-Hill.

Graham, Stephen, and Simon Marvin. 1996. *Telecommunications and the City: Electronic Spaces, Urban Places*. New York: Routledge.

Grasmuck, Sherri, and Patricia R. Pessar. 1991. *Between Two Islands: Dominican International Migration*. Berkeley: University of California Press.

Groth, Paul. 1990. Parking Garden. In *The Meaning of Gardens: Idea, Place, and Action*, edited by M. Francis and R. T. J. Hester. Cambridge: MIT Press.

Hayden, Dolores. 1984. *Redesigning the American Dream: The Future of Housing, Work, and Family Life*. New York: W. W. Norton and Company.

———. 1991. *The Grand Domestic Revolution*. 5th ed. Cambridge, MA: MIT Press.

————. 1995. *The Power of Place: Urban Landscape History*. Cambridge, MA: MIT Press.

————. 2003. *Building Suburbia: Green Fields and Urban Growth, 1820–2000*. New York: Pantheon Books.

Hear, Nicholas van. 1998. *New Diasporas: The Mass Exodus, Dispersal and Regrounding of Migrant Communities*. Edited by R. Cohen. Global Diaspora. Seattle: University of Washington Press.

Here and There 3–1. 1998. *New York Times*, July 19.

Here and There 3–2. 1998. *New York Times*, July 20.

Here and There 3–3. 1998. *New York Times*, July 21.

Hester, Randolph T. Jr. 1996. Wanted: Local Participation with a View. Paper read at EDRA/27, at The Public and Private Places, at Salt Lake City.

Hester, Randolph T., Jr., and Shenglin Chang. 2002. Impacts of Status Seeking on Local Culture and Place: Some Preliminary Observations and Strategies for Community Designers. Paper read at Fourth Annual Pacific Rim Participatory Community Design Conference, at Hong Kong.

Him, Mark Lai. 1992. *From Chinese Immigrants to Chinese Americans: A Social History of Chinese Americans in the Twentieth Century*. Hong Kong: Joint Publishing (H.K.) Co.

Hirokazu, Kore-eda. 1998. *After Life*, edited by K.-e. Hirokazu. New Yorker Video.

Horton, John. 1995. *The Politics of Diversity: Immigration, Resistance, and Change in Monterey Park, California*. Philadelphia: Temple University Press.

Hsiao, Michael. 1994. The Transformations and Brain Re-drain of Taiwanese Immigrants in the United States: Case Studies of Los Angeles and New York. Taipei: Overseas Chinese Affairs Commission, Republic of China.

Hsinchu Science Park. 2004a. *Housing, Land, and Factory Sep. 2004*. Hsinchu Science Park. http://service.sipa.gov.tw/WEB/Jsp/Page/index.jsp?thisRootID=497.

————. 2004b. *Employee Education Background Sep. 2004* Hsinchu Science Park. http://service.sipa.gov.tw/WEB/Jsp/Page/index.jsp?thisRootID=496.

————.2004c. *Establishment of Enterprises Sep. 2004*. Hsinchu Science Park. http://www.sipa.gov.tw/en/seconde/hsip/hsi00092_09_03.htm.

Hsu, Jinn-Yuh. 1997. A Late-industrial District? Learning Network in the Hsinchu Science-based Industrial Park, Taiwan. Ph.D. diss., Department of Geography, University of California, Berkeley.

Hsu, Madeline Yuan-Yin. 2000. *Dreaming of Gold, Dreaming of Home: Transnationalism and Migration Between the United States and South China, 1882–1943*. Edited by G. H. Chang. Asian American. Stanford, CA: Stanford University Press.

Hsu, Zueng-Mao. 1998a. The Rise and Fall of Singapore's Suchou Since Park Development (Part 1). *China Times*, February 4.

————. 1998b. The Rise and Fall of Singapore's Suchou Since Park Development (Part 2). *China Times*, February 5.

International Association of Science Parks. 2003. *Statistics: Number of IASP members—Evolution (Nov. 2002)*, International Association of Science Parks. http://www.iaspworld.org/information/statistics.php.

Jackson, Kenneth T. 1985. *Crabgrass Frontier: The Suburbanization of the United States*. New York: Oxford University Press.

Jacobs, Jane. 1992. *The Death and Life of Great American Cities*. New York: Vintage Books.

Jaggar, Alison M., and Susan R. Bordo, eds. 1989. *Gender/body/knowledge: Feminist Reconstructions of Being and Knowing*. New Brunswick, NJ: Rutgers University Press.

Jen, Gish. 1991. *Typical American*. New York: Plume.

Johnson, Don Hanlon. 1983. *Body: Recovering Our Sensual Wisdom*. Berkeley: North Atlantic Books and Somatic Resources.

Johnson, Lesley. 1999. As Housewives We Are Worms: Women Modernity, and the Home Question. In *Feminism and Cultural Studies: Oxford Reading in Feminism*, edited by M. Shiach. New York: Oxford University Press.

Jones, Richard C. 1995. *Ambivalent Journey: U.S. Migration and Economic Mobility in North-Central Mexico*. Tucson: University of Arizona Press.

Juang, Ming-Ren. 1999. Grand Opening of Tai-mao Shopping Mall—The Grandest Shopping Center in Taiwan. *China Time*, July 5.

Jung, C. G. 1989. *Memories, Dreams, Reflections*. Translated by Richard Winston and Clara Winston. Revised ed. New York: Vintage Books.

Jurgens, Jeffery. 2001. Shifting Spaces: Complex Identities in Turkish-German Migration. In *New Transnational Social Spaces: International Migration and Transnational Companies in the Early Twenty-first Century*, edited by L. Pries. London: Routledge.

King, Julia. 2003. IT's Global Itinerary: Offshore Outsourcing Is Inevitable. *Computerworld* 2003. http://www.computerworld.com/managementtopics/outsourcing/story/0,10801,84861,00.html.

Kinkead, Gwen. 1992. *Chinatown: A Portrait of a Closed Society*. New York: Harper-Perennial.

Kurien, Prema. 1998. Becoming American by Becoming Hindu: Indian Americans Take Their Place at the Multicultural Table. In *Gatherings in Diaspora: Religious Communities and the New Immigration*, edited by R. S. Warner and J. G. Wittner. Philadelphia: Temple University Press.

Laguerre, Michael S. 1999. *Minoritized Space: An Inquiry into the Spatial Order of Things*. Berkeley: Institute of Governmental Studies Press.

Lee, Ang. 1995. *Eat Drink Man Woman (Yin-Shi-Nan-Nu)*, edited by A. Lee. Los Angeles: Hallmark Home Entertainment, Image Entertainment.

Lee, Ding-Zan, et al. 1997. *Community History of Jin-shan-mian*. Hsinchu City, Taiwan: Hsinchu City Culture Center.

Lee, Guan-Chien. 1998. Coming to America—The Life of Taiwanese Seniors in the US. *Sinorama*, May 1998, 24–43.

Lerner, Gerda. 1993. *The Creation of Feminist Consciousness*. Vol. 2. New York: Oxford University Press.

Leu, Ching-Song. 1997. The Debate About the Science Park's Impact on Local Developments and Taiwan's Evidence: A Case Study of Science-Based Industrial Park in Shin Chu. Master's thesis, Graduate Institute of Urban Planning, National Chong-sing University, Taichong.

Levitt, Peggy. 2001. *The Transnational Villagers*. Berkeley: University of California Press.

Lima, Fernando H. 2001. Transnational Families: Institutions of Transnational Social Space. In *New Transnational Social Spaces*, edited by L. Pries. London: Routledge.

Lippard, Lucy. 1997. *The Lure of the Local: Sense of Place in a Multicentered Society*. New York: New Press.

Liu, Chia-Chung. 1970. My Home Is There. Taipei.

Liu, John K. C. 1980. Housing Transformation: A Study of Family Life and Built Form in Taiwan. Ph.D. diss., Department of Architecture, University of California, Berkeley.

———. 2002. Notes for the Pu-yu New City Project. Unpublished manuscript, Taipei.

Low, Setha M. 2003. *Behind the Gates: Life, Security, and the Pursuit of Happiness in Fortress America*. New York: Routledge.

Lowenthal, David. 1985. *The Past Is a Foreign Country*. Cambridge: Cambridge University Press.

Lubman, Sarah. 1999. A World Apart: A Look into the Lives of Silicon Valley's Long-Distance Commuters. *San Jose Mercury News*, August 22, 1A.

Lyman, Stanford M. 1974. *Chinese Americans*. Edited by P. I. Rose. 7 vols., *Ethnic Groups in Comparative Perspective*. New York: Random House.

Lyndon, Donlyn, and Charles W. Moore. 1994. *Chambers for a Memory Palace*. Cambridge, MA: MIT Press.

Ma, Ai-Hsuan. 1998. Cultural Aspect of Migration Decisions: A Study of Scientists in the United States from China and Taiwan. Paper read at American Sociological Association 93rd Annual Meeting, at San Francisco, CA.

Mahler, Sarah J. 1995. *Salvadorans in Suburbia: Symbiosis and Conflict*. Boston: Allyn and Bacon.

Malkki, Liisa H. 1995. *Purity and Exile: Violence, Memory, and National Cosmology Among Hutu Refugees in Tanzania*. Chicago: University of Chicago Press.

Marcus, Clare Cooper. 1974. House as a Symbol of Self. In Land et. al. (eds.) *Designing for Human Behavior*. Stroudsberg: Dowden, Hutchinson and Ross.

———. 1978. Remembrance of Landscape Past. Berkeley: Institute of Urban and Regional Development.

———. 1979. Environmental Autobiography. Berkeley: Institute of Urban and Regional Development.

———. 1986. Home-as-Haven, Home-as-Trap: Explorations in Experience of Dwelling. Berkeley: Center for Environmental Design Research.

———. 1992. Environmental Memories. In *Place Attachment*, edited by I. Altman and S. M. Low. New York: Plenum.

———. 1995. *House as a Mirror of Self*. Berkeley: Conari Press.

Mark, Jane. 1999. The Sacred or Profane Use of *Feng Shui* in Residential Communities. Master's Thesis, Department of Landscape Architecture and Environmental Planning, University of California, Berkeley, Berkeley.

Martin, Biddy, and Chandra Talpade Mohanty. 1999. Feminist Politics: What's Home Got to Do with It? In *Feminism and Cultural Studies: Oxford Reading in Feminism*, edited by M. Shiach. New York: Oxford University Press.

Martinson, Tom. 2000. *American Dreamscape: The Pursuit of Happiness in Postwar Suburbia*. New York: Carroll and Graf Publishers.

Massey, Doreen. 1994a. Double Articulation: A Place in the World. In *Displacements: Cultural Identities in Question*, edited by A. Bammer. Bloomington: Indiana University Press.

———. 1994b. *Space, Place, and Gender*. Minneapolis: University of Minnesota Press.

Mathews, John A., and Dong-sung Cho. 2000. *Tiger Technology: The Creation of a Semiconductor Industry in East Asia*. New York: Cambridge University Press.

Matless, David. 1995. The Art of Right Living: Landscape and Citizenship, 1918–39. In *Mapping the Subject: Geographies of Cultural Transformation*, edited by S. Pile and N. Thrift. London: Routledge.

Matthews, Kim C. 2002. Boundaries of Diaspora Identity: The Case of Central and East African–Asians in Canada. In *Communities Across Borders: New Immigrants and Transnational Cultures*, edited by P. Kennedy and V. Roudometof. London: Routledge.

Miles, Ann. 2004. *From Cuenca to Queens: An Anthropological Story of Transnational Migration*. Austin: University of Texas Press.

Mill, Sara. 2003. Gender and Colonial Space. In *Feminist Postcolonial Theory: A Reader*, edited by R. Lewis and S. Mills. New York: Routledge.

Miller, Daniel, Peter Jackson, Nigel Thrift, and Michael Rowlands. 1998. *Shopping, Place, and Identity*. London: Routledge.

Ministry of Education in Taiwan. 1999. *1998 Annual Report*. Taipei: Ministry of Education in Taiwan.

———. 2005. *2004 Annual Report / Higher Education Students as a Share of Population*. Ministry of Education in Taiwan 2002. http://140.111.1.22/english/home_statistics.htm.

Ministry of the Interior. 1998. *Taiwan-Fukien Demography Quarterly, Republic of China*. Taipei: Ministry of the Interior, ROC.

———. 2003. *Population Affairs Monthly: December 2003*. Ministry of the Interior, ROC. http://www.moi.gov.tw/W3/stat/home.asp.

Mirochnik, Elijah. 2002. The Possibilities of Passion. In *Passion and Pedagogy: Relation, Creation, and Transformation in Teaching*, edited by E. Mirochnik and D. C. Sherman. New York: Peter Lang.

Mitchell, Joni. 1971. California. In *Blue*. Burbank (CA); New York: Reprise Records.

MOI Statistical Information Service. 2003. *Taiwan-Fukien Demography Quarterly, Republic of China*. Ministry of the Interior, ROC 2002. Available from http://www.moi.gov.tw/W3/stat/home.asp.

Morse, Edward S. 1961. *Japanese Homes and Their Surroundings*. New York: Dover Publications.

Mozingo, Louise A. 2003. Campus, Estate, and Park: Lawn Culture Comes to the Corporation. In *Everyday America: Cultural Landscape Studies After J. B. Jackson*, edited by C. Wilson and P. Groth. Berkeley: University of California Press.

Naquin, Susan, and Evelyn S. Rawski. 1987. *Chinese Society in the Eighteenth Century*. New Haven, CT: Yale University Press.

National Taiwan University Building and Planning Foundation. 1997. Preservation and Reuse of the Lee Family Compound: From Historic Preservation to Cultural Regeneration. Taipei: National Taiwan University Building and Planning Foundation.

Ong, Aihwa. 1992. Limits to Cultural Accumulation: Chinese Capitalists on the American Pacific Rim. Paper read at Toward a Transnational Perspective on Migration: Race, Class, Ethnicity, and National Reconsidered, at New York.

———. 1993. On the Edge of Empires: Flexible Citizenship Among Chinese in Diaspora. *Positions* 1, no. 3 (Winter 1993): 745–78.

———. 1999. *Flexible Citizenship*. Durham, NC: Duke University Press.

Ong, Paul, Edna Bonacich, and Lucie Cheng. 1994. *The New Asian Immigration in Los Angeles and Global Restructuring*. Edited by S. Chan and D. Palumbo-

Liu. Asian American History and Culture. Philadelphia: Temple University Press.

Packard, Vance. 1961. *The Status Seekers*. 15th ed. New York: Pocket Books.

Population Affairs Administration. 2003. *Population by Age in Taiwan-Fuchien Area*. Ministry of Interior ROC 2003. http://www.moi.gov.tw/stat/.

Portes, Alejandro, and Ruben G. Rumbaut. 1990. *Immigrant America: A Portrait*. Berkeley: University of California Press.

Pu-yu Project Working Group. 2002. The Hsinchu County Pu-yu Project: Taiwan Knowledge-based-economy New City Plan. Taipei: Hsinchu County.

Qian, Ning. 1997. *Studying in U.S.A.* Taipei: Mei-tien Publishers.

Rapport, Nigel, and Andrew Dawson, eds. 1998. *Migrants of Identity*. In *Ethnicity and Identity*, edited by S. Ardener, T. Dragadze, and J. Webber. Oxford: Berg.

Relph, E. 1976. *Place and Placelessness*. London: Point Limited.

Rorty, Richard. 1989. *Contingency, Irony, and Solidarity*. New York: Cambridge University Press.

———. 2001. Redemption from Egotism: James and Proust as Spiritual Exercises. *Telos* 3, no. 3: 243–63.

Rosenthal, Elisabeth. 1998. Middle America in China: Funny, I Moved to Beijing and Wound Up in Pleasantville. *New York Times*, November 15.

———. 2003. North of Beijing, California Dreams Come True. *New York Times*, February 3.

Roth, Rodris. 1998. Scrapbook Houses: A Late Nineteenth-Century Children's View of the American Home. In *The American Home: Material Culture, Domestic Space, and Family Life*, edited by E. M. Thompson. Winterthur, DE: Henry Francis du Pont Winterthur Museum.

Sachs, Aaron. 1999. Virtual Ecology: A Brief Environmental History of Silicon Valley. *World Watch Magazine*, January/February.

San Jose Starlite Court. 1997. *Chinese New Home Buyer's Guide*, 17.

Saxenian, AnnaLee. 1997. Transnational Entrepreneurs and Regional Industrialization: The Silicon Valley–Hsinchu Connection. Paper read at Conference on Social Structure and Social Change: International Perspectives on Business Firms and Economic Life, at Taipei.

———. 1999. *Silicon Valley's New Immigrant Entrepreneurs*. San Francisco: Public Policy Institute of California.

Saxenian, AnnaLee, and Jumbi Edulbehram. 1998. Immigrant Entrepreneurs in Silicon Valley. *Berkeley Planning Journal* 12 (1998): 32–49.

Saxenian, AnnaLee, Yasuyuki Motoyama, and Xiaohong Quan. 2002. Local and Global Networks of Immigrant Professionals in Silicon Valley. San Francisco: Public Policy Institute of California.

Scott, Allen J. 1993. *Technopoles: High-Technology Industry and Regional Development in Southern California*. Berkeley: University of California Press.

———. 1996. High-Technology Industrial Development in the San Fernando Valley and Ventura County: Observations on Economic Growth and the Evolution of Urban Form. In *The City: Los Angeles and Urban Theory at the End of the Twentieth Century*, edited by Allen J. Scott and Edward W. Soja. Berkeley: University of California Press.

Seamon, David. 1985. Reconciling Old and New Worlds: The Dwelling-journey Relationship as Portrayed in Vilhelm Moberg's "Emigrant" Novels. In *Dwelling, Place, and Environment: Toward a Phenomenology of Person and World*, edited by David Seamon and Robert Mugerauer. New York: Columbia University Press.

Sha, Yin-Chih. 1994. Cover Stories: Taiwanese Immigrants. *Business Weekly (Taipei)*, July 7, 18–38.

Smith, Michael P., and Luis E. Guarnizo. 1998. *Transnationalism from Below*. New Brunswick, NJ: Transaction Publishers.

Soja, Edward W. 1996. *Thirdspace: Journeys to Los Angeles and Other Real-and-Imagined Places*. Oxford: Blackwell Publishers.

Sopher, David E. 1979. The Landscape of Home. In *The Interpretation of Ordinary Landscapes: Geographical Essays*, edited by D. W. Meinig. New York: Oxford University Press.

Sørensen, Ninna Nyberg, and Karen Fog Olwig, eds. 2002. *Work and Migration: Life and Livelihoods in a Globalizing World*. Edited by S. Vertovec. Vol. 4, *Transnationalism*. London: Routledge.

Starr, Kevin. 1985. *Inventing the Dream: California Through the Progressive Era*. Oxford: Oxford University Press.

Taipei Modern Dance Theater. 1982. Taipei Modern Dance Theater. Taipei: Cloud Gate Dance Theater.

Takaki, Ronald. 1989. *Strangers from a Different Shore: A History of Asian Americans*. New York: Penguin Books.

———. 1993. *A Different Mirror: A History of Multicultural America*. Boston: Little, Brown and Company.

Teyssot, Georges, ed. 1999. *The American Lawn*. New York: Princeton Architectural Press.

The Top-ten Model Community Award. 1995. *China Times*, September 21.

Tsai, Cheng-Shong. 2003. Bilingual Job Title Does Not Improve Communication in English. *China Times*, June 3. http://news.chinatimes.com/Chinatimes/newslist/newslist-list/0,3545,110514,00.html.

Tseng, Sue-Yah. 1995. The Aesthetics of Daily Life and Community. Master's thesis, Department of Socio-Anthropology, Ching-Hwa University, Hsinchu, Taiwan.

TSMC. 2003a. *TSMC* Hsinchu Science-based Industrial Park 2003. http://www. sipa.gov.tw/1/searcher/index-searcher.htm.

———. 2003b. *TSMC Worldwide*. TSMC 2003. http://www.tsmc.com/chinese/ tsmcinfo/c01.htm.

Tu, Wenling, ed. 2003. *Hsinchu Science-based Industrial Park News Clips from 1970 to March 3, 2003*. Berkeley: Tu, Wenling.

Tuan, Yi-Fu. 1974. *Topophilia: A Study of Environmental Perception, Attitudes, and Value*. Englewood Cliffs, NJ: Prentice-Hall.

———. 1977. *Space and Place: The Perspective of Experience*. Minneapolis: University of Minnesota Press.

———. 1996. *Cosmos and Hearth: A Cosmopolite's Viewpoint*. Minneapolis: University of Minnesota Press.

U.S. Bureau of the Census. 2003. *Census 2000*. U.S. Bureau of the Census, 2000. www.census.gov.

Wang, Hwie-Min. 1998. Silicon Valley and Taiwan Competing for Hi-tech Engineers: The Brain Drain Indicator. *United Daily*, May 1.

Ward, Stephen V. 1998. *Selling Places: The Marketing and Promotion of Towns and Cities 1850–2000*. Edited by A. Sutcliffe. 23 vols. Vol. 23, *Studies in History, Planning and the Environment*. New York: E & FN Spon.

Warner, R. Stephen, and Judith G. Wittner, eds. 1998. *Gatherings in Diaspora: Religious Communities and the New Immigration*. Philadelphia: Temple University Press.

Wellmeier, Nancy J. 1998. Santa Eulalia's People in Exile: Maya Religion, Culture, and Identity in Los Angeles. In *Gatherings in Diaspora: Religious Communities and the New Immigration*, edited by R. S. Warner and J. G. Wittner. Philadelphia: Temple University Press.

Welsch, Wolfgang. 1999. Transculturality: The Puzzling Form of Cultures Today. In *Spaces of Culture*, edited by M. Featherstone and S. Lash. London: Sage.

Welty, Eudora. 1984. *One Writer's Beginning*. Cambridge, MA: Harvard University Press.

Wright, Gwendolyn. 1981. *Building the Dream: A Social History of Housing in America*. Cambridge, MA: MIT Press.

Wu, Ching-Jie, ed. 1997. *Jin-shan-mian District News Clips, from September, 25th, 1994, to September 14th, 1997*. Hsinchu, Taipei: Wu, Ching-Jie, photocopy.

———. 1998. *The Orchid in Silicon Valley—Jin-shan-mian*. Hsinchu City, Taiwan: Chin-shan-main Cultural Historical Research Studio and the East Hsinchu City Chin-shan-main Community Development Association.

Wu, Kang-Li. 1997. Employment and Housing Development and Their Impacts on Metropolitan Commuting: An Empirical Study of the Development of the Silicon Valley Region of the San Francisco Bay Area. Ph.D. diss., Department of City and Regional Planning, University of California, Berkeley.

Wu, Kang-Li Tony. 1998a. Place, Homeplace Identity, Image, Environmental Design. Paper read at Third Asian Design Conference, October 15, at Taiwan.

————. 1998b. A Study of the Impact of Science Park Development on Housing Development: A Case Study of Silicon Valley and Its Implications for Taiwan's Science Park Planning. Paper read at Third Annual Conference of the Asian Real Estate Society, at Taiwan.

Yang, Yeou-Ren. 1998. Hsinchu to Tainan: The Political Economy of Science Park, New Industry, and Local Development. Master's thesis, Graduate Institute of Building and Planning, National Taiwan University, Taipei.

Yip, Christopher Lee. 1985. San Francisco's Chinatown: An Architectural and Urban History. Ph.D. diss., Department of Architecture, University of California, Berkeley.

Zhou, Min. 1992. *Chinatown: The Socioeconomic Potential of an Urban Enclave*. Philadelphia: Temple University Press.

Zia, Helen. 2000. *Asian American Dream: The Emergence of an American People*. New York: Farrar, Straus and Giroux.

Zukin, Sharon. 2004. *Point of Purchase: How Shopping Changed American Culture*. New York: Routledge.

Index

In this index an "f" after a number indicates a separate reference on the next page, and an "ff" indicates separate references on the next two pages. A continuous discussion over two or more pages is indicated by a span of page numbers, e.g., "57–59." *Passim* is used for a cluster of references in close but not consecutive sequence.

adapt stem families, *see* family structure
adulthood, 31. *See also* cheng-jia
Afterlife, 221. *See also* Hirokazu Kore-eda
agricultural landscape, 132, 158, 160
air transportation, 19, 23, 95. *See also* global commuting; trans-Pacific commuters
ambiguity: of identity, xviii, 85–89 *passim,* 100, 194, 205, 208
American citizenship, 48, 51, 97, 147, 169, 216. *See also* jin-yi; U.S. citizenship
American colonial town, *see* Bamboo Village; Hsinchu Science Park
American lifestyle, *see* lifestyles: American
American style, 86, 103, 105, 125; home, 33–34, 68, 199, 201; transplanting in Taiwan and China, 132, 147, 149, 154, 161, 169, 175
American suburban landscape, xix, 11, 103, 158, 169, 171f, 234n2 (chap. 2)
American Taiwanese, *see* Taiwanese American
American-born Chinese (ABC), 72–73, 156
Americanization, 48

arrival, 45, 67, 80, 160, 221, 230. *See also* departure
Asian American, xxi, 19, 47, 72, 109, 114, 118, 181, 237n4; identity, 25–29 *passim,* 104–6, 220, 224
Asian shopping malls (in Silicon Valley, CA), 123; Lundy Street, 119; Pacific Rim Plaza, 119; San Jose Starlite Court, 119, 188–89, 225; Milpitas Square (*see* Ranch 99)

Bamboo Village (in Hsinchu, Taiwan), 103, 129, 151, 170 (table), 197, 212–13, 218–19, 233n2; Winnie's & Julie's homes, 27–32 *passim*; neighborhood characteristics, 135–43 *passim. See also* American style; Hwei-chu Housewife Club; lifestyles: American; quality of life: high
beautiful clothes, 3, 210–11, 215–16, 220–23 *passim*, 230; degree and American citizenship, 48, 57, 95, 97 (*see also* American citizenship); American suburban house and modern shopping mall, 95–100 *passim*,

ASIAN AMERICA

Before Internment: Essays in Pre-War Japanese American History

YUJI ICHIOKA, EDITED BY ARIF DIRLIK, EIICHIRO AZUMA, AND
GORDON CHANG, FORTHCOMING.

Sexual Naturalization: Asian Americans and Miscegenation

SUSAN KOSHY, FORTHCOMING.

*Better Americans in a Greater America: Japanese American Internment,
Redress, and Historical Memory*

ALICE YANG-MURRAY, FORTHCOMING.

Five Faces of Exile: The Nation and Filipino Intellectuals

AUGUSTO FAUNI ESPIRITU, 2005.

Dhan Gopal Mukerji, *Caste and Outcast*

EDITED AND PRESENTED BY GORDON H. CHANG, PURNIMA MANKEKAR,
AND AKHIL GUPTA, 2002.

*New Worlds, New Lives: Globalization and People of Japanese Descent in the
Americas and from Latin America in Japan*

EDITED BY LANE RYO HIRABAYASHI, AKEMI KIKUMURA-YANO, AND JAMES
A. HIRABAYASHI, 2002.

*Japanese Pride, American Prejudice: Modifying the Exclusion Clause of the
1924 Immigration Act*

IZUMI HIROBE, 2001.

Chinese San Francisco, 1850–1943: A Trans-Pacific Community

YONG CHEN, 2000.

Dreaming of Gold, Dreaming of Home: Transnationalism and Migration Between the United States and South China, 1882–1943

MADELINE Y. HSU, 2000.

Imagining the Nation: Asian American Literature and Cultural Consent

DAVID LEIWEI LI, 1998.

Morning Glory, Evening Shadow: Yamato Ichihashi and His Internment Writings, 1942–1945

EDITED, ANNOTATED, AND WITH A BIOGRAPHICAL ESSAY BY GORDON H. CHANG, 1997.

Mary Kimoto Tomita, *Dear Miye: Letters Home from Japan, 1939–1946*

EDITED, WITH AN INTRODUCTION AND NOTES, BY ROBERT G. LEE, 1995.

Beyond the Killing Fields: Voices of Nine Cambodian Survivors in America

USHA WELARATNA, 1993.

Making and Remaking Asian America

BILL ONG HING, 1993.

Righting a Wrong: Japanese Americans and the Passage of the Civil Liberties Act of 1988

LESLIE T. HATAMIYA, 1993.